Democracy, Governance, and Growth

Economics, Cognition, and Society

This series provides a forum for theoretical and empirical investigations of social phenomena. It promotes works that focus on the interactions among cognitive processes, individual behavior, and social outcomes. It is especially open to interdisciplinary books that are genuinely integrative.

Titles in the Series

Democracy, Governance, and Growth

Edited by Stephen Knack

with a Foreword by Charles A. Cadwell

THE UNIVERSITY OF MICHIGAN PRESS
Ann Arbor

Copyright © 2003 by the IRIS Center, University Research Corporation,
International, College Park, Maryland
All rights reserved
Published in the United States of America by
The University of Michigan Press
Manufactured in the United States of America
♾ Printed on acid-free paper

2006   2005   2004   2003   4   3   2   1

A CIP catalog record for this book is available from the British Library.

Library of Congress Cataloging-in-Publication Data

Democracy, governance, and growth / edited by Stephen Knack ; with a
    foreword by Charles Cadwell.
        p.   cm. — (Economics, cognition, and society)
    Results of research conducted at the Center on Institutional
Reform and the Informal Sector (IRIS) at the University of Maryland.
    Includes bibliographical references and index.
        ISBN 0-472-09823-3 (alk. paper) — ISBN 0-472-06823-7
    (pbk. : alk. paper)
        1. Economic development—Political aspects.   2. Democracy.
    3. Economic policy.   4. Political planning.   I. Knack, Stephen F.
    II. University of Maryland (College Park, Md.). Institutional Reform
    and the Informal Sector Center.   III. Series.

HD75 .D443   2002
338.9—dc21   2002010532

Foreword

In 1991 the idea that "institutions matter" was not so much new as not widely turned into practical effect. Scholars such as Mancur Olson and Douglass North had been writing about the role of institutions in development for some time. But much of the work by practitioners interested in economic growth or democratic development seemed to presume that simply increasing the supply of some factor of production such as labor, capital, or technology would lead to dramatic improvement in the lives of the world's poor. Institutions such as property rights and contract enforcement had not received much attention, and the relationship of governance to institutions even less. The work represented in this volume establishes that the supply of certain institutions is an essential explanation for the relative poverty or progress of nations. As a nuclear superpower and its ex-satellites undertook in the 1990s to transform themselves, the questions of how markets and how democracies evolve took on new urgency. How indeed is prosperity achieved? Even in parts of the persistently "developing" world, the object lesson represented by the collapse and transition in the postcommunist nations was noticed and brought useful new attention to these issues.

At the Center on Institutional Reform and the Informal Sector (IRIS) at the University of Maryland, this challenge formed the center of the agenda for Mancur Olson and his colleagues. With initial funding in 1990 from the U.S. Agency for International Development, Olson put together a team to fund research and work with reformers around the globe, developing the idea that "institutions matter" and testing these in practice.

For Olson, this was an opportunity to accelerate attention to the question of why some countries are rich and others poor. In his 1982 *Rise and Decline of Nations,* he had suggested that differences in the prosperity of countries or regions can be explained by the extent to which narrow interest groups exercise influence to advance policies that undermined the prosperity of the whole. He argued that the institutions and policies necessary to advance the interests of an entire nation emerged more reliably in places where politics gave voice to more encompassing interests. This insight laid open a concern for the details of governance and the processes by which good institutions emerge.

Olson's work put him in high demand as a lecturer, and he crisscrossed the globe presenting his ideas to various academic and other audiences. Other scholars traveled to Maryland to see him. The impact of this intellectual outreach can be found in the work of others. For example, a lengthy visit from Hernando de Soto in the 1980s is reflected in much of the approach to the organization of interests represented in de Soto's widely read book *The Other Path*. The academic progeny of Olson's work is seen in the thousands of citations to his books and articles, not only by economists but also by political scientists, sociologists, and legal scholars.

At the same time Olson resisted opportunities to climb on the bandwagon advising presidents and prime ministers of new nations. Though thoughtful on many topics, he was jealous of the demands of his research agenda and careful to advance his ideas in ways that would stand the test of time and the review of colleagues. Though Olson did much of his most focused work on airplanes, "drive-by" economic policy advice was not the market for him. This more patient view of how ideas interact with reform was based on an understanding that the ideas of a broader elite were more likely to lead to lasting change than would a type of advice that became known at IRIS by the shorthand of "whispering in ministers' ears." Targeting the right idea was the modest task Olson set for himself.

As Olson undertook the research effort, there were two basic questions facing his Center. Which institutions matter? How do you get more of the needed ones? Theory certainly suggested the nature of the needed institutions. A research agenda authored by Olson at the time outlined the logic of how property rights and contract enforcement institutions were necessary for modern markets and why democracies seemed more likely to produce these institutions. Subsequent work conducted and sponsored by IRIS addressed many of these issues.

But was there a way to measure the sophistication of these institutions, an empirical indicator that would either capture the overall level of institutional development or suggest areas of needed institutional reform? Such a measure might draw attention to the salience of concern for institutions and might also address issues of priority or sequencing in the reform agendas of various countries. In 1991 I posed this question to Stephen Knack who responded with a memorandum describing the then-extant measures of various institutions and some ideas for what might be done to improve upon them. That exchange and the ambition it describes led to much of the work collected in the present volume. The challenge of course fit well within the ambition of Olson's own ongoing work, and soon a team of economists led by Olson but including Christopher Clague, Philip Keefer, Stephen Knack, and several graduate students were hard at work on several projects to test and develop a measure or set of measures. Inside IRIS the project was known as the "IRIS Index" project, even after the idea of a single direct index had been abandoned in favor of more fruitful work (chapter 1 describes the effort to develop an objective measure of institutional development).

The work took several directions. One was the effort to simply document institutional development in a credible way, a way that also took account of the causal relationship of institutions and levels of development. The other was to consider what types of regimes produced good institutions. In all cases the effort was to explore the empirical relationship between governance, economic institutions, and growth. The effort was indeed a team effort, and as in most research, the exchange of ideas, the exploration of blind alleys, and formulation and testing of hypotheses consumed the scholars here, even as they were working on specific reforms in countries around the globe. While Olson was clearly the intellectual leader, the momentum and energy to produce a coherent body of work owes much to the leadership of Knack, Clague, and Keefer as well.

The results of the work are evident first of all in the articles included here. They are also evidenced by the now widespread use of some of the measures of institutional development first used by the Index team. In searching for existing cross-country accounting of institutions, Knack and Keefer came across several investor-focused country risk rating services and initiated their use by a range of researchers and donor agencies. Of course there are now many people who have turned to these questions, inspired in part by the work begun here, and Knack's opening and closing chapters in this volume describe much of this ongoing work.

The main conclusions of this volume, that governance matters and that good governance emerges from both formal and informal institutions, are significant and form both the theoretical base and empirical starting point for work under way now to establish how it is that certain governance institutions interact with economic behavior and how these institutions emerge. Two other volumes being published by the University of Michigan Press are logical companions here. In *Market-Augmenting Government: The Institutional Foundations for Prosperity,* Omar Azfar and Charles Cadwell organize a series of essays asking the question of how it is that certain state institutions augment markets. In *Assessing the Value of Law in Transition Economies,* Peter Murrell has challenged a series of authors to demonstrate empirically how legal institutions interact with the economic behavior of actors in the postcommunist societies.

The articles in this book offer an accessible and practical examination of how governance matters to development. For anyone responsible for considering the likely course of events in emerging democracies, resistant dictatorships, or failing states the insights here offer a valuable framework, if not specific instructions. More than simply asking whether a regime has consolidated its control to the extent of becoming a "stationary" or a "roving bandit," the work here will help us think in much more useful detail about the incentives of various regimes to produce a variety of public goods. Indeed, the transition from a predatory state to a market-augmenting one is a challenge that will rely on broader understanding of the issues tackled by Knack and the other authors here. As this book is published in 2002, events in Afghanistan and its neighboring states make these lessons seem particularly urgent.

—*Charles A. Cadwell*

Contents

Acknowledgments

Prior to his untimely death, Mancur Olson had enthusiastically agreed with my idea of producing a volume such as this one, containing empirical studies produced by the "IRIS Index" project with the addition of some of his related individual works. Mancur very likely would have been a coeditor of the volume were he still living, and the introductory chapter borrows liberally from his ideas. I was fortunate enough to benefit for 12 years as Mancur's student, research assistant, and colleague from his brilliance, enthusiasm, and generosity—it is likely no coincidence that he was born in North Dakota, the highest-ranked state on "social capital."

I benefited enormously from the stimulating intellectual environment at IRIS created by Mancur, and from pleasant and productive collaborations with many other colleagues there, including contributors to this volume. I owe large debts to three of them. Chris Clague first hired me for IRIS, on Olson's recommendation and despite my lack of training in institutional economics, to help edit a set of papers for a conference volume. As Research Director at IRIS, Chris was a wonderful mentor and colleague, and I continue to benefit from his comments on drafts of papers. The IRIS Index project began when Charles Cadwell asked me to investigate the possibilities for constructing quantitative indicators of institutional arrangements and the quality of governance, and Chas was a strong and consistent supporter of the project, even when it sometimes traveled down paths he had not envisioned. Phil Keefer was instrumental in arranging my appointment at the World Bank, and I continue to benefit from our collaborations—in part because he actually does have training in institutional economics.

The Index project benefited over the years from valuable research assistance by Suzanne Gleason, Gary Anderson, Christos Kostopoulos, Jennifer Mellor, Ricardo Sanhueza, Sushenjit Bandyopadhyay, and Asta Zviniene.

Wallace Oates brought our group's attention to the existence of the International Country Risk Guide data, which was used in many of the studies contained in this volume, and subsequently by dozens of other researchers around the globe. Jon Isham alerted me to the existence of the World Values Survey, used in two of these studies.

Ellen McCarthy of the University of Michigan Press and Timur Kuran, editor of the series on Economics, Cognition, and Society, encouraged me to produce and complete this volume. I am also thankful to two anonymous referees for their helpful comments. I also thank Ann Schultz and Kevin Rennells of the University of Michigan Press for their assistance.

Susheela Jonnakuty and Imran Hafiz of the World Bank provided excellent help in constructing the indexes, reformatting a diverse set of word processing files, and typing several chapters for which electronic files no longer existed.

Most of the work reflected in this volume was financially supported by the U.S. Agency for International Development, under a cooperative agreement with IRIS. The views expressed are not necessarily those of USAID, nor are they intended to represent the views of the World Bank, its Executive Directors, or the countries they represent.

Stephen Knack
The World Bank

Predation or Production? The Impact of Political, Legal, and Social Institutions

Stephen Knack

> Societies . . . offer men two essentially different ways of acquiring wealth. One is by producing it directly or indirectly through the work and services of the capital they possess. The other is by acquiring the wealth thus produced by others. These two methods have at all times been employed. . . . the second method . . . is a general and enduring phenomenon.
>
> — *Vilfredo Pareto (Les Systèmes Socialistes, 1902)*

1. Introduction

An emerging consensus among development and growth economists views good governance as a prerequisite to sustained increases in living standards. The difference between developmental success and failure in this view has little to do with natural resource availability, climate, foreign aid, or luck. It is, rather, largely a function of whether incentives within a given society steer wealth-maximizing individuals toward *producing* new wealth or toward *diverting* it from others.

In most societies throughout history and in much of the underdeveloped world today, incentives have favored predation over production, or "taking" instead of "making" (Usher 1987; North 1990, 9, 78). Where social and legal mechanisms for enforcing contracts and property rights are weak or absent, the private returns to redistributive efforts will generally exceed the private returns to production.

Beginning with Hobbes, theorists have emphasized the key role of governmental coercion in preventing predation by private parties. However, the government is itself often a source of predation. John Stuart Mill noted the problem of establishing both "protection by the government, and protection against the government" (1848, Book I, chap. vii, 70; emphasis in original) and argued: "The latter is the more important" because "against all other depredators there is a hope of defending oneself."[1]

North (1990, 35) and Olson (chapter 5, this volume) point out that a government with sufficient power to enforce contracts between private agents and to prevent violations of property rights is a potential source of insecurity. Such a government can abrogate its own contracts with private citizens, default on its debts, debase the currency, and seize assets directly. Arguably, one of the most critical issues in all of social science is understanding how governments can emerge that simultaneously act as effective third-party enforcers yet are inhibited from violating individual rights.

The essays in this volume, written by Mancur Olson and his IRIS Center colleagues with financial support from USAID, all bear in one way or another on these fundamental issues. Each chapter provides theoretical and/or empirical underpinnings for the emerging consensus that differences in the way governments and societies are organized have enormous implications for the structure of incentives faced by politicians, bureaucrats, investors, and workers, which in turn determines the level of a nation's material well-being.

The essays comprising part 1 provide evidence that good governance matters for development. Specifically, poor societies are poor because institutions and policies in those societies fail to discourage redistribution of wealth from others, and fail to encourage sufficiently the production of new goods and services that others value. These chapters contribute to the theoretical discussion of how governance is critical to economic performance. However, the contribution of most of these chapters is primarily empirical, introducing and testing important new measures of the quality of governance.

Beginning with the premise from part 1 that good governance matters, the chapters comprising part 2 attempt to contribute to our understanding of how good governance emerges. This question, as well as the related one of how to improve the quality of governance through reforms, is far more problematic than the task of demonstrating that governance matters.

Part 3 extends the discussion of governance to include social institutions and informal mechanisms for enforcing agreements. The relative payoffs of production and predation (or "making" versus "taking") are determined not only by legal mechanisms for enforcing contracts and protecting property rights, but also by social norms that facilitate interpersonal trust. These social institutions, where they are effective, complement the effect of government institutions in reducing uncertainty and transaction costs, enhancing the efficiency of exchange, encouraging specialization, and encouraging investment in ideas, human capital, and physical capital. Where social and legal mechanisms for the efficient resolution of Prisoner's Dilemma and principal-agent games are weak or absent—that is, where most potential pairs of economic transactors cannot trust each other—the private returns to predation increase while the private returns to production fall.

Both of the chapters in part 3 are consistent with part 2 in treating institutions as endogenous. They both analyze informal mechanisms for enforcing rules and contracts. Clague's (chapter 9) is a theoretical exposition, while chapter 10 by Knack and Keefer is largely empirical, but they both explore the implications of informal institutions for the performance of economies and governments.

Part 4 concludes with a discussion of the prospects for reforming institutions, in light of their demonstrated importance for economic performance, but also in the context of Olson's (1982) well-known work on the destructive effects of special interests. Olson is remarkably optimistic regarding the feasibility and effectiveness of reform efforts in less-developed and transition economies. Is institutional reform simply a matter of "wising up," as Olson seems to imply in chapter 2, if powerful interests have a stake in preventing institutional and policy reform? Are ideas and the power of example influential enough to overcome narrow interests opposing reform? Evidence suggesting that the quality of governance is determined largely by cultural and religious heritage and accidents of climate and geography provides some grounds for cautious expectations regarding impacts of reform.

The remainder of this introductory chapter provides an overview of issues that turn up often throughout the subsequent chapters of the volume, including *modeling* institutions in the context of growth theories and *measuring* institutions in empirical tests. Section 2 discusses the absence of the quality of governance from the standard theories of economic growth. It argues that while an important role for governance is not inconsistent with either theory, these theories by emphasizing more proximate sources of growth tend to divert attention away from the more crucial issue of governance. Section 3 summarizes how the problem of measuring political, legal, and social institutions has been dealt with in the chapters contained in this volume, and in other recent work. That section concludes by summarizing recent developments in the empirical investigation of governance and development, including ongoing data collection efforts.

2. Modeling Institutions

The debate between neoclassical and endogenous growth (or old and new growth) theories has dominated the study of economic growth in the last several years. However, neither of these theories (or sets of theories) provides much insight into what is arguably the most interesting and important question about growth, namely, why some less developed economies have grown rapidly while others have stagnated or shrunk. Moreover, the most striking and robust new empirical evidence on the determinants of growth—pointing to the crucial role of the quality of governance—bears only tangentially on the debate between new and old growth theorists. The quality of governance is central to neither of the two major theories, as Olson notes in chapter 2 of this volume. Capital intensity and diminishing returns occupy center stage in the neoclassical theory, as do externalities, increasing returns, and learning-by-doing in endogenous growth theory. To be sure, neither theory explicitly precludes a decisive role for the quality of governance, but the view that governance is unimportant is also perfectly consistent with either theory.

Neoclassical growth models predict that poorer countries will grow more rapidly than rich ones. Poor countries have less capital, and therefore higher marginal products of capital. Higher resulting investment rates in poor than in rich countries should tend to reduce over time the cross-country dispersions in capital per worker, and thus in income per worker.

The growth potential of poorer countries should exceed that of rich countries for another reason noted by Gerschenkron (1952). The productivity growth of nations already on the technological frontier is constrained by their ability to push out that frontier. Countries well inside the frontier can borrow technology at low cost from more advanced nations, moving rapidly toward the frontier.

Unfortunately for these theories, observation seems to contradict their predictions. On average, poor countries have actually grown somewhat more *slowly* than wealthier ones since 1960, the period for which relatively reliable data are available for most nations. Figure 1.1 illustrates the weak, positive relationship between 1960 per capita income and its average annual rate of growth over the 1960–98 pe-

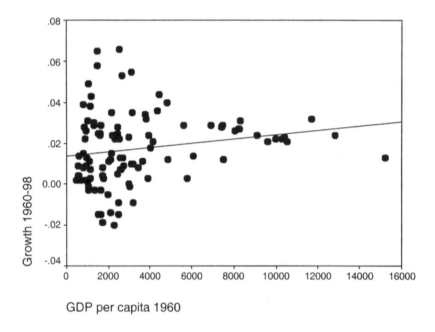

Fig. 1.1. Growth and initial income

riod, using data from the Penn World Tables (Summers and Heston 1991). Some poor nations grew more rapidly than the developed nations, but the majority did not. The most striking pattern is the huge dispersion in growth rates among the initially poor countries, with many economies actually shrinking in per capita terms. Also difficult to reconcile with the neoclassical theory is the observation that physical and human capital often flow from nations where it is scarce (and the marginal product is higher) to nations where it is already abundant (and the marginal product is lower).

The "new growth theory" or "endogenous growth theory" arose at least in part as a response to these gaps between observation and existing theory (Romer 1994). In theories of endogenous growth, externalities associated with investments in tangible or human capital allow for nondecreasing returns, explaining why rich countries can grow as fast or faster than poor ones. The new growth theory is thus consistent with the absence of a general tendency for poorer nations as a group to grow more rapidly than richer nations.[2] As Olson notes in chapter 2, however, the new growth theory cannot easily explain another striking empirical finding: the fastest-growing countries at any point in time are never those with the highest per capita incomes, but are always a subset of the lower-income countries.[3]

Neither do endogenous growth theories predict the huge observed disparities in growth rates among poor countries depicted in figure 1.1. Nothing in the theory tells us why some, but not all, poor countries successfully take advantage of the opportunities presented by relative backwardness. Table 1.1 lists the most dramatic examples of successful catch-up growth, and the most abysmal failures.[4] Values in the table are per capita incomes as a proportion of the U.S. level, for 1960 and for 1998. Three nations—Hong Kong, Japan, and Singapore—closed most of the gap over this period. Two others—Ireland and Taiwan—closed half of the gap. However, for quite a few nations in Latin American and Africa with incomes comparable to those of Singapore and Hong Kong in 1960, incomes had fallen to a tiny fraction of Singapore's by 1998. Several other Latin American nations—Argentina, Uruguay, and Venezuela—had incomes four or five times as large as those of Korea and Taiwan in 1960, but by 1998 had fallen far behind.

The new growth theory is relatively pessimistic in its predictions for convergence: increasing returns may prevent poorer nations from ever catching up to the rich, even if all nations have the same preferences and technology. It is primarily an explanation of why rich nations can continue growing indefinitely, however, and has little to say about whether poor nations will grow rapidly, slowly, or not at all.

Extensions of the neoclassical theory in recent years emphasize the concept of "conditional convergence," by which nations converge to their own steady state income levels, as determined by their tastes for saving, fertility rates, levels of human capital, and other variables, rather than to the level of the technological leaders (Barro and Sala-i-Martin 1992; Mankiw, Romer, and Weil 1992). This view of convergence also has pessimistic implications, by focusing on convergence to (often low) country-specific steady states rather than catching up to rich nations, and by treating the determinants of steady state income levels as being largely exogenously determined rather than as choice variables. Unlike the new growth theory, this extension of the neoclassical theory can also account for the many observed cases of negative growth, as steady state income levels can be lower than current levels, given (for example) sufficiently unfavorable rates of savings or fertility or levels of human capital.

Based more on empirical observation than on theory, Baumol et al. (1989, 204) are even more pessimistic regarding the prospects for the poorest countries. Citing evidence that most successful cases of catch-up involved middle-income rather than extremely poor nations, they conclude that "a bit of backwardness may contribute to a high growth rate, but beyond some point it seems clearly to become pure handicap."

However, the data suggest that middle-income status is neither necessary nor sufficient for catch-up growth. Successful cases of catch-up growth by nations such as Korea, Taiwan, and Botswana that were extremely poor in 1960 contradict the thesis of Baumol et al. In

TABLE 1.1.   Per Capita Income/U.S. Per Capita Income

	1960	1998
"Catch-Up" Countries		
Singapore	.20	.99
Hong Kong	.24	.79
Japan	.35	.74
Ireland	.38	.69
Taiwan	.11	.55
Spain	.34	.53
Greece	.29	.44
Korea	.12	.42
Malaysia	.17	.26
Thailand	.09	.19
Botswana	.08	.21
"Fall-Back" Countries		
Argentina	.58	.37
Uruguay	.47	.33
Venezuela	.45	.20
South Africa	.38	.24
Namibia	.30	.14
Nicaragua	.25	.07
Peru	.25	.15
Equatorial Guinea	.24	.09
Guinea	.23	.09
Jamaica	.21	.12
Guyana	.20	.11
Angola	.19	.04
Bolivia	.19	.09
Central African Republic	.18	.03
Mozambique	.16	.04
Senegal	.15	.05
Zambia	.14	.03
Niger	.13	.03
Ghana	.13	.05
Madagascar	.12	.03
Nigeria	.08	.03

1960, Korea was anything but middle income: its per capita GDP was similar to those of Angola, Haiti, and Ghana (see table 1.1). Taiwan was only marginally better off, with incomes similar to Mozambique, Madagascar, and Bolivia. Botswana was among the most destitute, ranking below all of these and just ahead of Zaire.[5] Just as poverty did not prevent Taiwan, Botswana, or Korea from tripling or even quadrupling their fractions of U.S. income levels between 1960 and 1990, a "bit of backwardness" seems to have done little for growth in middle-income nations such as Argentina, Venezuela, or Iran.

The evidence strongly suggests that relative backwardness presents an *opportunity* for nations that are not among the group of technological leaders. The lower a nation's per capita income, the greater is this opportunity to grow rapidly through borrowed technology and new investment. Whether nations successfully exploit these opportunities is a matter of economic policies and institutions rather than of starting-income levels — as empirical findings in several of the chapters in this volume indicate.

Poverty itself should not be an important constraint on the ability to exploit these opportunities. Royalties and licensing fees for foreign technology constitute only a minute percentage of the national income of a developing nation such as Korea, as Olson shows in chapter 2. The ability to fully absorb the most modern technology may in some industries require experience with intermediate technologies; these, however, can be borrowed from middle-income nations. Some modern production processes require large-scale production to be profitable, but poverty does not imply a small market if the economy is open to foreign trade. Lack of credit in poor nations can prevent many workers from investing in schooling (Galor and Zeira 1993), but underdeveloped markets for credit are neither universal in, nor peculiar to, poor nations, but are sensitive to government policies underlying sound financial institutions such as enforceability of long-term contracts between strangers.

To the extent that growth is a function of factor accumulation, this begs the question of why countries differ so much in this respect. Neither the neoclassical theory nor the new growth theory appropriately emphasizes the crucial role of economic policies and institutions in creating incentives conducive to investing in productive technology and in physical and human capital. Although many trades are self-enforcing, so that the gains from them can be obtained irrespective of what governments do, much economic activity is highly sensitive to governmental policies. The gains from many trades, such as those in capital markets, are generally not self-enforcing and depend on third-party enforcement of contracts (see chapter 4, this volume). Capital-intensive production depends over the long run on secure property rights, which can rarely be provided entirely through private mechanisms. Innovation in new technologies depends on government-enforced rights to intellectual property and to tangible property such as machinery and equipment in which technology is often embodied.

While human capital is more difficult to steal or expropriate than physical capital, the returns to investments in education and training are nevertheless influenced by governmental institutions and policies. Third-party enforceability of contracts furthers specialization, which raises the value of specialized knowledge. Frequent changes in economic policies create uncertainty about the returns on specialized knowledge, reducing its value to risk-averse workers. The governing elite often finds it in its own interest to overinvest in higher education and underinvest in primary and secondary education. Even if policymakers allocate resources for basic schooling, corrupt and incompetent public administrators can waste them or divert them to other purposes (Reinikka and Ablo 1998).

The quality of economic policy also matters for growth, as shown in numerous empirical studies published since the late 1980s. Openness to foreign trade, combined with an environment receptive to foreign direct investment, improves the ability of poor countries to learn about advanced production processes and management practices as well as to acquire high-technology machinery and other capital. Overvalued exchange rates and other barriers to imports and foreign investment significantly impair the access of poor countries to the ideas and capital necessary to fully exploit the opportunities presented by relative backwardness. Openness also tends to force the adoption of other policies favorable to economic activity, to better compete in international markets.

For a variety of reasons, then, narrowing the income gap between developing and developed nations is crucially dependent on the choices of governments. A recurring theme in every chapter of part 1 of this volume is that "good governance" is key to the ability of poor societies to take advantage of the opportunities presented by relative backwardness. This emphasis on the quality of governance, while missing from the usual formulations of neoclassical and endogenous growth theories, can be incorporated into either of these theories, in the absence of any formal theory that is premised on a central role for policies and institutions.

A straightforward extension of the neoclassical model to incorporate a role for governance would endogenize total factor productivity and factor accumulation. The steady state capital stock—and the investment rate during the transition to the steady state—can be modeled as a function of the quality of institutions that protect property rights and enforce contracts. In chapter 3, Knack and Keefer test the relationship between the quality of governance and investment rates across countries, finding a very strong empirical relationship. The hypothesis that the quality of governance influences investment rates receives additional support in chapter 4, where Clague et al. employ an alternative, objective proxy for the quality of governance.

For reasons previously discussed, investment in human capital can also be viewed as a function of the quality of governance. Indirect evidence for this hypothesis is provided in chapter 4. The partial correlation between the quality of governance and growth strengthens when schooling variables are omitted from growth regressions. This result is consistent with the conjecture that the quality of governance influences growth in part through decisions regarding investment in human capital.

Country-specific rates of technological advance can also be modeled as a function of governmental policies and institutions. Olson, Sarna, and Swamy (2000) empirically link changes in total factor productivity to quality-of-governance indicators.

Even the labor supply is potentially influenced by the quality of governance, through migration, labor force participation, fertility, and health. In general terms, then, the production function can be written as:

$$Y = f[A(G),K(G)^\alpha,H(G)^\beta,L(G)^\gamma]$$

where A is TFP, K is physical capital, H is human capital, L is labor, and G is the quality of governance. With the usual restrictions on the parameters, this production function is entirely consistent with the neoclassical theory.

By treating the quality of governance as a choice variable, rather than as a constraint, the analyses in part 1 can support an optimistic view on convergence in incomes across countries. Those chapters, however, largely abstract from the question of who makes these choices and what incentives they face. Those problematic issues are addressed in part 2, particularly in chapters 5 and 6. In most societies over most of recorded time, decision makers have not faced incentives for establishing a strong rule of law, for opening markets fully to trade with foreigners (or even internally), or for educating all of their citizens.

3. Measuring Institutions

In most of the chapters of this volume, the authors attempt to quantify governmental and social institutions, however imperfectly, to conduct statistical tests of hypotheses about their causes and their consequences for economic performance. Such quantification appears to defy the judgments of two Nobel Prize winners. Douglass North has argued that "we cannot see, feel, touch, *or even measure* institutions" (1990, 107; emphasis added). Robert Solow is sympathetic to the idea of social capital, but notes that if it is to be more than a "buzzword" its stock "should somehow be measurable, even inexactly," but "measurement seems very far away" (1995, 36).

The indicators of social capital and of the quality of governance employed in this volume are all highly inexact, as the authors of each chapter acknowledge. They go to great lengths, however, to demonstrate that these indicators are reasonable and useful proxies, and that they have greater validity than others previously used in the cross-country empirical literature on institutions and growth. Despite the measurement error that is unavoidable in these indicators, they turn out to be strongly linked to economic outcomes in ways predicted by theory.

In "Big Bills Left on the Sidewalk" (chapter 2) Mancur Olson employs a process-of-elimination argument against more traditional views of why some countries are rich and others poor. He convincingly argues that neither differential access to technology nor differences in factor endowments (natural resources, human capital, and physical capital) can explain the bulk of cross-country variation in economic performance: "The only remaining plausible explanation is that the great differences in the wealth of nations are mainly due to differences in the quality of their institutions and economic policies." Olson further notes that differences in the factor endowments that are related to growth—physical and human capital—are not exogenously given to societies but are themselves the products of countries' policies and institutions.

As elegantly constructed as it is, Olson's argument nevertheless highlights the need for more direct quantitative evidence regarding the impact on growth of differences in the quality of governance. This task is central to the subsequent chapters of part 1. Chapter 3 ("Institutions and Economic Performance") employs subjective indicators of property rights, contract enforceability, and bureaucratic inefficiency and corruption, obtained from firms that provide assessments of country risk to overseas investors. In chapter 4, Clague, Keefer, Knack, and Olson introduce an objective measure of contract enforceability and property rights, which they call contract-intensive money. These quantitative indicators of the quality of governance, along with others, are used as dependent variables in chapter 6, in an empirical analysis of some political determinants of the quality of policies and institutions. Quantifying informal social mechanisms for enforcing agreements raises additional measurement issues for Knack and Keefer in chapter 10. They test several hypotheses concerning various aspects of social capital using cross-country data, with social capital measures constructed by aggregating survey responses.

Measuring the Quality of Governance

Despite his assertion that "we cannot ... measure institutions," North encourages quantification of their effects on transaction costs and actually suggests several proxies for institutional inefficiency, including interest rates or the length of time required to get a telephone or spare parts. Another possible indicator is the size of the public sector, as the greater the share of society's resources influenced by government decisions, the greater is the incentive to devote resources to rent seeking instead of producing (North 1990, 134–35, 43, 69, 65, 135, 87). However, government expenditure is an extremely crude indicator of the share of social resources influenced by government, particularly in poorly governed countries. For example, government expenditures are unaffected when corrupt government officials allocate business permits, monopoly rights, or scarce foreign exchange on the basis of bribes, personal ties, or political support.[6]

The earliest cross-country growth studies that attempted to test the importance of property rights and contract enforcement used the Freedom House indices of political freedoms and civil liberties (Kormendi and Meguire 1985; Grier and Tullock 1989) and frequencies of various forms of political violence such as coups, revolutions, and assassinations (Alesina et al. 1996; Barro 1991; Gupta 1990).

As explained by Knack and Keefer in chapter 3, there are several major drawbacks in using these measures as institutional proxies. These deficiencies, coupled with the increasing prominence of "new institutional" explanations for underdevelopment (e.g., North 1990), created a demand for more direct and comprehensive measures of the quality of governance. In independent but simultaneous efforts, Mauro (1995) and Knack and Keefer (chapter 3, this volume) introduced the use of subjective ratings marketed to international investors by firms specializing in political risk evaluation. These ratings services include Business International (BI), the International Country Risk Guide (ICRG), and Business Environmental Risk Intelligence (BERI).

The ICRG rates the institutional environments of countries on many dimensions. Knack and Keefer (chapter 3) construct an index from the five they viewed as being of greatest relevance to the security of private property and the enforceability of contracts: "Corruption in Government," the "Rule of Law," "Expropriation Risk," "Repudiation of Contracts by Government," and "Quality of the Bureaucracy." From BERI, they construct a similar index from the variables "Contract Enforceability," "Nationalization Risk," "Bureaucratic Delays," and "Infrastructure Quality."

Adding the ICRG index to a Barro-type growth regression, Knack and Keefer find that a standard-deviation increase in the index (about 12 points on a 50-point scale) increases the annual rate of growth in per capita income by 1.2 percentage points on average. Substituting the BERI index for the ICRG index produces a similar association with growth. These indices (particularly BERI) prove to have strong explanatory power for private investment also. Moreover, in growth or investment regressions that include the violence counts or Freedom House indices as well as the Knack and Keefer property rights indices, only the latter prove statistically significant.

Mauro (1995) tested three variables constructed from BI indicators: (1) "Corruption," (2) a bureaucratic efficiency index constructed from three measures: "Corruption," "Bureaucracy and Red Tape," and the quality of the "Legal System and Judiciary," and (3) a "political stability" index constructed from six indicators representing the likelihood of changes in government, terrorist acts, labor unrest, other domestic conflict, or conflict with neighboring countries. He found these indices to be positively and significantly related to growth and investment in Barro-type regressions.

These measures are not perfect, of course. Reverse causality is one potential problem. Causality is always an issue in growth studies, particularly where independent variables are measured at the end of the growth period. For example, Mauro's (1995) BI indicators are averages over the 1980–83 period, while investment and growth are measured over 1960–85. Bureaucratic efficiency and political stability are likely to be a function of per capita income; while initial per capita income is controlled for, final per capita income is not. More important, biases in subjective ratings of institutions could be correlated with economic performance, as one cannot rule out the possibility that BI's experts (or those of ICRG or BERI) surmise that corruption must not be too severe in a particular country, because it is observed to be attracting foreign investment or growing rapidly.

Mauro dealt with the reverse causation issue by using an index of ethnic fractionalization and a set of colonial heritage dummies as exogenous instruments for the BI indicators. In general, his two-stage least-squares estimates of the association between the BI indicators and economic performance remain positive and significant. Knack and Keefer attempt to minimize reverse causation problems by measuring institutions as far back in time as possible and measuring their dependent variables farther forward in time. They focus primarily on growth and investment rates over the 1974–89 period and use the first available observation for each country for their institutional indicators, 1982 for ICRG and 1972 for BERI for most countries. Subsequently, Chong and Calderon (2000) employed a more rigorous approach to causality using the BERI and ICRG data. They find evidence of significant causation in both directions: growth increases the value of the institutional indicators, but higher values of ICRG and BERI increase growth rates.

A second potential drawback of the political risk indicators used in chapter 3 is that these measures likely better represent conditions facing foreign investors—the paying clients of the risk assessment firms—than conditions confronting domestic investors. Given the crucial importance of foreign technology and capital for successful catch-up growth in poor countries, conditions facing would-be foreign investors are by no means irrelevant, but unless those conditions are perfectly correlated across countries with conditions facing domestic investors, subjective political risk evaluations remain only partial indicators.

These subjective governance indicators have attained wide usage in the growth and development literature, however, and are even used by the World Bank and other donors and aid agencies to assess the state of governance in developing economies.[7] Because of its much better cross-country coverage relative to BI and BERI, the ICRG indicators have been the most widely used governance indicators in the cross-country empirical literature on economic performance.

In response to the imperfections of subjective ratings, Clague and his colleagues introduced an objective measure called contract-intensive money (CIM), equal to the proportion of M_2 not comprised of currency outside banks (chapter 4). The data coverage over time and across countries for CIM, calculated from standard monetary indicators, is superior to the subjective measures. Because CIM is objectively measured, it is not subject to contamination by knowledge of recent economic performance by country experts or by surveyed entrepreneurs, removing an important potential source of endogeneity.

The logic behind CIM is that for numerous reasons, individuals will hold a larger proportion of their financial assets in the form of currency in environments where third-party enforcement of contracts is unreliable. Money lent to financial institutions (i.e., bank deposits) is less safe where contracts cannot be relied upon. Not only are banks more likely to default on their obligations, but governments unable or unwilling to enforce contracts between private parties are unlikely to respect private property themselves, for example, by refraining from expropriating bank depositors. The CIM ratio is the outcome of choices by wealth-maximizing firms and individuals: the ratio will increase where governments better enforce and respect contracts and private property rights. Where property and contract rights are less clearly defined and secure, borrowers will find it more difficult to offer collateral as security against default, inhibiting the development of financial institutions and sophisticated financial instruments, and limiting the availability of money other than currency. Clague et al. show in chapter 4 that CIM is significantly and positively correlated with growth rates and (even more strongly) with investment's share of GDP over the 1970–92 period.

Despite its virtues as an easily measured, objective indicator with broad coverage over time and across countries, CIM clearly only partially captures variations in the institutional environment. It measures the trade-off between holding assets in only one of two forms: currency and bank deposits. Ideally, a broader measure could be constructed which captured holdings of foreign currencies, gold, and other assets (which should constitute a higher proportion of assets in nations with poor contract enforcement). Unfortunately, available data do not permit construction of such indicators for a reasonable-sized sample of countries.

Although CIM and subjective measures, such as those from the

ICRG, each undoubtedly measure the quality of governance across countries only with substantial error, these errors have different and independent sources. Thus, it is reassuring that tests using CIM in chapter 4 yield very similar findings as tests using the subjective measures in chapter 3.

Measuring Time Horizons and Regime Stability

Chapters 5 and 6 describe important relationships between the quality of governance and the time horizons of autocrats. It is impossible to construct any more than a rough proxy for time horizons to use in empirical tests. The approach introduced in chapter 6 is to take tenure to date (in years) of leaders and regimes as horizon indicators. Arguably, the first few years of an autocrat's reign are especially crucial for the consolidation of power, so the natural log of years in power is the particular specification used. Consistent with this assumption, coup attempts decline in frequency as time in power increases, up to about six years in power and leveling off thereafter. One might expect that past some point, horizons must decrease with tenure to date as autocrats reach old age. However, even at very advanced ages, remaining life expectancy is surprisingly high (exceeding five years for an eighty-year-old male in the United States). Moreover, the prospect of natural death is less likely to generate predatory policies than the prospect of exit by coup: even for an autocrat, you can't take it with you.

Chapter 6 hypothesizes that property and contract rights strengthen as democracies are expected to last longer into the future, that is, as they become more durable. Durability of democracy is assumed to increase the longer a country has continuously remained a democracy. Consistent with this assumption, coup attempts against democratic regimes decline in frequency with the age of democracies. Expectations about the future survival of democracy should eventually encounter diminishing returns to further increases in the current age of democracy; thus the log of the age of democracy is used in empirical tests.

Measuring Trust

Informal and nongovernmental institutions, as well as formal and governmental institutions, can help solve the problem of social order by overcoming collective action problems. Norms and trust produced by common values, informal networks, and associational memberships can be viewed as analogous to legally enforced property and contract rights: they potentially reduce uncertainty and transaction costs, enhancing the efficiency of exchange, encouraging specialization, and encouraging investment in ideas, human capital, and physical capital.

Ideally, one could separately measure governmental and nongovernmental, or formal and informal, mechanisms for enforcing contracts, protecting property rights, and keeping public officials honest. Both conceptual and practical problems arise, however. Important interdependencies between governmental and social institutions make it very difficult to separately measure their effects. The effectiveness of informal institutions relies ultimately on the existence of a coercive power such as a government, as Clague et al. argue in chapter 6. On the other hand, governmental institutions clearly are not exogenous, and their effectiveness is influenced in turn by civil society (Putnam 1993; Knack 2002), as argued by Clague in chapter 9. Indicators of governance and social trust available for reasonably large samples of countries do not reliably distinguish between the two concepts. For example, subjective measures of corruption may incorporate the effects of informal as well as formal restraints on dishonesty by public officials. Similarly, trust inspired by social cohesion could lead individuals to hold a higher proportion of their financial assets in the form of contract-intensive money, the governance measure employed in chapter 4. Survey-based measures of social trust (discussed later) are likely influenced by the efficiency of the legal system, as principals will expect fewer violations of trust by their agents where untrustworthy behavior is detected and punished by the authorities.

In chapter 10, Knack and Keefer demonstrate an empirical link between economic performance and the level of social trust, using survey measures of trust available from the World Values Survey (WVS) for twenty-nine market economies.[8] They also show that higher trust is associated with better ratings on subjective measures of governmental efficiency, corruption, and infrastructure quality. Trust is also correlated with survey measures of confidence in governmental institutions, constructed from WVS data. These findings are consistent with Putnam's (1993) results, in which Italian regions scoring higher on social capital indicators showed superior governmental performance.

Conceptually, the type of trust that should be unambiguously beneficial to a nation's economic performance is trust between strangers, or more precisely between two randomly matched residents of a country. Particularly in large and mobile societies where personal knowledge and reputation effects are limited, a sizable proportion of potentially mutually beneficial transactions will involve parties with no prior personal ties. In societies where strangers can trust each other to act in the collective interest, people not only can leave their bicycles unattended and unlocked on the street, they can contract with a wide range of parties without extended written agreements, or run a business without devoting substantial time to monitoring employees, partners, and suppliers. They may also be more likely than members of low-trust societies to support efficient economic policies, whether or not they increase one's personal income.

Within-family trust, intraethnic trust, or other forms of "particularized trust" or "specific trust" may well be corrosive to "generalized trust" (trust in strangers). Strong intraethnic trust in an ethnically heterogeneous society may restrict the scope for transacting and lead to segmented markets, reducing gains from specialization, and perhaps from economies of scale (Greif 1994). The WVS question on trust used in chapter 10 is ambiguous with respect to the issue of generalized vs. particularized trust, asking simply whether "most people" can be trusted. There are several pieces of evidence, however, which taken together substantially validate its use as a proxy for trust in strangers (chapter 10). First, Knack and Keefer find that this trust measure is not correlated with trust in family members. Second, they show that it is strongly correlated ($r = .67$) across countries with the percentage of "lost" wallets returned in experiments conducted by *Reader's Digest* (see chapter 10). Trust's high correlation with returned wallets reassuringly indicates that it is capturing "generalized" trust (trust in strangers) rather than "specific" or "particularized" trust placed in people with whom one has repeated interactions or who belong to the same groups. The correlation with returned wallets also suggests that translation differences or less-than-fully-random samples do not generate gross measurement error in country-level estimates of trust derived from the WVS. Third, Knack and Keefer find that the trust-in-people measure is strongly correlated at the country level with an indicator of trustworthiness based on other items in the WVS. Their index of trustworthiness, or of the strength of "civic norms," is constructed from responses to five questions about whether various forms of cheating are ever justifiable.[9] Compared to the trust question, these "civic norms" items are relatively unambiguous in describing what are effectively encounters with strangers. As with trust in people, this civic norms index is positively and significantly related to investment and growth rates across countries.

Recent Developments in Measuring Governance and Institutions

There are several recent noteworthy developments in improving the quantity and quality of governance and institutional indicators available at the country level. These include surveys of businesses, citizens, and public officials; aggregated indices of the quality of governance constructed from indicators collected from various sources; data sets characterizing political systems, including electoral rules and timing of elections; and objective measures of government processes and performance.

Expanding on surveys designed and implemented by Borner, Brunetti, and Weder (1995), the World Bank, as part of the 1997 World Development Report, sponsored surveys of entrepreneurs (both foreign and domestic) in more than seventy-five countries, inquiring about corruption, the quality of government-provided services, and the predictability of laws and policies (Brunetti, Kisunko, and Weder 1997).[10] This survey work is continuing with the Bank's ongoing World Business Environment Survey (WBES) and the more detailed Firm Analysis and Competitiveness (FACS) surveys. The latter have been conducted recently in eight developing nations and will permit detailed firm-level analyses of the impact of the legal and regulatory environment, and provision of infrastructure and other public services, on market structure and investment decisions. Such microlevel analyses can provide a useful complement to the cross-country studies contained in this volume. Other surveys undertaken by the World Bank and other agencies are designed to provide information about perceptions of corruption, quality of public services, and other aspects of governance from citizens and public officials.

A second advance is represented in Transparency International's (TI) Corruption Perceptions Index[11] and in similar indices subsequently constructed by Kaufmann, Kraay, and Zoido-Lobaton (1999). These indices aggregate various governance indicators from numerous sources, including expert assessments such as the ICRG, and surveys of businesses and citizens. The plausible assumption behind these aggregation efforts is that the more information an index of the quality of governance contains, the greater its expected accuracy. The Kaufmann et al. (1999) "Graft" index is the key dependent variable used in chapter 8, which finds that corruption levels are reduced by allowing more women to play prominent roles in government.

The surveys of businesses, public officials, and citizens and the aggregated governance indices are valuable for improving the accuracy of cross-country comparisons. Because they rely entirely on very recent assessments, however, they are less useful as independent variables in studying the determinants of past economic performance. Even as dependent variables in analyses of the determinants of the quality of governance, the lack of time-series data can be a major limitation of these new indicators. For example, the empirical work in chapter 6 relies heavily on time-series variation in the data on institutions and the quality of governance.

A third area of recent progress in measurement is the construction of much richer data sets on political institutions. The largest and most impressive of these is the Database of Political Institutions (DPI) compiled by Beck et al. (2001). Using various editions of the *Europa Yearbook* and the *Political Handbook of the World,* they code more than 100 variables for 177 countries, from 1975 to the present. Variables provide detailed information about election outcomes, the timing of elections, electoral rules, type of political system, party composition of the opposition and government coalitions, and other topics. Indices of checks and balances and of political stability are constructed from several of these variables, using an objective coding system.

The DPI is designed to permit more thorough empirical investigations of issues such as the determinants of democratic consolidation, the political conditions for successful economic reform, and the political and institutional roots of corruption. Using variables on the timing of elections, Shi and Svensson (2002) study the issue of electoral budget cycles for a much larger sample of developing nations than were available to previous researchers. They find that deficits are larger in election years (legislative elections in parliamentary systems, and executive elections in presidential systems), and that this effect is much stronger in less developed than in more developed nations.

These and other advances in measurement not only are useful in permitting more sophisticated research inquiry, but can also help in guiding practical efforts at reform. Broad indicators of the quality of governance, such as the ICRG ratings, have been invaluable in drawing attention to the crucial role of good governance for successful development and to the need for public-sector reform. In part because of research findings based on these indicators, the fundamental importance of good governance for successful development has recently attained the status of conventional wisdom. For example, "good and clean government" and "an effective legal and judicial system" are two of the pillars in the World Bank's Comprehensive Development Framework. However, empirical findings linking ICRG-type ratings to economic performance provide only limited guidance toward particular reforms in the way government is structured or in the way it operates. To date, public-sector reform programs tend to be based on a set of plausible but largely untested assumptions regarding the institutional mechanisms conducive to good governance and a strong rule of law. More specific measures of government performance, coupled with more specific measures of governmental processes or institutional arrangements, are needed to permit tests that provide more indication of which reforms are likely to be effective. For example, increasing civil service pay and reducing overstaffing are standard parts of the usual package of reforms pushed by donor agencies. Improvements in the quality and cross-country coverage of data on civil service pay and employment can allow informative tests of the proposition that low pay encourages bureaucratic corruption and worsens the quality of public services.[12] Progress in identifying, collecting, and testing more operationally relevant governance indicators is likely to be slow, however.

Notes

1. The quote from J. S. Mill introducing part 1 foreshadows Olson's arguments in chapter 5 on roving and stationary bandits: "Where a person known to possess anything worth taking away, can expect nothing but to have it torn from him, with every circumstance of tyrannical violence, by the agents of a rapacious government, it is not likely that many will exert themselves to produce much more than necessities" (1848, Book I, chap. vii, 70).

2. A few models couple endogenous growth with diminishing returns to capital (and thus with convergence). For example, with appropriate parameter restrictions, constant-elasticity-of-substitution models generate a marginal product of capital that declines, but approaches some positive constant instead of 0 (Barro and Sala-i-Martin 1995, 41–46). The lack of observed convergence, however, was a major inspiration behind the emergence of endogenous growth models.

3. Romer (1986) notes in support of his model that mean growth among OECD members from 1950 through 1980 exceeded mean growth among developing nations. However, incomes in 1950 for OECD members, and their subsequent growth rates, varied substantially. The poorer members

were far from the technological frontier in 1950, and they were the rapid growers. The richer half of the OECD grew at a 2.3 percent rate from 1950 through 1985, while the poorer half grew at 3.7 percent (Dowrick and Nguyen 1989).

4. "Catch-up" nations are ranked by 1998 per capita income. "Fall-back" countries are ranked by 1960 income. These cases were selected from a sample of nations that were underdeveloped (per capita income less than .4 of the U.S. level) either ex ante (1960) or ex post (1998).

5. Botswana's success is sometimes attributed to its diamonds and other natural resources. The recent experience of mineral-rich underdeveloped nations such as Angola, Nigeria, and Zaire calls this view into question. Theoretical and empirical work by Sachs and Warner (1995), Lane and Tornell (1996), and others emphasizes the growth disadvantages of windfalls from natural resources or favorable terms of trade shifts.

6. Barro (1991) and others have investigated the relation of different types of government spending to economic growth. Barro finds that a measure of government spending that nets out education, defense, and public investment is negatively associated with growth across countries.

7. Similarly, the subjective nature of the Freedom House indicators does not prevent USAID from citing them as indicators of its effectiveness in promoting democratization. See "USAID Accomplishments" at <http://www.usaid.gov/about/accompli.html>.

8. Zak and Knack (2001) later found even stronger links for a larger sample of forty countries.

9. The items include "cheating on taxes," "claiming government benefits which you are not entitled to," "avoiding a fare on public transport," "failing to report damage you've done accidentally to a parked vehicle," and "keeping money that you have found." Taxpayers collectively are the "victims" in the first three items; "victims" in the last two items will be individuals who are unlikely to be known by the respondent except in small towns with few visitors.

10. By not including would-be entrepreneurs deterred from operating by poor policies and institutions, these surveys are administered to a censored sample and likely understate the true cross-country variation in the quality of governance.

11. See <http://www.transparency.de>.

12. The World Bank's civil service pay and employment data base can be found at <http://www1.worldbank.org/publicsector/civilservice/>.

References

Alesina, Alberto, Sule Ozler, Nouriel Roubini, and Phillip Swagel. 1996. "Political Instability and Economic Growth." *Journal of Economic Growth* 1:189–211.

Barro, Robert J. 1991. "Economic Growth in a Cross Section of Countries." *Quarterly Journal of Economics* 106:407–33.

Barro, Robert, and Xavier Sala-i-Martin. 1992. "Convergence." *Journal of Political Economy* 100:223–32.

———. 1995. *Economic Growth.* New York: McGraw-Hill.

Baumol, William J., Sue Ann Batey Blackman, and Edward N. Wolff. 1989. *Productivity and American Leadership: The Long View.* Cambridge: MIT Press.

Beck, Thorsten, George Clarke, Alberto Groff, Philip Keefer, and Patrick Walsh. 2001. "New Tools in Comparative Political Economy: The Database on Political Institutions." *World Bank Economic Review* 15 (1): 165–76.

Borner, Silvio, Aymo Brunetti, and Beatrice Weder. 1995. *Political Credibility and Economic Development.* London: Macmillan.

Brunetti, Aymo, Gregory Kisunko, and Beatrice Weder. 1997. "Credibility of Rules and Economic Growth." World Bank Policy Research Working Paper 1760.

Chong, Alberto, and Cesar Calderon. 2000. "On the Causality and Feedback between Institutional Measures and Economic Growth." *Economics and Politics* 12 (1): 69–81.

Dowrick, Steve, and Duc-Tho Nguyen. 1989. "OECD Comparative Economic Growth 1950–80: Catch-Up and Convergence." *American Economic Review* 79:1010–30.

Galor, Oded, and J. Zeira. 1993. "Income Distribution and Macroeconomics." *Review of Economic Studies* 40:35–52.

Gerschenkron, Alexander. 1952. "Economic Backwardness in Historical Perspective." In Bert F. Hoselitz, ed., *The Progress of Underdeveloped Areas.* Chicago: University of Chicago Press.

Greif, Avner. 1994. "Cultural Beliefs and the Organization of Society: A Historical and Theoretical Reflection on Collectivist and Individualist Societies." *Journal of Political Economy* 102 (5): 912–50.

Grier, Kevin B., and Gordon Tullock. 1989. "An Empirical Analysis of Cross-National Economic Growth, 1951–80." *Journal of Monetary Economics* 24:259–76.

Gupta, D. K. 1990. *The Economics of Political Violence: The Effect of Political Instability on Economic Growth.* New York: Praeger.

Kaufmann, Daniel, Aart Kraay, and Pablo Zoido-Lobaton. 1999. "Aggregating Governance Indicators." World Bank Policy Research Working Paper 2196.

Knack, Stephen. 2002. "Social Capital and the Quality of Government: Evidence from the States." *American Journal of Political Science* 46 (4): 772–85.

Kormendi, Roger C., and Philip G. Meguire. 1985. "Macroeconomic Determinants of Growth." *Journal of Monetary Economics* 16:141–63.

Lane, Philip, and Aaron Tornell. 1996. "Power, Growth, and the Voracity Effect." *Journal of Economic Growth* 1 (2): 213–41.

Mankiw, N. Gregory, David Romer, and David N. Weil. 1992. "A Contribution to the Empirics of Economic Growth." *Quarterly Journal of Economics* 107:407–37.

Mauro, Paolo. 1995. "Corruption and Growth." *Quarterly Journal of Economics* 110:681–712.

Mill, John Stuart. 1848. *Principles of Political Economy.* London: John W. Parker.

North, Douglass. 1990. *Institutions, Institutional Change and Economic Performance.* Cambridge: Cambridge University Press.

Olson, Mancur. 1982. *The Rise and Decline of Nations.* New Haven: Yale University Press.

Olson, Mancur, Naveen Sarna, and Anand Swamy. 2000. "Governance and Growth: A Simple Hypothesis Explaining Cross-Country Differences in Productivity Growth." *Public Choice* 102:341–64.

Putnam, Robert, with Robert Leonardi and Raffaella Y. Nanetti. 1993. *Making Democracy Work.* Princeton: Princeton University Press.

Reinikka, Ritva, and Emmanuel Ablo. 1998. "Do Budgets Really Matter? Evidence from Public Spending on Education and Health in Uganda." World Bank Policy Research Working Paper 1926.

Romer, Paul M. 1986. "Increasing Returns and Long-Run Growth." *Journal of Political Economy* 94 (5): 1002–37.

———. 1994. "The Origins of Endogenous Growth." *Journal of Economic Perspectives* 8 (1): 3–22.

Sachs, Jeffrey, and Andrew Warner. 1995. "Natural Resource Abundance and Economic Growth." HIID Development Discussion Paper No. 517a, Harvard University.

Shi, Min, and Jakob Svensson. 2002. "Conditional Political Budget Cycles." CEPR Discussion Paper, no. 3352.

Solow, Robert. 1995. "But Verify." *New Republic,* September 11: 36.

Summers, Robert, and Alan Heston. 1991. "The Penn World Tables (Mark V): An Extended Set of International Comparisons, 1950–88." *Quarterly Journal of Economics* 106:327–68.

Usher, Dan. 1987. "Theft as a Paradigm for Departures from Efficiency." *Oxford Economic Papers* 39:235–52.

Zak, Paul J., and Stephen Knack. 2001. "Trust and Growth." *Economic Journal* 111:295–321.

PART I

Governance and Growth

> Where a person known to possess anything worth taking away, can expect nothing but to have it torn from him, with every circumstance of tyrannical violence, by the agents of a rapacious government, it is not likely that many will exert themselves to produce much more than necessities.
>
> —*John Stuart Mill (Principles of Political Economy, 1848)*

"Big Bills Left on the Sidewalk" (chapter 2) was first published in the spring 1996 *Journal of Economic Perspectives.* Mancur Olson reported that this essay generated more favorable responses from readers than almost any other essay he had ever written. Because the first version of the essay[1] was written before much progress had been made in identifying direct measures of institutional quality, it relies on a clever use of indirect evidence for the "overwhelming importance of institutions and economic policies." Via a process-of-elimination style of argument, he convincingly makes the case that "the large differences in per capita income across countries cannot be explained by differences in access to the world's stock of productive knowledge or to its capital markets, by differences in the ratio of population to land or natural resources, or by differences in the quality of marketable human capital or personal culture." Olson concludes in chapter 2 that "the best thing a society can do to increase its prosperity is to wise up." However, he also notes that eliminating incentives for predatory behavior is dependent on successfully resolving large-scale collective action problems. Picking up the "big bills" that many societies leave on the sidewalk cannot be accomplished through uncoordinated individual actions.

"Institutions and Economic Performance" (chapter 3) was first published in *Economics and Politics* in November 1995. This essay was one of several written by Stephen Knack and Philip Keefer that introduced more direct measures of institutional quality than had been previously used in the development and growth literature.[2] These indicators—from the International Country Risk Guide (ICRG) and Business Environmental Risk Intelligence (BERI)—have since been used by scores of researchers and by many donor agencies. In chapter 3, Knack and Keefer show that these indicators are strongly associated with investment and growth rates across countries. These results are robust to the inclusion of measures of political violence and of political and civil liberties, which had been used as proxies for institutional quality by other researchers.

"Contract-Intensive Money" by Christopher Clague, Philip Keefer, Stephen Knack, and Mancur Olson (chapter 4) was first published in the June 1999 *Journal of Economic Growth*. An early version was presented at the Eastern Economic Association meetings in March 1994, and it became available as an IRIS Center Working Paper in April 1995. This essay introduced an objective measure of the enforceability of contracts, based on the form in which individuals choose to hold their assets. The premise behind contract-intensive money (CIM) is that assets held in banks can be effectively confiscated by governments or banks—as Russian depositors found to their dismay in August 1998. The proportion of financial assets held in banks is therefore an indicator of trust in the government's willingness and ability to restrain itself and banks from reneging on promises. Ideally, the authors of chapter 4 would have been able to collect data on various forms of asset holdings, including gold and foreign currency as well as domestic currency. The latter, however, is the only form of asset holding for which data are available for a large sample of countries. Thus, CIM is defined as the proportion of a country's broad money supply not held in the form of currency. The authors do not claim that CIM is a more accurate measure of the quality of governance than available subjective measures, but rather that it can provide important corroborating evidence, as any measurement error in CIM should be independent of the errors in the ICRG or BERI indices. They show that CIM is indeed positively related to investment and growth rates, controlling for inflation, financial development, and other variables.

Notes

1. This was a 1993 IRIS Center Working Paper titled "Why Are Differences in Per Capita Income So Large and So Persistent?"

2. In articles first appearing as IRIS Center Working Papers written in 1993, Keefer and Knack ("Why Don't Poor Countries Catch Up? A Cross-Country Test of an Institutional Explanation," *Economic Inquiry* 35, no. 3

[1997]: 590–602) and Knack ("Institutions and the Convergence Hypothesis: The Cross-National Evidence," *Public Choice* 87 [1996]: 207–28) showed that catch-up growth among poor countries was strongly conditional on institutional quality.

CHAPTER 2

Big Bills Left on the Sidewalk: Why Some Nations Are Rich, and Others Poor

Mancur Olson

1. Introduction

There is one metaphor that not only illuminates the idea behind many complex and seemingly disparate articles, but also helps to explain why many nations have remained poor while others have become rich. This metaphor grows out of debates about the "efficient markets hypothesis" that all pertinent publicly available information is taken into account in existing stock market prices, so that an investor can do as well by investing in randomly chosen stocks as by drawing on expert judgment. It is embodied in the familiar old joke about the assistant professor who, when walking with a full professor, suddenly reaches for the $100 bill he sees on the sidewalk. But he is held back by his senior colleague, who points out that, if the $100 bill were real, it would have been picked up already. This story epitomizes many articles showing that the optimization of the participants in the market typically eliminates opportunities for supranormal returns: big bills aren't often dropped on the sidewalk, and if they are, they are picked up very quickly.

Many developments in economics in the last quarter century rest on the idea that any gains that can be obtained are in fact picked up. Though primitive early versions of Keynesian macroeconomics promised huge gains from activist fiscal and monetary policies, macroeconomics in the last quarter century has more often than not argued that rational individual behavior eliminates the problems that activist policies were supposed to solve. If a disequilibrium wage is creating involuntary unemployment, that would mean that workers had time to sell that was worth less to them than to prospective employers, so a mutually advantageous employment contract eliminates the

involuntary unemployment. The market ensures that involuntarily un-
employed labor is not left pacing the sidewalks.

Similarly, profit-maximizing firms have an incentive to enter exceptionally profitable industries, and this reduces the social losses
from monopoly power. Accordingly, a body of empirical research
finds that the losses from monopoly in U.S. industry are slight: Harberger triangles are small. In the same spirit, many economists find
that the social losses from protectionism and other inefficient government policies are only a minuscule percentage of the GDP.

The literature growing out of the Coase theorem similarly suggests
that even when there are externalities, bargaining among those involved can generate socially efficient outcomes. As long as transaction costs are not too high, voluntary bargaining internalizes externalities, so there is a Pareto-efficient outcome, whatever the initial
distribution of legal rights among the parties. Again, this is the idea
that bargainers leave no money on the table.

Some of the more recent literature on Coasian bargains emphasizes that transaction costs use up real resources and that the value of
these resources must be taken into account in defining the Pareto
frontier. It follows that, if the bargaining costs of internalizing an externality exceed the resulting gains, things should be left alone. The
fact that rational parties won't leave any money on the table automatically ensures that laissez-faire generates Pareto efficiency.

More recently, Gary Becker (1983, 1985) has emphasized that government programs with deadweight losses must be at a political disadvantage. Some economists have gone on to treat governments as
institutions that reduce transaction costs and applied the Coase theorem to politics. They argue, in essence, that rational actors in the polity
have an incentive to bargain politically until all mutual gains have
been realized, so that democratic government, though it affects the
distribution of income, normally produces socially efficient results
(Stigler 1971, 1992; Wittman 1989, 1995; Thompson and Faith 1981;
Breton 1993). This is true even when the policy chosen runs counter
to economists' prescriptions: if some alternative political bargain
would have left the rational parties in the polity better off, they would
have chosen it! Thus, the elemental idea that mutually advantageous
bargaining will obtain all gains that are worth obtaining—that there
are no bills left on the sidewalk—leads to the conclusion that, whether
we observe laissez-faire or rampant interventionism, we are already in
the most efficient of all possible worlds.[1]

The idea that the economies we observe are socially efficient, at least to an approximation, is not only espoused by economists who follow their logic as far as it will go, but is also a staple assumption behind much of the best-known empirical work. In the familiar aggregate-production-function or growth-accounting empirical studies, it is assumed that economies are on the frontiers of their aggregate production functions. Profit-maximizing firms use capital and other factors of production up to the point where the value of the marginal product equals the price of the input, and it is assumed that the marginal private product of each factor equals its marginal social product. The econometrician can then calculate how much of the increase in social output is attributable to the accumulation of capital and other factors of production and treat any increases in output beyond this—"the residual"—as due to the advance of knowledge. This procedure assumes that output is as great as it can be, given the available resources and the level of technological knowledge.

If the ideas invoked here are largely true, then the rational parties in the economy and the polity ensure that the economy cannot be that far from its potential, and the policy advice of economists cannot be especially valuable. Of course, even if economic advice increased the GDP by just 1 percent, that would pay our salaries several times over. Still, the implication of the preceding ideas and empirical assumptions is that economics cannot save the world, but at best can only improve it a little. In the language of Keynes's comparison of professions, we are no more important for the future of society than dentists.

2. The Boundaries of Wealth and Poverty

How can we find empirical evidence to test the idea that the rationality of the individuals in societies makes them achieve their productive potential? This question seems empirically intractable. Yet there is one type of place where evidence abounds: the borders of countries. National borders delineate areas of different economic policies and institutions, and so—to the extent that variations in performance across countries cannot be explained by the differences in their endowments—they tell us something about the extent to which societies have attained their potentials.

Income levels differ dramatically across countries. According to the best available measures, per capita incomes in the richest countries are more than 20 times as high as in the poorest. Whatever the causes of high incomes may be, they are certainly present in some countries and absent in others. Though rich and poor countries do not usually share common borders, there are cases of vast differences of per capita income on opposites sides of the same boundary. Sometimes there are great differences in per capita income on opposite sides of a meandering river, like the Rio Grande, or where opposing armies happened to come to a stalemate, as between North and South Korea, or where arbitrary lines were drawn to divide a country, as not long ago in Germany.

At the highest level of aggregation, there are only two possible types of explanations of the great differences in per capita income across countries that can be taken seriously. The first possibility is that, as the aggregate-production-function methodology and the preceding theories suggest, national borders mark differences in the scarcity of productive resources per capita: the poor countries are poor because they are short of resources. They might be short of land and natural resources, or of human capital, or of equipment that embodies the latest technology, or of other types of resources. On this theory, the Coase theorem holds as much in poor societies as in rich ones: the rationality of individuals brings each society reasonably close to its potential, different as these potentials are. There are no big bills on the footpaths of the poor societies, either.

The second possibility is that national boundaries mark the borders of public policies and institutions that are not only different, but in some cases better and in other cases worse. Those countries with the best policies and institutions achieve most of their potential, while other countries achieve only a tiny fraction of their potential income. The individuals and firms in these societies may display rationality, and often even great ingenuity and perseverance, in eking out a living in extraordinarily difficult conditions, but this individual achievement does not generate anything remotely resembling a socially efficient outcome. There are hundreds of billions or even trillions of dollars that could be—but are not—earned each year from the natural and human resources of these countries. On this theory, the poorer countries do not have a structure of incentives that brings forth the productive cooperation that would pick up the big bills, and the reason they don't have it is that such structures do not emerge automatically as a consequence of individual rationality. The structure of incentives depends not only on which economic policies are chosen in each period, but also on the long-run or institutional arrangements: on the legal systems that enforce contracts and protect property rights and on political structures, constitutional provisions, and the extent of special-interest lobbies and cartels.

How important are each of these two possibilities in explaining economic performance? This is an extraordinarily important question. The answer must not only help us judge the theories under discussion, but also tell us about the main sources of economic growth and development.

I will attempt to assess the two possibilities by aggregating the productive factors in the same way as in a conventional aggregate-production-function or growth-accounting study and then consider each of the aggregate factors in turn. That is, I separately consider the relative abundance or scarcity of "capital," of "land" (with land standing for all natural resources), and of "labor" (with labor including not only human capital in the form of skills and education, but also culture). I will also consider the level of technology separately and find some considerations and evidence that support the familiar assumption from growth-accounting studies and Solow-type growth theory that the same level of technological knowledge is given exogenously to all countries.[2] With this conventional taxonomy and the assumption that societies are on frontiers of their aggregate neoclassical production functions, we can derive important findings with a few simple deductions from familiar facts.

The following section shows that there is strong support for the familiar assumption that the world's stock of knowledge is available at little or no cost to all the countries of the world. I next examine the degree to which the marginal productivity of labor changes with large migrations, and evidence on population densities, and show that diminishing returns to land and other natural resources cannot explain much of the huge international differences in income. After that, I borrow some calculations from Robert Lucas on the implications of the huge differences across countries in capital intensity—and relate them to facts on the direction and magnitude of capital flows—to show that it is quite impossible that the countries of the world are anywhere near the frontiers of aggregate neoclassical production functions. I then examine some telling natural experiments with migrants from poor to rich countries to estimate the size of the differences in endowments of human capital between the poor and rich countries, demonstrating that they are able to account for only a small part of the international differences in the marginal product of labor. Since neither differences in endowments of any of the three classical aggregate factors of production nor differential access to technology explain much of the great variation in per capita incomes, we are left with the second of the two (admittedly highly aggregative)

possibilities set out above: that much of the most important explanation of the differences in income across countries is the difference
in their economic policies and institutions. There will not be room
here to set out many of the other types of evidence supporting this
conclusion, nor to offer any detailed analysis of what particular institutions and policies best promote economic growth. Nonetheless, by
referring to other studies—and by returning to something over-
looked by the theories with which we began—we shall obtain some
sense of why variations in institutions and policies are surely the
main determinants of international differences in per capita incomes.
We shall also obtain a faint glimpse of the broadest features of the institutions and policies that nations need to achieve the highest possible income levels.

3. The Access to Productive Knowledge

Is the world's technological knowledge generally accessible at little
or no cost to all countries? To the extent that productive knowledge
takes the form of unpatentable laws of nature and advances in basic
science, it is a nonexcludable public good available to everyone without charge. Nonpurchasers can, however, be denied access to many
discoveries (in countries where intellectual property rights are enforced) through patents or copyrights, or because the discoveries are
embodied in machines or other marketable products. Perhaps most
advances in basic science can be of use to a poor country only after
they have been combined with or embodied in some product or
process that must be purchased from firms in the rich countries. We
must, therefore, ask whether most of the gains from using modern
productive knowledge in a poor country are mainly captured by firms
in the countries that discovered or developed this knowledge.

Since those third world countries that have been growing exceptionally rapidly must surely have been adopting modern technologies
from the First World, I tried (with the help of Brendan Kennelly) to
find out how much foreign technologies had cost some such countries. As it happens, there is a study with some striking data for South
Korea for the years from 1973 to 1979 (Koo 1982). In Korea during
these years, royalties and all other payments for disembodied technology were minuscule—often less than one-thousandth of GDP.
Even if we treat all profits on foreign direct investment as solely a
payment for knowledge and add them to royalties, the total is still less
than 1.5 percent of the *increase* in Korea's GDP over the period. Thus

the foreign owners of productive knowledge obtained less than a fiftieth of the gains from Korea's rapid economic growth.[3]

The South Korean case certainly supports the long-familiar assumption that the world's productive knowledge is, for the most part, available to poor countries, and even at a relatively modest cost.[4] It would be very difficult to explain much of the differences in per capita incomes across countries in terms of differential access to the available stock of productive knowledge.[5]

4. Overpopulation and Diminishing Returns to Labor

Countries with access to the same global stock of knowledge may nonetheless have different endowments, which in turn might explain most of the differences in per capita income across countries. Accordingly, many people have supposed that the poverty in the poor countries is due largely to overpopulation, that is, to a low ratio of land and other natural resources to population. Is this true?

There is some evidence that provides a surprisingly persuasive answer to this question. I came upon it when I learned through Bhagwati (1984) of Hamilton and Whalley's (1984) estimates about how much world income would change if more workers were shifted from low-income to high-income countries. The key is to examine how much migration from poorer to richer countries *changes* relative wages and the marginal productivities of labor.

For simplicity, suppose that the world is divided into only two regions, North and South, and stick with the conventional assumption that both are on the frontiers of their aggregate production functions. As we move left-to-right from the origin of figure 2.1 we have an ever-larger work force in the North until, at the extreme right end of this axis, all of the world's labor force is there. Conversely, as we move right-to-left from the right-hand axis, we have an ever-larger work force in the South. The marginal product of labor or wage in the rich North is measured on the vertical axis at the left of figure 2.1.

The curve MPL_N gives the marginal product or wage of labor in the North, and, of course, because of diminishing returns, it slopes downward as we move to the right. The larger the labor force in the South, the lower the marginal product of labor in the South, so MPL_S, measured on the right-hand vertical axis, slopes down as we move to the left. Each point on the horizontal axis will specify a distribution of the world's population between the North and the South. A point

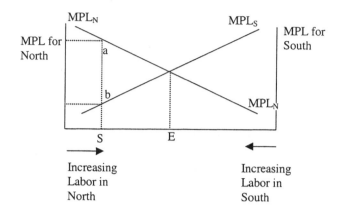

Fig. 2.1. Population distribution and relative wages

like S represents the status quo. At S, there is relatively little labor and population in relation to resources in the North, and so the Northern marginal product and wage is high. The marginal product and wage in the overpopulated South will be low, and the marginal product of labor in the North exceeds that in the South by a substantial multiple.

This model tells us that when workers migrate from the low-wage South to the high-wage North, world income goes up by the difference between the wage the migrant worker receives in the rich country and what that worker earned in the poor country, or by amount ab.

Clearly, the world as a whole is not on the frontier of its aggregate production, even if all of the countries in it are: some big bills have not been picked up on the routes that lead from poor to rich countries.[6] Of course, the argument that has just been made is extremely simple, and international migration involves many other considerations. We can best come to understand these considerations—as well as other matters—by staying with this simple factor-proportions story a while longer.

5. The Surprising Results of Large Migrations

This elementary model reminds us that, if it is diminishing returns to land and other natural resources that mainly explain international differences in per capita incomes, then large migrations from poorer to richer societies will, if other things (like the stocks of capital) remain equal, necessarily reduce income differentials. Such migration obviously raises the resource-to-population ratio in the country of emigration and reduces it in the country of immigration and if carried far enough will continue until wages are equalized, as at point E in figure 2.1.

Now consider Ireland, the country that has experienced much the highest proportion of outmigration in Europe, if not the world. In the census of 1821, Ireland had 5.4 million people and Great Britain a population of 14.2 million.[7] Though the Irish have experienced the same rates of natural population increase that have characterized other European peoples since 1821, in 1986 Ireland had only 3.5 million people. By this time, the population of Great Britain had reached 55.1 million. In 1821, the population density of Ireland was greater than that of Great Britain; by 1986, it was only about a fifth as great.[8]

If overpopulation or the lack of "land" is decisive, Ireland ought to have enjoyed an exceptionally rapid growth of per capita income, at least in comparison with Great Britain, and the outmigration should eventually have ceased. Not so. Remarkably, the Irish level of per capita income is still only about five-eighths of the British level and less than half of the level in the United States, and the outmigration from Ireland is still continuing.[9] As we shall see later, such large disparities in per capita income cannot normally be explained by differences in human capital, and it is clear that in the United States, Britain, and many other countries, immigrants from Ireland tend to earn as much as other peoples, and any differences in human capital could not explain the *increase* in wage that migrants receive when they go to a more productive country. Thus we can be sure that it is not the ratio of land to labor that has mainly determined per capita income in Ireland.

Now let us look at the huge European immigration to the United States between the closing of the U.S. frontier in about 1890 and the imposition of U.S. immigration restrictions in the early 1920s. If diminishing returns to labor were a substantial part of the story of economic growth, this vast migration should have caused a gradual reduction of the per capita income differential between the United States and Europe. In fact, the United States had a bigger lead in per capita income over several European countries in 1910 and 1920 than it had in the nineteenth century. Although many European countries did *not* narrow the gap in per capita incomes with the United States in the nineteenth century when they experienced a large outmigration to the United States, many of these same countries did nearly close that gap in the years after 1945, when they had relatively little emigration to the United States, and when their own incomes ought to have been lowered by a significant inflow of migrants and guest workers. Similarly, from the end of World War II until the construction of the Berlin Wall, there was a considerable flow of population from East to West Germany, but this flow did not equalize income levels.

Consider also the irrepressible flow of documented and undocumented migration from Latin America to the United States. If diminishing returns to land and other natural resources was the main explanation of the difference in per capita incomes between Mexico and the United States, these differences should have diminished markedly at the times when this migration was greatest. They have not.

Several detailed empirical studies of relatively large immigration to isolated labor markets point to the same conclusion as the great migrations we have just considered. Card's (1990) study of the Mariel boatlift's effect on the wages of natives of Miami, Hunt's (1992) examination of the repatriation of Algerian French workers to southern France, and Carrington and De Lima's (1996) account of the repatriates from Angola and Mozambique after Portugal lost its colonies all suggest that the substantial inmigration did not depress the wages of natives.[10]

Perhaps in some cases the curves in figure 2.1 would cross when there was little population left in a poor country. Or maybe they would not cross at all: even that last person who turned the lights out as he left would obtain a higher wage after migrating.

6. Surprising Evidence on Density of Population

Let us now shift focus from changes in land/labor ratios due to migration to the cross-sectional evidence at given points in time on ratios of land to labor. Ideally, one should have a good index of the natural resource endowments of each country. Such an index should be adjusted to take account of changes in international prices, so that the value of a nation's resources index would change when the prices of the resources with which it was relatively well-endowed went up or down. For lack of such an index, we must here simply examine density of population. Fortunately, the number of countries on which we have data on population and area is so large that population density alone tells us something.

Many of the most densely settled countries have high per capita incomes, and many poor countries are sparsely settled. Argentina, a country that fell from having one of the highest per capita incomes to third world status, has only 11 persons per square kilometer; Brazil, 16; Kenya, 25; and Zaire, 13. India, like most societies with a lot of irrigated agriculture, is more densely settled, with 233 people per square kilometer. But high-income West Germany, with 246 people per square kilometer, is more densely settled than India. Belgium and Japan have half-again more population density than India, with 322 and 325 people per square kilometer, and Holland has still more density with 357. The population of Singapore is 4,185 per square kilometer; that of Hong Kong, over 5,000 persons per square kilometer (United Nations 1986). These two densely settled little fragments of land also have per capita incomes ten times as high as the poorest countries (and as of this writing they continue, like many other densely settled countries, to absorb migrants, at least when the migrants can sneak through the controls).

These cases could be exceptions, so we need to take all countries for which data are available into account and summarily describe the overall relationship between population density and per capita income. If we remember that the purpose is description and are careful to avoid drawing causal inferences, we can describe the available data with a univariate regression in which the natural log of real per capita income is the left-hand variable and the natural log of population per square kilometer is the "explanatory" variable. Obviously, the per capita income of a country depends on many things, and any statistical test that does not take account of all important determinants is misspecified and thus must be used only for descriptive and heuristic purposes. It is nonetheless interesting—and for most people surprising—to find that there is a *positive* and even a statistically significant relationship between these two variables: the *greater* the number of people per square kilometer, the *higher* per-capita income.[11]

The law of diminishing returns is indisputably true: it would be absurd to suppose that a larger endowment of land makes a country poorer. This consideration by itself would, of course, call for a negative sign on population density. Thus, it is interesting to ask what might account for the "wrong" sign and to think of what statistical tests should ultimately be done. Clearly, there is a simultaneous two-way relationship between population density and per capita income: the level of per capita income affects population growth, just as population, through diminishing returns to labor, affects per capita income.

The argument offered here suggests that perhaps countries with better economic policies and institutions come to have higher per capita incomes than countries with inferior policies and institutions, and that these higher incomes bring about higher population growth through more immigration and lower death rates. In this way, the effect of better institutions and policies in raising per capita income swamps the tendency of diminishing returns to labor to reduce it. This hypothesis also may explain why many empirical studies have not been able to show a negative association between the rate of population growth and increases in per capita income.

One reason why the ratio of natural resources to population does not account for variations in per capita income is that most economic activity can now readily be separated from deposits of raw materials and arable land. Over time, transportation technologies have certainly improved, and products that have a high value in relation to their weight, such as most services and manufactured goods like computers and airplanes, may have become more important. Silicon Valley is not important for the manufacture of computers because of deposits of silicon, and London and Zurich are not great banking centers because of fertile land. Even casual observation suggests that most modern manufacturing and service exports are not closely tied to natural resources. Western Europe does not now have a high ratio of natural resources to population, but it is very important in the export of manufactures and services. Japan has relatively little natural resources per capita, but it is a great exporter of manufactures. Certainly the striking successes in manufactures of Hong Kong and Singapore cannot be explained by their natural resources.

7. Diminishing Returns to Capital

We have seen that large migrations of labor do not change the marginal productivities of labor the way that they would if societies were at the frontiers of aggregate neoclassical production functions, and there is even evidence that labor is on average more highly paid where it is combined with less land. We shall now see that the allocation of capital across countries—and the patterns of investment and migration of capital across countries of high and low capital intensities—contradict the assumption that countries are on the frontiers of aggregate neoclassical production functions in an even more striking way.

This is immediately evident if we return to figure 2.1 and relabel its coordinates and curves. If we replace the total world labor supply given along the horizontal axis of figure 2.1 with the total world stock of capital, and assume that the quantity of labor as well as natural resources in the North and South do not change, we can use figure 2.1 to analyze diminishing returns to capital in the same way we used it to consider diminishing returns to labor.

As everyone knows, the countries with high per capita incomes have incomparably higher capital intensities of production than do those with low incomes. The countries of the Third World use relatively little capital, and those of the First World are capital rich: most of the world's stock of capital is crowded into North America, Western Europe, and Japan.

If the countries of the world were on the frontiers of neoclassical production functions, the marginal product of capital would therefore be many times higher in the low-income than in the high-income countries. Robert Lucas (1990) has calculated, albeit in a somewhat different framework,[12] the marginal product of capital that should be expected in the United States and in India. Lucas estimated that, if an Indian worker and an American worker supplied the same quantity and quality of labor, the marginal product of capital in India should be *fifty-eight times* as great as in the United States. Even when Lucas assumed that it took *five* Indian workers to supply as much labor as one U.S. worker, the predicted return to capital in India would still be a multiple of the return in the United States.

With portfolio managers and multinational corporations searching for more profitable investments for their capital, such gigantic differences in return should generate huge migrations of capital from the high-income to the low-income countries. Capital should be struggling at least as hard to get into the Third World as labor is struggling to migrate into the high-wage countries. Indeed, since rational owners of capital allocate their investment funds across countries so that the risk-adjusted return at the margin is the same across countries, capital should be equally plentiful in all countries. (As we know from the Heckscher-Ohlin-Stolper-Samuelson discovery, if all countries operate on the same aggregate production functions, free trade alone will equalize factor price ratios and thus factor intensities even in the absence of capital flows.)

Obviously, the dramatically uneven distribution of capital around the world contradicts the familiar assumption that all countries are on the frontiers of aggregate neoclassical production functions. A country could not be Pareto efficient and thus could not be on the frontier of its aggregate production unless it had equated the marginal product of capital in the country to the world price of capital.[13]

If it were not meeting this law-of-one-price condition, it would be passing up the gains that could come from borrowing capital abroad at the world rate of interest, investing it at home to obtain the higher marginal product of capital, and pocketing the difference — it would be leaving large bills on the sidewalk. Accordingly, the strikingly unequal allocation of the world's stock of capital across the nations of the world proves that the poor countries of the world cannot be anywhere near the frontiers of their aggregate production functions.

Sometimes the shortcomings of the economic policies and institutions of the low-income countries keep capital in these countries from earning rates of return appropriate to its scarcity, as we may infer from Harberger's (1978) findings and other evidence. Sometimes the shortcomings of the economic policies and institutions of poor countries make foreign investors and foreign firms unwelcome, or provoke the flight of locally owned capital, or make lending to these countries exceedingly risky. Whether the institutional and policy shortcomings of a country keep capital from having the productivity appropriate to its scarcity, or discourage the investments and lending that would equalize the marginal product of capital across countries, they prevent it from achieving its potential.

On top of all this, it is not rare for capital and labor to move *in the same direction:* both capital and labor are sometimes trying to move out of some countries and into some of the same countries. Of course, in a world where countries are on the frontiers of their aggregate production functions, capital and labor move in opposite directions.[14]

Given the extraordinarily uneven allocation of capital across the countries of the world and the strong relationship between capital mobility and the economic policies and institutions of countries, the stock of capital cannot be taken to be exogenous in any reasonable theory of economic development.

8. Distinguishing Private-Good and Public-Good Human Capital

The adjustment of the amount of human capital per worker in Lucas's (1990) foregoing calculation for India and the United States raises a general issue: can the great differences in per capita income be mainly explained by differences in the third aggregate factor, labor? that is, by differences in the *human* capital per capita, broadly understood as including the cultural or other traits of different peoples as well as their skills? The average level of human capital in the form of occupational skills or education in a society can obviously influence the level of its per capita income.

Many people also argue that the high incomes in the rich countries are due in part to cultural or racial traits that make the individuals in these countries adept at responding to economic opportunities: they have the Protestant ethic or other cultural or national traits that are supposed to make them hard workers, frugal savers, and imaginative entrepreneurs. Poor countries are alleged to be poor because they lack these traits.[15] The cultural traits that perpetuate poverty are, it is argued, the results of centuries of social accumulation and cannot be changed quickly. Unfortunately, the argument that culture is important for economic development, though plausible, is also vague: the word *culture,* even though it is widely used in diverse disciplines, has not been defined precisely or in a way that permits comparison with other variables in an aggregate production function.

We can obtain conceptions of culture that are adequate for the present purpose by breaking culture down into two distinct types of human capital. Some types of human capital are obviously marketable: if a person has more skill, or a propensity to work harder, or a predilection to save more, or a more entrepreneurial personality, this will normally increase that individual's money income. Let us call these skills, propensities, or cultural traits that affect the quality or the quantity of productive inputs that an individual can sell in the marketplace *marketable human capital* or, synonymously, *personal culture.* Max Weber's analysis of what he called the Protestant ethic was about marketable human capital or personal culture.

The second type of culture or human capital is evident when we think of knowledge that individuals may have about how they should vote, for example, about which public policies will be successful. If enough voters acquire more knowledge about what the real consequences of different public policies will be, public policies will improve and thereby increase real incomes in the society. But this better knowledge of public policy is usually not marketable: in a society with *given* economic policies and institutions, the acquisition of such knowledge would not in general have any effect on an individual's wage or income. Knowledge about what public policy should be is a public good rather than a private or marketable good. Thus this second kind of human capital is *public-good human capital* or *civic culture.* Whereas marketable human capital or personal culture increases an individual's market income under given institutions and public policies, public-good human capital or civic culture is not normally marketable and only affects incomes by influencing public policies and institutions.

With the aid of the distinction between marketable and public-good human capital, we can gain important truths from some natural experiments.

9. Migration as an Experiment

As it happens, migration from poor to rich countries provides researchers with a marvelous (and so far strangely neglected) natural experiment. Typically, the number of individuals who immigrate to a country in any generation is too small to bring about any significant change in the electorate or public policies of the host country. But the migrant who arrives as an adult comes with the marketable human capital or personal culture of the country of origin; the Latin American who swims the Rio Grande is not thereby instantly baptized with the Protestant ethic. Though the migrant may in time acquire the culture of the host country, the whole idea behind the theories that emphasize the cultural or other characteristics of peoples is that it takes time to erase generations of socialization: if the cultural or other traits of a people could be changed overnight, they could not be significant barriers to development. Newly arrived immigrants therefore have approximately the same marketable human capital or personal culture they had before they migrated, but the institutions and public policies that determine the opportunities that they confront are those of the host country. In the case of migration to the United States, at least, the data about newly arrived migrants from poor countries are sufficient to permit some immediate conclusions.

Christopher Clague (1991), drawing on the work of Borjas (1987), has found that individuals who had just arrived in the United States from poor countries, in spite of the difficulties they must have had in adjusting to a new environment with a different language and conditions, earned about 55 percent as much as native Americans of the same age, sex, and years of schooling.[16] New immigrants from countries where per capita incomes are only a tenth or a fifth as large as in the United States have a wage more than half as large as comparable American workers.[17] Profit-maximizing firms would not have hired these migrants if they did not have a marginal product at least as large as their wage. The migrant's labor is, of course, combined with more capital in the rich than the poor country, but it is not an accident that the owners of capital chose to invest it where they did: as the foregoing argument showed, the capital-labor ratio in a country is mainly determined by its institutions and policies.

Migrants might be more productive than their compatriots who did not migrate, so it might be supposed that the preceding observations on immigrants are driven by selection bias. In fact, no tendency for the more productive people in poor countries to be more likely to emigrate could explain the huge increases in wages and marginal products of the *migrants themselves*. The migrant earns and produces much more in the rich country than in the poor country, so no tendency for migrants to be more productive than those who did not migrate could explain the *increase* in the migrant's marginal product when he or she moves from the poor to the rich country.[18] In any event, developing countries often have much more unequal income distributions than developed nations, so the incentive to migrate from these countries is greatest in the least successful half of their income distributions. In fact, migrants to the United States are often drawn from the lower portion of the income distribution of underdeveloped countries (Borjas 1990).

It is also instructive to examine the differences in productivity of migrants from poor countries with migrants from rich countries and then to see how much of the difference in per capita incomes in the countries of origin is likely to be due to the differences in the marketable human capital or personal culture of their respective peoples. Compare, for example, migrants to the United States from Haiti, one of the world's least successful economies, with migrants from West Germany, one of the most successful. According to the 1980 U.S. Census, self-employed immigrants from Haiti earned $18,900 per year, while those from West Germany earned $27,300; salaried immigrants from Haiti earned $10,900, those from West Germany, $21,900. Since the average Haitian immigrants earned only two-thirds or half as much as their West German counterparts in the same American environment, we may suspect that the Haitians had, on average, less marketable human capital than the West Germans.

So now let us perform the thought experiment of asking how much West Germans would have produced if they had the same institutions and economic policies as Haiti, or conversely how much Haitians would have produced had they had the same institutions and economic policies as West Germany. If we infer from the experience of migrants to the United States that West Germans have twice as much marketable capital as Haitians, we can then suppose that Haiti with its present institutions and economic policies, but with West German levels of marketable human capital, would have about twice the per capita income that it has. But the actual level of Haitian per capita income is only about a tenth that of the West German level, so Haiti would still under our thought experiment have less than one-fifth of the West German per capita income. Of course, if one imagines Haitian levels of marketable human capital operating with West German institutions and economic policies, one comes up with about half of the West German per capita income, which is again many times larger than Haiti's actual per capita income.

Obviously, one of the reasons for the great disparity implied by these thought experiments is the different amounts of tangible capital per worker in the two countries. Before taking this as given exogenously, however, the reader should consider investing his or her own money in each of these two countries. It is also possible that different selection biases for immigrants from different countries help account for the results of the foregoing thought experiments. Yet roughly the same results hold when one undertakes similar comparisons of migrants from Switzerland and Egypt, Japan and Guatemala, Norway and the Philippines, Sweden and Greece, the Netherlands and Panama, and so on.[19] If, in comparing the incomes of migrants to the United States from poor and rich countries, one supposes that selection bias leads to an underestimate of the differences in marketable human capital between the poor and rich countries, then makes a larger estimate of this effect than anyone is likely to think plausible, one still ends up with the result that the rich countries have vastly larger leads over poor countries in per capita incomes than can possibly be explained by differences in the marketable human capital of their populations. Such differences in personal culture can explain only a small part of the huge differences in per capita income between the rich and the poor countries.

History has performed some other experiments that lead to the same conclusion. During most of the postwar period, China, Germany, and Korea have been divided by the accidents of history, so that different parts of nations with about the same culture and group traits have had different institutions and economic policies. The economic performances of Hong Kong and Taiwan, West Germany, and South Korea have been incomparably better than the performances of mainland China, East Germany, and North Korea. Such great differences in economic performance in areas of very similar cultural characteristics could surely not be explained by differences in the marketable human capital of the populations at issue.

It is important to remember that the preceding experiments in-volving migration do not tell us anything about popular attitudes or prejudices in different countries regarding what public policy should be. That is, they do not tell us anything about the public-good human capital or civic cultures of different peoples. As we know, the mi-grants from poor to rich countries are normally tiny minorities in the countries to which they migrate, so they do not usually change the public policies or institutions of the host countries. The natural ex-periments that we have just considered do not tell us what would happen if the civic cultures of the poor countries were to come to dominate the rich countries. For example, if traditional Latin Ameri-can or Middle Eastern beliefs about how societies should be orga-nized came to dominate North America or western Europe, insti-tutions and economic policies—and then presumably also economic performance—would change.

10. The Overwhelming Importance of Institutions and Economic Policies

If what has been said so far is correct, then the large differences in per capita income across countries cannot be explained by differences in access to the world's stock of productive knowledge or to its capital markets, by differences in the ratio of population to land or natural re-sources, or by differences in the quality of marketable human capital or personal culture. Albeit at a high level of aggregation, this elimi-nates each of the factors of production as a possible explanation of most of the international differences in per capita income. The only re-maining plausible explanation is that the great differences in the wealth of nations are mainly due to differences in the quality of their institutions and economic policies.

The evidence from the national borders that delineate different institutions and economic policies not only contradicts the view that societies produce as much as their resource endowments per-mit, but also directly suggests that a country's institutions and eco-nomic policies are decisive for its economic performance. The very fact that the differences in per capita incomes across countries— the units with the different policies and institutions—are so large in relation to the differences in incomes across regions of the same country supports my argument. So does the fact that national bor-ders sometimes sharply divide areas of quite different per capita incomes.

11. The Old Growth Theory, the New Growth Theory, and the Facts

The argument offered here also fits the relationships between levels of per capita income and rates of growth better than either the old growth theory or the new one does. As has often been pointed out, the absence of any general tendency for the poor countries with their opportunities for catch-up growth to grow faster than the rich countries argues against the old growth theory. The new or endogenous growth models feature externalities that increase with investment or with stocks of human or tangible capital and can readily explain why countries with high per capita incomes can grow as fast or faster than low-income countries.

But neither of these growth theories predicts the relationship that is actually observed: *the fastest-growing countries are never the countries with the highest per capita incomes but always a subset of the lower-income countries.* At the same time that low-income countries as a whole fail to grow any faster than high-income countries, a subset of the lower-income countries grows far faster than *any* high-income country does. The argument offered here suggests that poor countries on average have poorer economic policies and institutions than rich countries, and therefore, in spite of their opportunity for rapid catch-up growth, they need not grow faster on average than the rich countries.

But any poorer countries that adopt relatively good economic policies and institutions enjoy rapid catch-up growth: since they are far short of their potential, their per capita incomes can increase not only because of the technological and other advances that simultaneously bring growth to the richest countries, but also by narrowing the huge gap between their actual and potential income (Barro 1991). Countries with the highest per capita incomes do not have the same opportunity.

Thus the argument here leads us to expect what is actually observed: no necessary connection between low per capita incomes and more rapid rates of growth, but much the highest rates of growth in a subset of low-income countries—the ones that adopt better economic policies and institutions. During the 1970s, the four countries (apart from the oil-exporting countries) that had the fastest rates of growth grew on average 6.9 percentage points faster than the United States—more than five times as fast. In the 1980s the four fastest growers grew 5.3 percentage points faster than the United States— four times as fast. They outgrew the highest-income countries as a class by similarly large multiples. All four of the fastest growing countries in each decade were low-income countries.

In general, the endogenous growth models do not have anything in their structures that predicts that the most rapid growth will occur in a subset of low-income countries, and the old growth theory is contradicted by the absence of general convergence.

Note also that, as the gap in per capita incomes between the relatively poor and relatively rich countries has increased over time, poor countries have also fallen further behind their potential. Therefore, the argument offered here predicts that the maximum rate of growth that is possible for a poor country—and the rate at which it can gain on the highest per capita income countries—is increasing over time. This is also what has been observed. In the 1870s, the four continental European countries with the fastest growth of per capita incomes grew only 0.3 of 1 percent per annum faster than the United Kingdom. The top four such countries in the 1880s also had the same 0.3 percent gain over the United Kingdom. As we have seen, the top four countries in the 1970s grew 6.9 percentage points faster than the United States, and the top four in the 1980s, 5.3 percentage points faster. Thus the lead of the top four in the 1970s was *twenty-three times* as great as the lead of the top four in the 1870s, and the lead of the top four in the 1980s was more than *seventeen times* as great as the top four a century before.[20]

Thus neither the old growth theory nor the new one leads us to expect either the observed overall relationship between the levels and rates of growth of per capita incomes or the way this relationship has changed as the absolute gap in per capita incomes has increased over time. The present theory, by contrast, suggests that there should be patterns like those we observe.

12. Picking Up the Big Bills

The best thing a society can do to increase its prosperity is to wise up. This means, in turn, that it is very important indeed that economists, inside government and out, get things right. When we are wrong, we do a lot of harm. When we are right—and have the clarity needed to prevail against the special interests and the quacks—we make an extraordinary contribution to the amelioration of poverty and the progress of humanity. The sums lost because the poor countries obtain only a fraction of—and because even the richest countries do not reach—their economic potentials are measured in the trillions of dollars.

None of the familiar ideologies is sufficient to provide the needed wisdom. The familiar assumption that the quality of a nation's economic institutions and policies is given by the smallness, or the largeness, of its public sector—or by the size of its transfers to low-income people—does not fit the facts very well (Levine and Renelt 1992; Rubinson 1977; Olson 1986). But the hypothesis that economic performance is determined mostly by the *structure of incentives*—and that it is mainly national borders that mark the boundaries of different structures of incentives—has far more evidence in its favor. This essay has set out only one of the types of this evidence; there is also direct evidence of the linkage between better economic policies and institutions and better economic performance. Though it is not feasible to set out this direct evidence here, a fair amount is available in other writings (see chapters 3 and 4, this volume; Olson 1982, 1987a, 1987b, 1990).

We can perhaps obtain a glimpse of another kind of logic and evidence in support of the argument here—and a hint about what kinds of institutions and economic policies generate better economic performance—by returning to the theories with which we began. These theories suggested that the rationality of the participants in an economy or the parties to a bargain implied that there would be no money left on the table. We know from the surprisingly good performance of migrants from poor countries in rich countries, as well as from other evidence, that there is a great deal of rationality, mother wit, and energy among the masses of the poor countries: individuals in these societies can pick up the bills on the sidewalk about as quickly as we can.

The problem is that the really big sums cannot be picked up through uncoordinated individual actions. They can only be obtained through the efficient cooperation of many millions of specialized workers and other inputs: in other words, they can only be attained if a vast array of gains from specialization and trade are realized. Though the low-income societies obtain most of the gains from self-enforcing trades, they do not realize many of the largest gains from specialization and trade. They do not have the institutions that enforce contracts impartially, and so they lose most of the gains from those transactions (like those in the capital market) that require impartial third-party enforcement. They do not have institutions that make property rights secure over the long run, so they lose most of the gains from capital-intensive production. Production and trade in these societies is further handicapped by misguided economic policies and by private and public predation. The intricate social cooperation that emerges when there is a sophisticated array of markets requires far better institutions and economic policies than most countries have. The effective correction of market failures is even more difficult.

The spontaneous individual optimization that drives the theories with which I began is important, but it is not enough by itself. If spontaneous Coase-style bargains, whether through laissez-faire or political bargaining and government, eliminated socially wasteful predation and obtained the institutions that are needed for a thriving market economy, then there would not be so many grossly inefficient and poverty-stricken societies. The argument presented here shows that the bargains needed to create efficient societies are not, in fact, made. Though that is another story, I can show that in many cases such bargains are even logically inconsistent with rational individual behavior.[21] Some important trends in economic thinking, useful as they are, should not blind us to a sad and all-too-general reality: as the literature on collective action demonstrates (Olson 1965; Hardin 1982; Sandler 1992; and many others), individual rationality is very far indeed from being sufficient for social rationality.

Notes

This article was previously published under the same title as the Distinguished Lecture on Economics in Government in the *Journal of Economic Perspectives* 10 (2) (spring 1996): 3–24. It is reprinted with permission of the American Economic Association. The author is grateful to the U.S. Agency for International Development for supporting this research and many related inquiries through the IRIS Center at the University of Maryland. He is indebted to Alan Auerbach, Christopher Clague, David Landes, Wallace Oates, Robert Solow, Timothy Taylor, and especially to Alan Krueger for helpful criticisms, and to Nikolay Gueorguiev, Jac Heckelman, Young Park, and Robert Vigil for research assistance.

1. A fuller statement of this argument, with additional citations to the literature on "efficient redistribution," appears in Dixit and Olson 2000.

2. The different assumptions of endogenous growth theory are explored later.

3. My calculation leaves out that portion of the cost of new equipment that is an implicit charge for the new ideas embodied in it. We must also remember that by no means all of Korea's growth was due to knowledge discovered abroad.

4. It is sometimes said that developing countries do not yet have the highly educated people needed to use modern technologies, and so the world's stock of knowledge is not in fact accessible to them. This argument overlooks the fact that the rewards to those with the missing skills, when

other things are equal, would then be higher in the poor societies than in societies in which these skills were relatively plentiful. If difficulties of language and ignorance of the host country's markets can be overcome, individuals with the missing skills would then have an incentive to move (sometimes as employees of multinational firms) to those low-income countries in which they were most needed.

5. We shall see, when we later consider a heretofore neglected aspect of the relationship between levels and rates of growth of per capita incomes, that the new or endogenous growth theory objection to this assumption need not concern us here.

6. In other words, there has not been a Coase-style bargain between rich and poor regions. Given that income increases by, say, tenfold when labor moves from the poor to the rich countries, there would be a continuing incentive for the poor to migrate to the rich countries even if the rich countries took, for example, half of this increase and kept it for their citizens. The transaction costs of such a deal would surely be minute in relation to the gains.

7. At the time I wrote this I had not read Joel Mokyr's (1983) analysis of nineteenth-century Ireland. For a richer analysis of nineteenth-century Ireland see his *Why Ireland Starved*. After detailed quantitative studies, he concludes that "there is no evidence that pre-famine Ireland was overpopulated in any useful sense of the word" (64).

8. Northern Ireland is excluded from both Great Britain and Ireland. See Mitchell 1962, Mitchell and Jones 1971, Ireland Central Statistics Office 1986, and Great Britain Central Statistical Office 1988.

9. [Since Olson wrote this essay, the gap between Irish and British per capita incomes has closed and Ireland is experiencing net in-migration. Irish economic policies have also improved markedly in recent decades. — Editor]

10. I am grateful to Alan Krueger for bringing these studies to my attention.

11. Specifically, the regression results are: Per capita GDP = 6.986 + 0.1746 Population Density. The r^2 = .05, and the t-statistic is 2.7.

12. Lucas's calculations are set in the context of Solow's growth theory. To clarify the contradiction between the assumption that societies are on the frontiers of aggregate neoclassical production functions and what is actually observed, most starkly and simply, I have focused on a single point in time and used the framework Solow put forth for empirical estimation. It would add little insight to the present argument to look at the growth paths of different countries.

13. Since each third world economy is small in relation to the world economy, it is reasonable to assume that no one of them could change the world price of capital, so that the marginal cost of capital to the country is equal to its price.

14. In a neoclassical world with only capital and labor, they would nec-

essarily move in opposite directions, but when there is a disequilibrium with respect to land or other natural resources, capital and labor could both move to correct this disequilibrium.

15. In his Ely lecture, Landes (1990) made an argument along these lines.

16. Clague takes the intercept of Borjas's regression about how the migrants' wages increase with time in the United States as the wage on arrival.

17. Apparently, somewhat similar patterns can be found when there is migration from areas of low income to other high-income countries. The increases in the wages that migrants from low-wage countries like Turkey, or from the German Democratic Republic, have received in West Germany are well known and in accord with the argument I am making. As Krueger and Pischke (1995) show, after German unification, East German workers who work in West Germany earn more than those who work in East Germany. By my reading of their numbers, the increase from this migration is less than it was before German unification. If Germany is succeeding in its efforts to create the same institutional and policy unification environment in East as in West Germany, the gains from East to West migration in Germany should diminish over time. The structures of incentives in East and West Germany are not yet by any means identical.

18. To account for this result in terms of selection bias, one would have to argue that those workers who remained in the poor countries would not have a similar increase in marginal product had they migrated.

19. I am thankful to Robert Vigil for help in studying the incomes of migrants from other countries to the United States.

20. Germany was the fastest-growing European country in the 1870s, but its borders changed with the Franco-Prussian war, and so the "1870s" growth rate used for Germany is that from 1872 to 1882. Angus Maddison's estimates were used for the nineteenth century; World Bank data for the twentieth. The top four qualifying growth countries in each decade were: for the 1980s, Korea, China, Botswana, and Thailand; for the 1970s, Botswana, Malta, Singapore, and Korea; for the 1880s, Germany, Finland, Austria, and Denmark; for the 1870s, Germany, Belgium, the Netherlands, and Austria. Those countries that still had open frontiers in the nineteenth century or, in some cases, even until World War I, or that were major oil-exporting countries at the times of the oil shocks, are not apt countries for the comparisons at issue now. It would be going much too far to extend the argument here (about the limited importance of land and natural resources to growth) to countries that are in major disequilibrium because of open frontiers or huge changes in their terms of trade. That is why I excluded the oil-exporting countries and compared the fastest-growing continental European countries with Britain in order to analyze the speed of catching up after the Industrial Revolution. I am thankful to Nikolay Gueorguiev for gathering and analyzing the data on this issue.

21. The logic at issue is set out in Dixit and Olson 2000.

References

Barro, Robert J. 1991. "Economic Growth in a Cross Section of Countries." *Quarterly Journal of Economics* 106 (2): 407–43.

Becker, Gary. 1983. "A Theory of Competition among Pressure Groups for Political Influence." *Quarterly Journal of Economics* 98:371–400.

———. 1985. "Public Policies, Pressure Groups, and Dead Weight Costs." *Journal of Public Economics* 28 (3): 329–47.

Bhagwati, Jagdish. 1984. "Incentives and Disincentives: International Migration." *Weltswirtschaftliches Archiv* 120:678–701.

Borjas, George. 1987. "Self-selection and the Earnings of Immigrants." *American Economic Review* 77:531–53.

———. 1990. *Friends or Strangers: The Impact of Immigrants on the U.S. Economy.* New York: Basic Books.

Breton, A. 1993. "Toward a Presumption of Efficiency in Politics." *Public Choice* 77:53–65.

Card, David. 1990. "The Impact of the Mariel Boatlift on the Miami Labor Market." *Industrial and Labor Relations Review* 43 (2): 245–57.

Carrington, William J., and Pedro J. F. De Lima. 1996. "The Impact of 1970s Repatriates from Africa on the Portuguese Labor Market." *Industrial and Labor Relations Review* 49 (2): 330–47.

Clague, Christopher. 1991. "Relative Efficiency Self-Containment and Comparative Costs of Less Developed Countries." *Economic Development and Cultural Change* 39 (3): 507–30.

Dixit, Avinash, and Mancur Olson. 2000. "Does Voluntary Participation Undermine the Coase Theorem?" *Journal of Public Economics* 76 (3): 309–35.

Great Britain Central Statistical Office. 1988. *Annual Abstract of Statistics.* London: HMSO.

Hamilton, R., and J. Whalley. 1984. "Efficiency and Distributional Implications of Global Restrictions on Labour Mobility: Calculations and Policy Implications." *Journal of Development Economics* 14 (1–2): 61–75.

Harberger, Arnold. 1978. "Perspectives on Capital and Technology in Less Developed Countries." In *Contemporary Economic Analysis,* ed. M. Artis and A. Nobay. London: Croom Helm.

Hardin, Russell. 1982. *Collective Action.* Baltimore: Johns Hopkins University Press.

Hunt, Jennifer. 1992. "The Impact of the 1962 Repatriates from Algeria on the French Labor Market." *Industrial and Labor Relations Review* 45 (3): 556–72.

Ireland Central Statistics Office. 1986. *Statistical Abstract.* Dublin: Stationery Office.

Koo, Bohn-Young. 1982. "New Forms of Foreign Direct Investment in Korea." Korean Development Institute Working Paper 82-02 (June).

Krueger, Alan B., and Jorn-Steffen Pischke. 1995. "A Comparative Analysis of East and West German Labor Markets." In Richard Freemand and Lawrence Katz, eds., *Differences and Changes in Wage Structures.* Chicago: University of Chicago Press.

Landes, David. 1990. "Why Are We So Rich and They So Poor?" *American Economic Review* 80:1–13.

Levine, Ross, and David Renelt. 1992. "A Sensitivity Analysis of Cross-Country Growth Regressions." *American Economic Review* 82:942–63.

Lucas, Robert. 1990. "Why Doesn't Capital Flow from Rich to Poor Countries?" *American Economic Review* 80:92–96.

Mitchell, Brian R. 1962. *Abstract of British Historical Statistics.* Cambridge: Cambridge University Press.

Mitchell, Brian R., and H. G. Jones. 1971. *Second Abstract of British Historical Statistics.* Cambridge: Cambridge University Press.

Mokyr, Joel. 1983. *Why Ireland Starved: A Quantitative and Analytical History of the Irish Economy, 1800–1850.* London and Boston: Allen and Unwin.

Olson, Mancur. 1965. *The Logic of Collective Action.* Cambridge: Harvard University Press.

———. 1982. *The Rise and Decline of Nations.* New Haven: Yale University Press.

———. 1986. "Supply-side Economics, Industrial Policy, and Rational Ignorance." In *The Politics of Industrial Policy,* ed. Claude E. Barfield and William A. Schambra. Washington, DC: American Enterprise Institute for Public Policy Research.

———. 1987a. "Diseconomies of Scale and Development." *Cato Journal* 7 (1): 77–97.

———. 1987b. "Economic Nationalism and Economic Progress: The Harry Johnson Memorial Lecture." *World Economy* 10 (3): 241–64.

———. 1990. "The IRIS Idea." IRIS, University of Maryland.

Rubinson, Richard. 1977. "Dependency, Government Revenue, and Economic Growth." *Studies in Comparative Institutional Development* 12:3–28.

Sandler, Todd. 1992. *Collective Action.* Ann Arbor: University of Michigan Press.

Stigler, George J. 1971. "The Theory of Economic Regulation." *Bell Journal of Economics and Management Science* 2 (spring): 3–21.

———. 1992. "Law or Economics?" *Journal of Law and Economics* 35 (2): 455–68.

Thompson, Earl, and Roger Faith. 1981. "A Pure Theory of Strategic Behavior and Social Institutions." *American Economic Review* 71 (3): 366–80.

United Nations. 1986. *Demographic Yearbook.* New York: United Nations.

Wittman, Donald. 1989. "Why Democracies Produce Efficient Results." *Journal of Political Economy* 97 (6): 1395–1424.

———. 1995. *The Myth of Democratic Failure: Why Political Institutions Are Efficient.* Chicago: University of Chicago Press.

CHAPTER 3

Institutions and Economic Performance: Cross-Country Tests Using Alternative Institutional Measures

Stephen Knack and Philip Keefer

Few would dispute that the security of property and contractual rights and the efficiency with which governments manage the provision of public goods and the creation of government policies are significant determinants of the speed with which countries grow. North (1990, 54) asserts, for example, that "the inability of societies to develop effective, low-cost enforcement of contracts is the most important source of both historical stagnation and contemporary underdevelopment in the Third World" because the absence of secure property and contractual rights discourages investment and specialization.[1] Conditional convergence in per capita incomes across nations, the object of an already large theoretical and empirical literature, is one natural platform for testing the importance of property rights to growth. This literature predicts that the lower the level of steady state income of countries, the slower is their rate of convergence to the steady state from a given initial level of income (see Barro and Sala-i-Martin 1992a). In countries with unprotected property rights, the steady state level of income to which they can aspire should be lower. Countries that make inefficient public investment and economic policy decisions would also be expected to have lower steady state levels of income.

Nevertheless, principally because of data limitations, empirical research into cross-country sources of growth and convergence has been restricted to a narrow examination of the role of institutions. This has hindered the development of a robust, cross-country test of North's proposition. Lacking data that directly bears on the security of property rights or on the institutions that protect property rights, researchers have relied upon measures of political stability (Barro 1991), such as coups, revolutions, and political assassinations, or on the Gastil (1983) measures of political freedoms and civil liberties (Kormendi and Meguire 1985; Grier and Tullock 1989; Scully 1988; McMillan, Rausser, and Johnson 1991). These sets of variables capture only incompletely many of the relevant threats to property and contractual rights.[2]

In addition, recent contributions to the growth literature have incorporated stylized notions of property rights and rent-seeking into formal growth models (see Tornell and Velasco 1992; Rama 1993). Rama models the relationship between rent seeking and economic growth. His tests of the model, using data on rent-seeking legislation from Uruguay, suggest an association between rent seeking and low growth. Empirical work in this area has not yet employed direct measures of the security of property rights, however.

This essay compares more direct measures of the institutional environment with both the instability proxies used in Barro 1991 and the Gastil indices, by comparing their effects both on growth and private investment. The results provide substantial support for the position that the institutional roots of growth and convergence are significant. The marked improvement that these new variables represent over existing proxies also suggests that there are substantial returns to future research into variables that reflect the security of property rights and the efficiency with which states determine economic policies and allocate public goods.

Ambiguities of Political Violence and the Gastil Indices

Political instability in previous studies is typically captured by two variables measuring political violence: (1) revolutions and coups and (2) assassinations. Barro 1991 employed averages of these measures over the 1960–85 period, to match the period for which growth data was then available from Summers and Heston 1991. In the present analysis, two different time periods are employed for revolutions and coups, in the variables $REVC6088$ and $REVC7488$. Both measure the average number of coups and revolutions per year, each over a different period. Two other variables measure the average number of assassinations per year per million population over two different periods, $ASSN6088$ and $ASSN7488$.

There are two seven-point Gastil indices, one for civil liberties and the other for political freedom. Both are averages for the period 1973 through 1986. Since the two indices are highly correlated with each other (the correlation coefficient is .97), they are added together to form the variable *FREE7386,* which ranges from two to fourteen. Higher values of all of these variables indicate fewer freedoms or greater political violence and, therefore, worsening conditions for investment.

The logic behind the use of political instability variables such as revolutions, coups, and political assassinations is straightforward. Leaders who fear replacement are more likely to expropriate because they expect to bear fewer of the future costs of their current expropriatory actions (see chapters 5 and 6, this volume). Moreover, during periods of political instability, particularly when instability is triggered by nonconstitutional events, institutional and noninstitutional mechanisms for protecting property and contractual rights are more fragile, and entrepreneurs are likely to reduce and to reallocate investment to avoid risk.

There are several reasons why such a variable only partially reflects the variation in property rights security among countries. First, leaders are averse to losing power whether or not their replacement is unconstitutional. However, the variables representing political instability contemplate only nonconstitutional political events, revolutions, coups, and assassinations. The actions of those leaders who face a higher risk of losing power constitutionally are not captured by this variable. Therefore, the success of this variable as a proxy for the effects of leadership tenure on property rights depends on whether short leadership tenure is correlated with expectations of unconstitutional replacement. There is little evidence on this point.

Second, the proxy itself may be misleading. Countries may experience few coups and revolutions but nevertheless exhibit insecure property rights. In fact, dictators who are most effective in the repression of dissent may be the most successful in avoiding coups, revolutions, and assassinations, but offer the worst protection for property rights. Malawi and Zambia, for example, exhibit very low frequencies of coups and revolutions; the leaders of these two countries survived or have survived in office for exceptionally long periods of time. Few would argue, however, that the absence of political violence endows these countries with more secure property rights than France, Italy, and even Germany, all of which score at least as poorly on the measures of political violence employed by Barro (1991). On the other hand, the victors in countries with frequent coups often do not make significant policy changes. Property rights that were vulnerable before a particular coup are likely to continue to be vulnerable. In these countries, political upheaval is likely to be symptomatic of an institutional environment that fails to protect property rights, just as it fails to ensure orderly political transitions. The new variables measure the inadequacies of the institutional environment directly, rather than through the proxies of the political violence variables.

The third limitation of the political violence indicators is that there are many margins on which institutions can affect property rights; instability is a relatively crude indicator of these, detracting from its usefulness for deriving policy prescriptions. Fourth, Londregan and Poole (1990) and others have shown, as Barro (1991) acknowledges, that political violence is in turn very sensitive to economic performance.[3] This sensitivity introduces problems of simultaneity into estimates of the effects of political violence on growth and investment.

For their part, the Gastil indices are aggregate measures that have been compiled without the explicit aim of measuring the security of property rights. Although they embody some consideration of the security of private property, they contain multiple and diverse other dimensions, including freedom of religion and rights of worker association. For many purposes these variables are of great importance. However, several of the dimensions are not closely related to property rights. Moreover, since the indices are not disaggregated and the implicit weights attached to the various dimensions may vary over time and between countries, these measures are likely to embody considerable measurement error in evaluating the particular institutions thought to affect property rights, contracting rights, and the efficiency with which public goods are allocated.[4]

The Institutional Data

The focus of this essay is on institutional indicators compiled by two private international investment risk services: International Country Risk Guide (ICRG) and Business Environmental Risk Intelligence (BERI). We use the first observations that these services have for any country. For BERI, the vast majority of observations are from 1972, and for ICRG, nearly all observations are from 1982. Unlike the Gastil data, these two sources provide detailed ratings for large samples on disaggregated dimensions of property rights that are closely related to those institutions emphasized by North (1990), Weingast (1993), Olson (1982), and others.

ICRG variables *Expropriation Risk,* measuring the risk of expropriation, and *Rule of Law,* measuring whether there are established peaceful mechanisms for adjudicating disputes, are interpreted here as proxies for the security of property and contract rights. If countries score low on these dimensions, they are likely to suffer a reduction in the quantity and efficiency of investment in physical and human capital. As the probability increases that investors will lose the proceeds from the investment, or the investment itself, investors reduce their investment and channel their resources to activities that are more secure from the threat of expropriation (trading rather than manufacturing, for example), although they may be less profitable.

Repudiation of Contracts by Government is another indicator of contract enforcement. It is likely that if private actors cannot count on the government to respect the contracts it has with them, they will also not be able to count on the government enforcing contracts between private parties. Without impartial enforcement of contracts by the state, only self-enforcing exchanges between private economic actors will occur—those in which the benefits of compliance exceed the gains from cheating or reneging. This restriction on economic activity severely limits the universe of possible Pareto-improving exchanges that would otherwise be undertaken.

Repudiation also measures government credibility. Regimes in which officials have the power unilaterally to modify or to repudiate contractual agreements will likely be unconstrained in other ways. In particular, entrepreneurs are likely to be suspicious about the institutional or other barriers on state officials that keep them from pursuing policies of confiscatory taxation (directly, or through inflation) or outright expropriation.[5]

The remaining two ICRG variables used in this essay are *Corruption in Government* and *Quality of Bureaucracy.* They are taken as proxies for the general efficiency with which government services are provided and for the extent and damage of rent-seeking behavior. When countries score poorly (low) on these dimensions, it is a strong indication that a bureaucracy lacks procedural clarity or technical competence and is likely to introduce criteria other than efficiency into the determination of government policies or the allocation of public goods. In particular, the bureaucracy is likely to award contracts, business and trade licenses, police protection, and so forth on the basis of criteria other than those of allocative and technical efficiency. In addition, bureaucracies where corruption is high or competence is low are less likely to provide a strong bulwark against infringements on property rights. The resulting distortions in investment and trade may reduce the quantity and efficiency of capital investment and foreign technology introduced into the country.

Theoretically, the use of corrupt allocation schemes in the political marketplace need not produce less efficient results than other forms of political allocation. However, in those countries where ICRG records high levels of corruption, entrepreneurs are also beset by greater uncertainty regarding the credibility of government commitments. That is, the same institutions that allow public officials to demand large and arbitrary bribes, such as failed law enforcement systems, also inhibit those officials from credibly pledging not to renege on their future commitments. This discourages investment and encourages forms of economic activity that are less vulnerable to expropriation.[6]

The measures from BERI that are used for this essay are *Contract Enforceability and Infrastructure Quality, Nationalization Potential,* and *Bureaucratic Delays.* The latter two parallel, respectively, the ICRG variables *Expropriation Risk* and *Quality of Bureaucracy.* The relevance of all the BERI variables is indicated by the foregoing discussion, with the exception of *Infrastructure Quality.* This variable allows some approximation to be made to the efficiency with which governments allocate public goods.[7]

Because of strong correlations among these separate indicators, with the consequent risk of multicollinearity, and in order to avoid omitting any of them from the equation, the five ICRG variables and the four BERI variables have been aggregated to form an ICRG index (*ICRG82*) and a BERI index (*BERI72*) of the security of contractual and property rights. Although the aggregation is accomplished through simple addition, the results reported later do not change significantly when individual components of these indices are used or when the indices are compiled with different weights.[8] Higher values of the ICRG and BERI indices indicate better conditions for investment.

Comparing Institutional Variables, Violence, and the Gastil Indices

The importance of institutional data that more precisely represent the security of property and contractual rights on growth is evaluated in a number of ways. First, we run correlations between the institutional variables and the political violence and Gastil indices. Second, we assess the relative explanatory power of the various measures in empirical growth equations. Third, we compare the coefficient on initial income with and without the institutional variables. If countries converge to their steady state incomes, and if institutions are significant determinants of the steady state incomes to which countries converge, then the coefficient on initial income should be higher when institutions are adequately controlled for. That is, if the convergence hypothesis is correct we should find that countries grow faster, the lower their initial income, if we control sufficiently for the quality of their institutions. Fourth, we compare the power of the variables in explaining private investment rates across countries.

Low correlations between the data are an indication that the institutional variables from the investor services contain information not in the other variables. High correlations suggest, on the other hand, that the new variables may add little additional information. The correlations in table 3.1 are negative, because higher values of the political violence and Gastil variables indicate worsening conditions for investment, while higher values of the ICRG and BERI indices indicate better conditions for investment.

In fact, the correlations are relatively low, as table 3.1 indicates. The ICRG index for 1982 has a Pearson correlation coefficient of only -0.23 with *ASSN7488* and -0.42 with *REVC7488*. The Pearson correlation with *FREE7386* is higher, at -0.66. Correlations with the political instability variables rise somewhat for the longer period, 1960–88, to -0.27 for *ASSN6088* and $-.51$ for *REVC6088*.

It may be argued that the ordinal information in the institutional variables is more meaningful than the intervals between observations. To account for this possibility, Spearman rank-correlation coefficients were also calculated. These were in most cases approximately the same as the Pearson coefficients. The ICRG index for 1982 has a Spearman correlation coefficient of only -0.25 with *ASSN7488* and -0.53 with *REVC7488*. The differences between the Spearman and Pearson calculations are greater for the longer periods. Spear-

TABLE 3.1.   Correlations between Institutional Variables

	ICRG82	BERI72
FREE7386	−0.661	−0.761
ASSN7488	−0.232	−0.240
ASSN6088	−0.270	−0.319
REVC7488	−0.424	−0.297
REVC6088	−0.514	−0.463

man correlations with the political instability variables for the period 1960–88 are −0.43 for *ASSN6088* and −.65 for *REVC6088*.

It is likely to be true that the longer a country's history of political violence, the lower its property rights indicators. The longer period identifies those countries better than the shorter period, and it increases somewhat the correlation between the property rights indicators and the political violence variables.[9] Regardless of the period or the variables, however, the correlations support the contention that the ICRG index conveys considerable additional information about the institutional environment that is not captured in the political violence or Gastil variables. The BERI index for 1972 exhibits a similar pattern of correlation, as table 3.1 shows, although it has a substantially higher correlation with *FREE7386,* at −.76.[10]

The extent of the complementarity can be seen by looking once again at Zambia, Malawi, France, and Italy. Zambia scores 20 on the ICRG index, and Malawi scores 25.6. Malawi averaged zero revolutions and coups per year over the period 1974–88, and .012 assassinations per million population per year. Zambia averaged .07 revolutions and coups over the period and zero assassinations. France and Italy have approximately the same scores for political violence as Zambia and Malawi (zero revolutions and coups and .006 assassinations in the case of France, and .07 revolutions and coups and .043 assassinations in the case of Italy). However, France and Italy score 46.5 and 38.2, respectively, on the ICRG index, demonstrating more precisely the possibility of breakdowns in the relationship between instability and the inadequate protection of property rights.

The Growth Equation

The principal motivation for searching for other institutional variables is not the low correlation among older and newer variables, but rather the additional insights that can be obtained regarding the sources of economic growth. Barro and Sala-i-Martin (1992a), Mankiw, Romer, and Weil (1992), and others examine the evolution of economic growth in countries, assuming that they are out of their steady state growth paths. That is, they explicitly model growth, taking into account rate of convergence of countries to their steady state. Equation (14) of Mankiw, Romer, and Weil 1992 and equation (8) of Barro and Sala-i-Martin 1992a describe the evolution of an economy as

$$\ln(y(t)) = (1 - e^{-\lambda t}) \ln (y^*) + e^{-\lambda t} \ln(y(0)) \tag{1}$$

where $y(t)$ is the level of income at time t, $y(0)$ is the initial level of income, and y^* is the steady state level of income. The rate of convergence is given by λ. Barro and Sala-i-Martin (1992a, 1992b) manipulate this to construct the equation

$$\ln \left(\frac{y_{iT}}{y_i(0)}\right) = a_i - (1 - e^{-\lambda}) \ln(y_i(0)) - g_i T) + \varepsilon_i \tag{2}$$

where $a_i = g_i + (1 - e^{-\lambda})\ln(y_i^*)$. The rate of technological progress, g_i, is assumed constant across countries.[11] This equation is similar to that employed by Barro (1991), the specification that is relied upon here to compare the effects of political violence and the Gastil and institutional indicators on growth:

$$GR6085 = \alpha + \beta_1 GDP60 + \beta_2 SEC60 + \beta_3 PRIM60$$

$$+ \beta_4 GOVCONS + \beta_5 REVCOUP$$

$$+ \beta_6 ASSASS + \beta_7 PPI60DEV + \varepsilon_i \tag{3}$$

Here, growth is a function of initial income,[12] secondary and primary school enrollment in 1960, the percentage of government consumption in GDP, frequencies of revolutions and assassinations, and the magnitude of the deviation of the Summers and Heston investment deflator (U.S. = 100) from the sample mean.[13] In the Barro model, then, the determinants of the steady state of income that vary across countries are (*SEC60, PRIM60, GOVCONS, REVCOUP, ASSASS, PPI60DEV*).

Unlike Mankiw, Romer, and Weil 1992 and others, Barro 1991 omits rates of factor accumulation, implicitly assuming that they should be the same across countries except to the extent that education and other idiosyncratic factors drive them apart. It is these idiosyncratic factors that he attempts to capture with government consumption, revolutions, price deviations, and so forth. Although the regressions that follow employ the Barro specification, the results derived are robust to adding rates of factor accumulation, following Mankiw, Romer, and Weil 1992.

Following Barro 1991, Barro and Sala-i-Martin 1992a, b, Mankiw, Romer, and Weil 1992, and others, we assume that the problem of omitted variables is not serious enough to require that ordinary least squares (OLS) be abandoned for another estimation procedure, such as fixed effects.[14] This is clearly a strong assumption. Growth depends on a multitude of factors, only some of which are captured by the included variables in any empirical investigation. If any of these omitted variables is correlated with included explanatory variables, the coefficients on those included variables will be biased. However, there are at least three reasons for retaining the OLS procedure.

First, the principal objective of this essay is to estimate the influence of institutions within the same framework that other effects, including those measured by the Gastil and political violence indicators, have been evaluated in the literature. Second, the new variables employed in this essay are significant, even in the presence of previously used institutional proxies, suggesting that they are capturing some of the effects omitted in previous work and, therefore, are reducing the influence of omitted variable bias. The third reason is eminently pragmatic: the institutional variables are relatively stable over time and would therefore drop out of a fixed-effects estimation.

Unlike Barro 1991, this essay focuses on growth over the period 1974–89 to mitigate the effects of possible measurement error in the ICRG and BERI indices that might have been introduced by evaluator bias. The evaluators of the investor services might be influenced by the level of income of the countries that they evaluate. Current levels of GDP are a product of past growth, naturally. To the extent that evaluators are influenced by the current level of GDP, estimates of the effect of property rights on growth might be biased upward. This is a problem that afflicts all such measures, including the Gastil measures. Our choice of period reduces problems of simultaneity that might cloud inferences about the effect of property rights.

Empirical Results—Growth

The following discussion indicates that the more specific ICRG and BERI indicators of the security of property and contractual rights offer additional insights into the sources of growth, beyond those provided by the instability and Barro variables. This section examines the performance of these indicators in growth equations, in which the ICRG index performs the best. The performance of these variables as explanations of private investment is also investigated in a subsequent section. The BERI index has the greatest explanatory power in those regressions. These findings are robust to changes in the sample period, sample size, and specification.

The regressions in tables 3.2, 3.3, and 3.4 compare the performance of political violence and Gastil variables with *ICRG82* and *BERI72*. Comparisons are made on the basis of several regressions. First, regressions are run with only political violence or Gastil variables (along with the other control variables in (3)) using the ICRG or BERI samples of countries.[15] Results from these tests are compared to regressions run using only ICRG or BERI as institutional indicators. Regressions are also run with the ICRG or BERI variables entering jointly with the political violence or Gastil variables.

The evaluation of the ICRG and BERI indices relative to the political violence and Gastil indices is made in three ways. Comparisons are made, first, of the statistical significance of the variables, when they enter alone and when they enter together; second, of their economic significance; and third, of the magnitude of the coefficient on *GDP70,* initial income. This coefficient reveals the extent of convergence after controlling for country-specific institutional, educational, and other factors that affect steady state income. When variables are used that capture more of these factors, the rate of conditional convergence, and therefore the coefficient on *GDP70,* should rise, provided that the underlying hypothesis of conditional convergence is correct.

Equations (1) of tables 3.2 and 3.3 are benchmark regressions for the ICRG and BERI samples, respectively, and include no institutional variables. Equations (2) add the political violence indicators, but not the ICRG and BERI indices. Three conclusions are noteworthy comparing equations (1) and (2). First, the explanatory power of the regressions is substantially higher when the political violence indicators are included.[16] Second, the political violence indicators are only marginally significant using the BERI sample; the same is true for *ASSN7489* for the ICRG sample. Third, both the statistical significance and the magnitude of the coefficient on *GDP70,* from which the rate of convergence is derived, increase notably.[17] Evidence for conditional convergence is significantly stronger when institutional determinants of steady state income are appropriately accounted for.

In equations (3) of tables 3.2 and 3.3 the ICRG and BERI indices, respectively, replace the political violence indicators. Both are more significant than the political violence indicators. Moreover, the magnitude and significance of the coefficient on *GDP70* rise dramatically. The coefficient on *GDP70* rises from −.482 with the Barro variables to −.692 with *ICRG82.* When *BERI72* replaces the political violence indicators, the coefficient rises from −.594 to −.694. These results once again support the conditional convergence hypothesis and suggest that *ICRG82* and *BERI72* better reflect the institutional determinants of steady state income. Both the magnitude and statistical significance of the convergence coefficient increase when these institutional variables are included in the estimated equation.

In the final equations of these two tables, the political violence indicators enter with either *ICRG82* or *BERI72*. In the regression with the ICRG index, the magnitude and statistical significance of the violence indicators drop substantially, and *ICRG82* remains significant. *BERI72* performs less well, but still exhibits at least as much economic and statistical significance as the political violence indicators.[18]

Comparing these variables in terms of their economic impact also reveals the greater explanatory power of the ICRG/BERI indices relative to the political violence indicators. Since the units of the variables are not comparable, standardized estimates of their regression coefficients were calculated. These denote the change in the dependent variable, in standard deviation units, for a one-unit change in the standard deviation of the dependent variable. For the ICRG case in table 3.2, the sum of the standardized estimates of *REVC7489* and *ASSN7489* in equation (2) is −0.36. The standardized estimate of

TABLE 3.2.   Growth, Institutions, and Political Violence: ICRG

	(1)	(2)	(3)	(4)
Intercept	1.980	3.028	0.254	1.345
	1.980	*2.851*	*0.237*	*1.091*
ICRG82			0.092	0.072
			3.420	*2.499*
REVC7489		−1.630		−1.115
		−1.904		*−1.302*
ASSN7489		−3.486		−2.278
		−1.695		*−1.108*
GDP70	−0.401	−0.482	−0.692	−0.683
	−2.564	*−3.141*	*−4.055*	*−4.030*
SEC70	6.083	6.284	5.051	5.411
	3.819	*4.083*	*3.286*	*3.524*
PRIM70	−0.690	−0.959	−0.532	−0.752
	−0.758	*−1.072*	*−0.617*	*−0.862*
GCON7489	−5.222	−6.388	−4.289	−5.286
	−1.213	*−1.527*	*−1.051*	*−1.293*
PPI74DEV	−0.920	−0.985	−0.892	−0.941
	−2.243	*−2.482*	*−2.3*	*−2.439*
R^2	0.198	0.270	0.291	0.318
N	97	97	97	97

Note: Dependent variable is average annual per capita GDP growth, 1974–89. Numbers in italics are *t*-statistics.

ICRG82 when it replaces these two variables in equation (3) of table 3.2, however, is 0.504: an increase of one standard deviation in *ICRG82* leads to an increase in growth equal to 0.504 of its standard deviation. The standard deviation of the growth variable *GR7489* is 2.465, indicating that an increase of one standard deviation in *ICRG82* (equal to approximately 12 points on the 40-point scale, or the difference between the *ICRG82* scores of Honduras [15] and Costa Rica [27], or of Argentina [25] and Italy [30]) increases growth by more than 1.2 percentage points. The importance of the effect of *ICRG82* can be seen by comparing its standardized coefficient to the standardized coefficient on secondary education enrollment (*SEC70*), which is not much higher at .57. When *ICRG82* and the political violence variables are all included in the same regression, the standardized estimate of *ICRG82* is 0.393, and the sum of the standardized estimates of the violence indicators is −0.235. In all cases, the economic impact of *ICRG82* is significant and greater than that of the political violence indicators.

A similar story can be told with regard to *BERI72*. Alone, the two political violence indicators have a combined standardized estimate of

TABLE 3.3.   Growth, Institutions, and Political Violence: BERI

	(1)	(2)	(3)	(4)
Intercept	1.022	0.356	−0.977	−0.627
	0.644	*0.205*	*−0.545*	*−0.336*
BERI72			0.376	0.263
			2.111	*1.357*
REVC7489		−1.653		−1.630
		−1.304		*−1.300*
ASSN7489		−23.015		−14.695
		−1.710		*−1.003*
GDP0	−0.501	−0.594	−0.694	−0.721
	−2.751	*−3.277*	*−3.520*	*−3.566*
SEC70	5.376	4.624	4.047	4.026
	2.805	*2.411*	*2.083*	*2.067*
PRIM70	0.653	2.793	0.580	2.018
	0.377	*1.389*	*0.349*	*0.976*
GCON7489	−1.145	−1.508	−2.968	−3.052
	−0.183	*−0.249*	*−0.489*	*−0.500*
PPI74DEV	−0.929	−0.894	−0.711	−0.748
	−1.921	*−1.938*	*−1.495*	*−1.595*
R^2	−0.276	0.375	0.350	0.405
N	46	46	46	46

Note: Dependent variable is average annual per capita GDP growth, 1974–89. Numbers in italics are *t*-statistics.

−0.47. When it replaces these variables, however, the BERI index has a standardized estimate of 0.54. When the three variables enter into the same regression, the combined political violence standardized estimate is −0.37, and the standardized estimate of $BERI72$ is 0.38.

These results were robust to a number of alternative specifications. The institutional variables were statistically and economically significant in growth regressions that included rates of factor accumulation (investment and labor force growth); that deleted OPEC members from the 1974–89 period regressions; that substituted $REVC6088$ and $ASSN6089$ for their 1974–89 counterparts in growth regressions; and that employed the log of initial income.[19]

The coefficients on the institutional variables were somewhat lower when investment was included. This is to be expected; one way that insecure property rights hinder growth is by deterring investment, an effect that is captured by investment itself when it enters the regression. However, it is noteworthy that the institutional variables were still significant, even in the presence of an investment term. This suggests that institutions measured by the BERI and ICRG indices matter not only because secure property rights encourage fixed investments, but also because they encourage the efficient allocation of factor inputs. In response to expropriatory threats of one kind or another, entrepreneurs not only reduce investment, they also invest in less specialized capital (human and physical), which can be moved more easily from one activity to another. This has static efficiency effects, but also discourages dynamic gains from innovation, since innovation is most likely to thrive when specialization is encouraged.

Table 3.4 summarizes parallel regression results for the index of the Gastil variables, $FREE7386$, for the period 1974–89. In no case is this variable significant.[20] The ICRG and BERI indices are in every case significant, however. Moreover, the coefficient on $GDP70$ shows the expected dramatic increase in magnitude when $ICRG82$ and $BERI72$ replace $FREE7386$. This again demonstrates the power of institutions and the extent of additional institutional information provided by these two variables.

Empirical Results—Investment

Another basis for comparing the different institutional variables is in their ability to explain investment. Barro excludes investment from his growth estimations at least implicitly because many of the variables in the growth equation, including institutional variables, operate,

TABLE 3.4. Growth, Institutions, and the Gastil Indices

	BERI			
	(1)	(2)	(3)	(4)
BERI72			0.376	0.381
			2.111	*2.067*
FREE7386		−0.042		0.018
		−0.287		*0.128*
GDP70	−0.501	−0.527	−0.694	−0.686
	−2.751	*−2.565*	*−3.520*	*−3.239*
R^2	0.276	0.277	0.350	0.350
N	46	46	46	46

	ICRG			
	(1)	(2)	(3)	(4)
ICRG82			0.092	0.089
			3.420	*3.234*
FREE7386		−0.111		−0.052
		−1.152		*0.563*
GDP70	−0.401	−0.482	−0.692	−0.720
	−2.564	*−2.815*	*−4.055*	*−4.032*
R^2	0.198	0.210	0.291	0.293
N	97	97	97	97

Note: Dependent variable: Average per capita GDP growth, 1974–89. For other control variables, see tables 3.1 and 3.2. Numbers in italics are *t*-statistics.

at least in part, through factor accumulation. The importance of institutions, then, can also be examined through empirical estimates of the determinants of investment. Barro 1991 estimates variants of the following equation for private investment, for which cross-country data are available beginning in the 1970s.

$$PINV7085 = \alpha + \beta_1 GDP60 + \beta_2 SEC60 + \beta_3 PRIM60$$

$$+ \beta_4 GOVCONS + \beta_5 REV + \beta_6 ASSASS$$

$$+ \beta_7 PPI60DEV + \beta_8 PPI60 + \varepsilon_i \qquad (4)$$

where *PINV7085* is the average ratio of real private investment to real GDP over the period, equal to the ratio of real total investment over real GDP less the same ratio for real public investment. The 1960 purchasing power parity investment deflator (from Summers and Heston 1991) is also employed.[21] Initial income, *GDP60*, enters as a proxy for initial capital stock. The higher the initial capital stock, the greater the effect of diminishing returns on investment, and the less investment that would be expected.

As before, the ICRG and BERI indices perform substantially better than the political violence or Gastil variables: their statistical and economic significance is greater and the explanatory power of models that contain only the ICRG and BERI indices is greater than those that contain the political violence or Gastil measures.

Table 3.5 summarizes the investment results comparing the political violence, ICRG, and BERI indicators. Contrary to the Barro 1991 results for the time period 1960–85, table 3.5 indicates that for the time period 1974–89 revolutions and assassinations are statistically insignificant, alone or in combination with *ICRG82* and *BERI72*, while the institutional indicators are statistically significant wherever they appear.[22] Economically, as well, the institutional indicators offer a more powerful explanation of growth. The sum of the standardized coefficients for *REVC7489* and *ASSN7489* in regression (4) of table 3.5 is −0.31. When the BERI variable enters alone, in regression (5), its standardized coefficient is .815. When the three variables enter together, the difference remains equally dramatic, −.08 versus .77. The ICRG results are qualitatively the same, although the magnitude of

TABLE 3.5.   Investment, Institutions, and Political Violence

	(1)	(2)	(3)	(4)	(5)	(6)
Intercept	0.160	0.112	0.125	0.159	0.124	0.123
	5.188	*3.443*	*3.404*	*2.678*	*2.487*	*2.174*
Institutional variable		0.002	0.001	0.263	0.014	0.014
		2.151	*1.741*	*1.357*	*3.087*	*2.554*
REVC7489	−0.017		−0.014	−0.011		−0.008
	−0.578		*−0.480*	*−0.216*		*−0.174*
ASSN7489	−0.083		−0.042	−0.560		−0.118
	−1.201		*0.072*	*−1.346*		*−0.281*
GDP70	−0.0002	−0.004	−0.004	−0.002	−0.009	−0.009
	−0.050	*−1.000*	*−0.942*	*−0.461*	*−1.754*	*−1.643*
SEC70	0.019	−0.002	0.528	0.033	0.007	0.005
	0.447	*−0.044*	*−0.002*	*0.528*	*0.131*	*0.085*
PRIM70	0.065	0.071	0.067	0.090	0.026	0.037
	2.529	*3.011*	*2.662*	*1.323*	*0.519*	*0.564*
GCON7489	0.005	0.043	0.048	−0.103	−0.215	−0.204
	0.043	*0.345*	*0.381*	*−0.527*	*−1.221*	*−1.105*
PPI74	−0.022	−0.019	−0.014	−0.014	−0.011	−0.011
	−2.549	*−2.325*	*−2.375*	*−1.329*	*−1.136*	*0.359*
R^2	0.312	0.338	0.345	0.215	0.356	0.359
N	69	69	69	38	38	38

Note: Dependent variable is average private investment/GDP, 1974–89. Numbers in italics are *t*-statistics.

the differences in absolute value is smaller: $-.20$ versus $.37$ when they enter in separate equations, and $-.12$ versus $.33$ when they enter in the same equation.[23]

Although variable *GDP70* does not attain high levels of significance, both the magnitude of its coefficient and its significance increase noticeably in the presence of the institutional variables. The low capital stock of countries with poor institutions does not attract investment, despite the possibility of high returns, while the high-capital-stock countries, benefiting from good institutions, continue to attract investment despite diminishing returns. This effect is identified when relatively precise institutional variables are used to explain investment.

Similar results, summarized in table 3.6, were obtained when the Gastil index was substituted for the political violence indicators.

TABLE 3.6.   Private Investment, Institutions, and the Gastil Indices

	BERI		
	(1)	(2)	(3)
BERI72		0.014	0.015
		3.087	*3.299*
FREE7386	0.002		0.005
	0.534		*1.247*
GDP70	−0.0001	−0.009	−0.007
	−0.019	*−1.754*	*−1.233*
PPI74	−0.016	−0.011	−0.014
	−1.444	*−1.136*	*−1.451*
R^2	0.166	0.350	0.388
N	38	38	38

	ICRG		
	(1)	(2)	(3)
ICRG82			0.002
			2.205
FREE7386	0.002	−0.111	0.002
	0.677	*−1.152*	*0.861*
GDP70	0.002	−0.482	−0.003
	0.396	*−2.815*	*−0.685*
PPI74	−0.022		−0.021
	−2.505		*−2.453*
R^2	0.293	0.338	0.345
N	69	69	69

Note: Dependent variable: Average private investment/GDP, 1974–89. For other control variables, see table 3.5. Numbers in italics are *t*-statistics.

FREE7386, entered alone or in combination with *ICRG82* or *BERI72,* is consistently insignificant. The institutional indices are statistically significant in every case and have an economic impact (as measured by standardized parameters) that substantially outweighs the effect of *FREE7386.* In combination with *FREE7386, ICRG82* has a standardized coefficient equal to .386. Alone, *ICRG82* has a standardized coefficient of .375. These not only exceed *FREE7386* (.152 and .123, respectively), but are comparable in magnitude to the other most powerful explanatory variable, enrollment in primary education, which has standardized coefficient estimates uniformly in the range of .35.

The BERI variable is even more impressive, with standardized coefficient estimates ranging as high as .88 compared to the estimate for the Gastil variable of .34, in the regression where they both appear. The BERI variable is the most statistically and economically significant explanatory variable in those investment equations in which it appears, for the sample of 38 countries for which BERI and private investment data is available. Finally, once again, the coefficient on initial income, *GDP70,* becomes larger and more significant in the presence of the institutional variables, demonstrating once again the importance of controlling for institutions in identifying diminishing returns to capital.

Conclusion

These results offer strong support for three propositions. First, political violence and the Gastil political and civil liberties indicators are insufficient proxies for the quality of the institutions that protect property rights. More direct indicators are needed to properly account for the influence of institutions. Second, institutions that protect property rights are crucial to economic growth and to investment. Some of the regressions point to effects that rival even those of education. Moreover, the effect of institutions on growth persists even after controlling for investment. This suggests that the security of property rights affects not only the magnitude of investment, but also the efficiency with which inputs are allocated. Third, when institutions are controlled for, stronger evidence emerges for conditional convergence. The coefficients on initial income, from which conditional convergence or diminishing returns to capital are evaluated, rise in both statistical and economic significance in the presence of the ICRG and BERI indices of institutional quality.

Notes

This chapter was originally published under the same title in *Economics and Politics* 7 (3) (November 1995): 207–27. It is reprinted with permission from Blackwell Publishing.

1. See also Olson 1982 and Weingast 1993.

2. Kormendi and Meguire (1985) and others assert that the Gastil indices are probably correlated with economic rights. They obtain very significant results using the Gastil civil liberties index as an explanation of rates of investment. We do not find the Gastil indices to be significant determinants of investment; the different results are likely due to their smaller sample, and to the fact that their Gastil index is from 1979, close to the end of their growth period, raising issues of simultaneity.

3. Alesina, Ozler, Roubini, and Swagel (1996) find no impact of growth on a broad measure of government turnover, but do find a significant impact of contemporaneous growth on coups.

4. Researchers using the Gastil data have found evidence that causality works from growth to better scores on the Gastil indices, rather than the reverse. See Bilson 1982 and Helliwell 1994.

5. See Weingast 1993 and Keefer 1993 for a discussion of the effects of government credibility on investment and growth.

6. The predominance of trading as the object of most new entrepreneurial effort in Russia during the transition is likely due not only to the high returns to trading, but also to the low returns to other forms of economic activity that are driven down by riskiness of investments and the difficulties of making credible deals with corrupt government officials.

7. Poorer countries are likely to score lower on this measure. The correlation coefficient for 1972 values of the infrastructure variable and income per capita in 1970 is .87.

8. For example, weighting by factor scores generated from factor analysis yields scales correlated at .99 with the simple additive indices for ICRG and BERI.

9. Barro and Lee (1993) similarly argue that political violence indicators averaged over a longer period may contain more information relevant to current investment decisions than do indicators averaged over more recent but shorter periods.

10. The Spearman rank correlation coefficients for the BERI data are substantially higher than the Pearson coefficients for the revolutions and coups variables. *BERI72* has a Spearman correlation of $-.60$ with *REVC7488* and $-.72$ with *REVC6088*.

11. Like Barro and others, we assume that institutions do not affect *g*, the rate of improvement in institutions and technology.

12. Other research has employed the log of initial GDP. The regressions reported later, employing initial GDP, were also run with the log of this vari-

able. In nearly all cases the qualitative findings, that the institutional variables add significant additional information that explains growth, remain unchanged (see note 19 for the exception).

13. Barro 1991 uses economic growth and investment data from Summers-Heston. For this essay, data on these variables come from the World Bank and are taken from Levine and Renelt 1992.

14. See McMillan, Rausser, and Johnson 1991, Islam 1993, and Knight, Loayza, and Villanueva 1993 for different econometric approaches to this problem in the context of cross-country growth equations.

15. To fully adjust to the use of the later period, the following other control variables are used: *PPIDEV74, GCON7489, PRIM70, SEC70,* and *GDP70. GCON7489* is from the World Bank (Levine and Renelt 1992) and includes education and defense expenditures. Government consumption in Barro 1991 does not include these expenditures.

16. The adjusted R^2 ratios are low by the standards of the literature on cross-country regressions because the sample only extends for sixteen years (1974–89). Similar results, with more typical R^2 ratios (in the .5 to .6 range), are obtained when the longer period (1960–89) is used. However, by focusing on the shorter period, we mitigate the causality issues that have arisen in earlier uses of the Gastil data, by Kormendi and Meguire (1985), Scully (1988), and others, in which growth periods beginning in 1950 or 1960 are examined despite the fact that the Gastil indices cover the period 1973–85.

17. The work of Mankiw, Romer, and Weil (1992) and others has already indicated that human capital is a significant determinant of conditional convergence.

18. Using log of initial income and the BERI sample of countries, and including the two political violence indicators along with *BERI72,* all three variables are statistically insignificant, although *BERI72* is more significant than *ASSN7489,* and the standardized estimate of *BERI72* is equal to the sum of the standardized estimates of the two political violence indicators.

19. These regressions were also run using the original Barro (1991) period of 1960–85. The results were similar in all respects. The institutional variables performed better, in terms of both statistical significance and economic impact, than the political violence variables. Moreover, the coefficients on initial income (*GDP60*) exhibited the expected increase in statistical significance and magnitude when the institutional variables were added, suggesting once again that the institutions that protect property rights are key determinants of the steady state of income that conditions rates of convergence.

20. Helliwell (1994) finds that the Gastil variable fails to predict growth for the 1960–85 period.

21. Barro runs this model with and without dummy variables for Africa and Latin America. These dummies remain significant even in the presence of the ICRG and BERI indices, suggesting either that our indices incompletely

describe the institutional characteristics that distinguish countries on these continents, or that there are noninstitutional idiosyncrasies that must also be taken into account. They might also become insignificant if we were better able to control possible endogeneity between the institutional indices and growth. Using a simultaneous equations methodology to examine the relationship of growth and political stability, Alesina et al. (1996) find that these dummies are insignificant in two of their three specifications.

22. The ICRG/BERI variables are much weaker at predicting total investment. This is consistent with the theory, however. We would not expect public investment to be sensitive to risks of expropriation.

23. Regressions comparing the institutional and the political violence indicators were also run using the original Barro 1991 specification (his regression [20]), covering investment over the period 1970–85, but independent variables from 1960. The results were unchanged; the ICRG and BERI variables were at least as significant as the political violence indicators, either in combination with them, or entered separately.

References

Alesina, A., S. Ozler, N. Roubini, and P. Swagel. 1996. "Political Instability and Economic Growth." *Journal of Economic Growth* 1:189–211.

Barro, R. 1991. "Economic Growth in a Cross Section of Countries." *Quarterly Journal qf Economics* 106:407–44.

Barro, R., and J. Lee. 1993. "International Comparisons of Educational Attainment." *Journal of Monetary Economics* 32 (3): 363–94.

Barro, R., and X. Sala-i-Martin. 1992a. "Convergence." *Journal of Political Economy* 100:223.

————. 1992b. "Convergence across States and Regions." In A. Cukierman et al., eds., *Political Economy, Growth, and Business Cycles.* Cambridge: MIT Press.

Bilson, J. 1982. "Civil Liberty: An Econometric Investigation." *Kyklos* 35: 94–114.

Gastil, R. D. 1983. *Freedom in the World.* Westport, CT: Greenwood.

Grier, Kevin B., and Gordon Tullock. 1989. "An Empirical Analysis of Cross-National Economic Growth, 1951–80." *Journal of Monetary Economics* 24:259–76.

Helliwell, J. F. 1994. "Empirical Linkages between Democracy and Economic Growth." *British Journal of Political Science* 24:225–48.

Islam, N. 1993. "Growth Empirics: A Panel Data Approach." Manuscript, Harvard University Department of Economics.

Keefer, P. 1993. "Institutions, Credibility and the Costs of Rent-seeking." Manuscript, the IRIS Center, University of Maryland.

Knight, M., N. Loayza, and D. Villanueva. 1993. "Testing the Neoclassical Theory of Economic Growth." *IMF Staff Papers* 40 (3): 512–32.

Kormendi, R. C., and P. G. Meguire. 1985. "Macroeconomic Determinants of Growth: Cross-Country Evidence." *Journal of Monetary Economics* 16:141–63.

Levine, R., and D. Renelt. 1992. "A Sensitivity Analysis of Cross-Country Growth Regressions." *American Economic Review* 82:942–63.

Londregan, J. B., and K. T. Poole. 1990. "Poverty, the Coup Trap, and the Seizure of Executive Power." *World Politics* 42:151–83.

Mankiw, N. G., D. Romer, and D. N. Weil. 1992. "A Contribution to the Empirics of Economic Growth." *Quarterly Journal of Economics* 107:407–37.

McMillan, J., G. Rausser, and S. Johnson. 1991. "Freedoms and Economic Growth." Working Paper, Institute for Policy Reform.

North, D. 1990. *Institutions, Institutional Change and Economic Performance.* Cambridge: Cambridge University Press.

Olson, M. 1982. *The Rise and Decline of Nations.* New Haven: Yale University Press.

Rama, M. 1993. "Rent-Seeking and Economic Growth: A Theoretical Model and Some Empirical Evidence." *Journal of Development Economics* 42:35–50

Scully, G. W. 1988. "The Institutional Framework and Economic Development." *Journal of Political Economy* 96:52–62.

Summers, R., and A. Heston. 1991. "The Penn World Table (Mark V): An Extended Set of International Comparisons, 1950–88." *Quarterly Journal of Economics* 106:327–36.

Tornell, A., and A. Velasco. 1992. "The Tragedy of the Commons and Economic Growth: Why Does Capital Flow from Poor to Rich Countries?" *Journal of Political Economy* 100 (6): 1208–31.

Weingast, B. 1993. "The Political Foundations of Democracy and the Rule of Law." IRIS Working Paper No. 54.

CHAPTER 4

Contract-Intensive Money: Contract Enforcement, Property Rights, and Economic Performance

Christopher Clague, Philip Keefer,
Stephen Knack, and Mancur Olson

1. Introduction

Markets are commonplace in all types of societies, including the poorest, and they exist even in remarkably unfavorable conditions. Herodotus, for example, describes Phoenician merchants who traded even with distant tribes with whom they shared no government or language. A long-standing literature on "silent trade" among those who cannot communicate directly includes accounts of tribes that traded when at war (Grierson 1904). Long experience with black markets in many countries confirms that markets persist even when they are prohibited. Nevertheless, some markets that are essential for economic development are less common and more easily repressed. These are markets in which economic actors make exchanges requiring significant and irreversible commitments in the present, whether in the form of goods manufactured and shipped or fixed investments made, in the expectation of payment or a stream of returns in the future.

These markets are less likely to exist when institutions for the protection of property rights and contract enforcement are absent. The importance of these institutions is now widely acknowledged, and emphasized in the work of North (1990), Rosenberg and Birdzell (1986), and others. Recent studies of growth have employed subjective indicators of contract enforcement and the security of property rights (see chapter 3, this volume, and Borner, Brunetti, and Weder 1995) to provide significant empirical support for the proposition that the absence of these institutions is a severe impediment to growth. This essay makes two contributions to the literature. First, it introduces a new, easily accessed, and objective measure of the enforceability of contracts and the security of property rights. Second, it uses this measure to provide additional and more direct evidence about the importance of secure property and contract rights for economic growth and investment. In the following analysis, we briefly review the arguments that link the quality of third-party contract enforcement to growth and investment. We then show how the new measure, which we call contract-intensive money, relates to the subjective measures employed in the literature. We test empirically the proposition that this variable, as a measure of the security of contract and property rights, is positively related to income, growth, and investment.

2. Why Does Government Enforcement of Contracts Matter?

The markets that are most likely to persist even in unfriendly environments are those in which exchange is simultaneous and self-enforcing. Such markets are common, either because many exchanges simply meet the conditions for self-enforcement or because they are so lucrative that even risky exchanges are worthwhile (despite the absence of self-enforcement). However, many transactions require a different kind of market, one more likely to need third-party enforcement. These are nonsimultaneous transactions, in which the quid is needed at one time or place and the quo at another. When there is lending and borrowing, capital is lent in expectation of a later return. When a demander and a supplier are some distance apart, someone must be at risk for the value of the goods in transit. When there is insurance, some parties must make payments now in hope of indemnification if specified contingencies occur. In all of these cases, the gains from trade cannot be realized unless the parties expect that the contracts they make will be carried out.

For example, we do not often see sophisticated capital markets where there is no third-party enforcement of loan contracts or of rules protecting agreements between shareholders and management, or between minority and majority shareholders (see La Porta et al. 1998). Firms in societies without third-party enforcement are usually restricted to capital that can be obtained through saving or family connections. Gains from either capital-intensive or large-scale production are accordingly lost in these societies. The absence of these exchanges hinders investment and growth. Since investment is usually required for innovation and the purchase of new technologies as well as capital deepening, contract enforcement also affects the rate of growth.

The contract-intensive money indicator of property rights enforcement that we introduce later indicates the countries and periods in which nonsimultaneous transactions are more difficult to enforce. Inadequacies in government-provided third-party enforcement are likely to be a principal reason for these difficulties.[1] It is true, even in societies with the best legal systems, that most disagreements are resolved without being taken to court (Williamson 1983, 1985). One reason, as David Hume noted long ago, is that a reputation for honoring commitments is valuable (see also Hayek 1948, and many others since). Other agreements are made self-enforcing by allowing valuables to be held hostage (as, most simply, in a pawnshop loan). It is not even the case that third-party resolution of disputes is solely the province of government, since arbitration and dispute settlement services are also available in the private sector. Moreover, countries are likely to vary in their capacity to support reputation and other self-enforcement mechanisms.[2]

Nevertheless, the market has clear limits in enforcing contracts. Reputation is of more limited utility for transactions in which the actors involved deal with each other infrequently. Neither reputation nor socially acceptable hostages are useful when transactions are exceptionally large or performance can only be verified over a long period of time. Private institutions that disseminate information on contract violations are less useful when the reasons for breach of contract cannot be conveyed; when firms that receive the information fail to impose the appropriate punishment strategy; when firms that breach contracts are able to mask their identities; and when the contractual arrangements that undergird the existence of the organization that collects and disseminates information about breaches of contract are themselves unenforceable.

Even after accounting for the effects of self-enforcement, then, the government still has four crucial roles to play in contract enforcement and the protection of property rights. First, it provides third-party enforcement when no self-enforcing mechanism exists. Second, it may itself constitute the entity that communicates breaches of contract. Third, it may enforce the arrangements that private actors use to constitute themselves as a formal group (such as a trade association). Fourth, and most elementally, the government ensures peace: if there is a Hobbesian anarchy, a reputation for effective violence is worth more than one for honoring commercial contracts. But whatever authority has the power to maintain peace also has the power to enforce or to abrogate contracts. It follows that even if private agents could, without recourse to governments or other third parties, engage in every profitable investment or exchange by relying on self-enforcement, they would still confront the possibility that the government could expropriate them. Differences in the behavior of governments therefore make for cross-country differences in property rights, contract enforcement, and levels of productivity and growth.

3. Testing the Theory: Contract-Intensive Money

In testing our argument that secure property and contract rights are crucial for productivity and growth, we take advantage of a fortuitous circumstance, that enforcement problems underlying the use of different forms of money and credit mirror enforcement problems underlying trade in goods and services in much the way a negative resembles a print. Though the gains from issuing money ensure that it is available everywhere, the types of money that are most widely used vary greatly from country to country. In some countries, currency is the only money that is widely used. In others, individuals and firms are more likely to use the types of money that are held in banks or invested in other financial institutions or instruments. Characteristics of third-party contract enforcement in countries are likely to explain much of the difference in firm and individual preferences governing the choice of money to use. This, and the fact that data on both types of money usage are regularly reported and widely available, make a monetary measure of the security of property and contract rights an attractive one to investigate.

There are several reasons why the same governmental deficiencies that require self-enforcement of transactions also lead economic actors to prefer currency. If contracts are generally unreliable, there can be no assurance that the money lent to financial institutions is safe. Moreover, when financial institutions cannot rely on third-party enforcement of loan contracts—and when property rights are not clear, so that lenders do not have secure rights to mortgaged assets in the event of borrowers' defaults—then they cannot earn as much with the depositors' money. This means in turn that there will be less financial intermediation and higher charges for banking services. Finally, where governments choose to prohibit many transactions, creating black markets in which contracts are inherently insecure, the discretion afforded by currency is likely to make it a favored medium of exchange.

In societies where contract and property rights are secure and well defined, on the other hand, even transactions that are heavily reliant on outside enforcement can be advantageous, and currency is normally used only for small transactions. In such environments, it is also profitable to provide extensive banking and financial intermediation services. Individuals and firms are increasingly able to invest their currency in bank deposits or financial instruments, and they are likely to prefer these to currency for several reasons. They are normally safer and more convenient than currency. These instruments are also more lucrative, since interest is generally paid on such deposits, unlike currency holdings. As is evident from the work of Townsend (1983), when more sophisticated forms of money and trade credit are available, individuals and firms not only can trade without a double coincidence of wants, but they are also spared much of the opportunity cost of significant intervals between the receipt and the spending of money. A final advantage of using monies in financial institutions is that this provides records that enhance the legal rights of the parties and thereby reduce their risks.

Thus the extent to which societies can capture not only the gains from self-enforcing transactions, but also those potential trades that are intensive in contract enforcement and property rights, can be approximated by the *relative* use of currency in comparison with contract-intensive money. We define contract-intensive money (CIM) as the ratio of noncurrency money to the total money supply, or $(M_2 - C)/M_2$, where M_2 is a broad definition of the money supply and C is currency held outside banks. Fortunately, there are data on the quantities of both currency and M_2 for almost all countries.[3] Each firm and individual can decide, after taking account of the type of governance in that society, in what form it wants to holds its assets. Where citizens believe that there is sufficient third-party enforcement, they are more likely to allow other parties to hold their money in exchange for some compensation, and CIM is correspondingly higher.

The discussion suggests the following set of hypotheses. First, if CIM is a good proxy for contractual enforcement more generally, then the higher a country's CIM ratio, the larger the share of GDP that should be generated by industries that are especially dependent on third-party enforcement, such as those involved with insurance and capital markets. Second, the higher CIM, the more gains from economies of scale and specialization a country should reap and thus the higher its capital stock, productivity, and per capita income. Third, the higher CIM, the greater the ability of firms to raise capital, the higher the rate of investment and (other things, like the opportunity for catch-up growth, equal) the faster the rate of economic growth. However, secure individual rights to contract enforcement and to property will help most in obtaining those gains from trade and specialization that can be completed only over a long period of time, such as those involving long-term loans. Therefore, CIM should be more closely associated with the gains from trade in the capital market than with the gains from trade in the economy as a whole, and thus better correlated with investment than with growth.

Note that we are *not* suggesting that the greater use of more sophisticated, noncurrency monies *causes* better economic performance; we are hypothesizing instead that better institutions, especially with respect to contract enforcement, enable a society to obtain a wider array of (real) gains from trade and, at the same time, facilitate the use of more sophisticated forms of money. Thus CIM is a reflection or measure of the type of governance that improves economic performance rather than a cause of that performance.

Before we turn to the statistical tests of our hypotheses, we examine, in section 4, some especially instructive country cases. Since the CIM ratio offers not only a precise test of our theory, but also a new measure of the quality of governance and institutions, we relate it, in section 5, to other measures of quality of governance. We then present in sections 6 through 8 a variety of evidence that stronger economic performance is associated with higher values of CIM. Sections 9 and 10 respond to possible objections to our tests. Section 11 concludes.

4. CIM Case Studies

If CIM is a good measure of the security of contract and property rights, dramatic political events or changes of regime affecting these rights should change the CIM ratio. They do, and in directions that are consistent with our argument. We looked for countries that experienced sharp and sudden political changes and present CIM time-series graphs, along with a brief summary of political events for each of these countries. Where data are available from IFS Yearbooks, we trace CIM from 1960 forward; for other countries, the beginning date is 1969.

Iran

The Shah ruled Iran from the 1950s until he was overthrown by a revolution led by Khomeini in 1978. The new regime had no respect for the rights of those who had been allied with the old regime or who did not fully support the new regime and follow its religious doctrine. There was a period of revolutionary turmoil and a dramatic change in the social order. Iraq launched a war against Iran in September 1980 that lasted until 1988. CIM was at relatively high and stable levels under the Shah, then dropped sharply with Khomeini's takeover, the revolutionary turmoil, and the attack by Iraq. As the new regime established a relatively stable order and as the war with Iraq came to an end, the CIM ratio increased and approached its former level (fig. 4.1).

The Gambia

Sir Dawda Jawara led Gambia from 1962 through 1992, winning re-election in several meaningful elections. In October 1980, however, the Gambian government had, out of fear of a coup by its own military, requested that Senegal station troops in the Gambia. In 1981, while Sir Dawda was out of the country, left-wing rebels staged a coup that was suppressed only with the help of Senegalese troops. The data indicate a substantial upward trend in the contract-intensive money ratio from 1969 to 1990 (consistent with the general stability of the regime) that is interrupted in the 1978–82 period (fig. 4.2).

Chile

Following a period of unsustainable expansionary policies, accelerating inflation, and some moves by the Allende government away from a market economy based on private property, a military government took over in 1973. Within a few years the new government dramatically changed economic management in the direction of economic orthodoxy in microeconomic, monetary, and fiscal policies. The late 1970s and early 1980s witnessed a degree of unorthodoxy in the use of exchange-rate policy to combat inflation, and these policies, perhaps combined with the explosion of the Mexican debt crisis in 1982, produced a banking crisis in 1982, followed by a severe recession. By 1985 the severe recession was over, macroeconomic policy seemed to be back on track, and the regime continued to pursue its economically orthodox policies including deregulation and privatization of the economy. The data show a marked decline in CIM in the early 1970s, followed by a dramatic rise in the ratio in the late 1970s, remaining at a very high level since the mid-1980s. The ratio exhibited

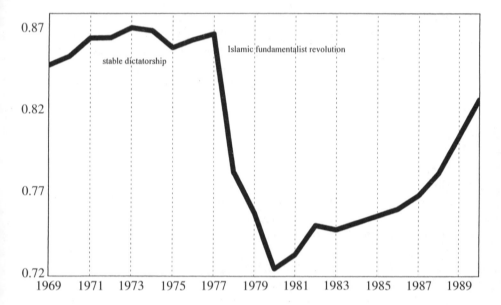

Fig. 4.1. The Republic of Iran (CIM vs. Time)

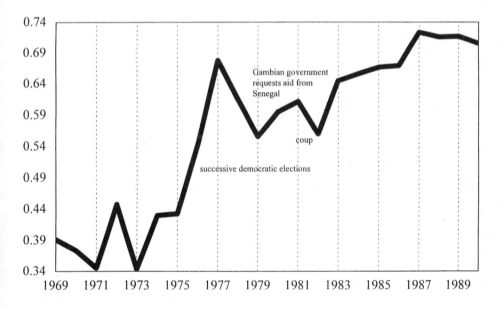

Fig. 4.2. The Gambia (CIM vs. Time)

only a moderate negative reaction to the macroeconomic and financial crisis of the early 1980s, suggesting that CIM was not very sensitive to the problems of the financial sector and that its increase in the late 1970s and its steadiness at a high level in the 1980s was mainly a consequence of the security of contract enforcement and property rights (fig. 4.3).

Brazil

There was a similar dramatic change in economic policy in Brazil after the military coup in 1964. Recession occurred in 1965 and 1966, as the new regime brought inflation down from the high level in the last years under Goulart. From 1967 to 1974 there was what has been described as "the economic miracle," and growth remained high during the 1970s, although it was based on excessive foreign borrowing and was ultimately unsustainable (fig. 4.4).

The data for Brazil from the IFS yearbooks do not correspond to the data on the IFS tapes for the years 1969–70. Thus there is a break in the series. The data in the earlier series show a fairly constant level of CIM during 1960 through 1964, followed by a jump in 1965 and a gradual rise in the late 1960s. The later series shows a further rise during the 1970s and 1980s. The data for Brazil stop in 1985.

Grenada

According to the *Europa Yearbook,* Grenada functioned as a democracy during its preindependence years in the 1960s and through independence in 1974. But Grenada was not a placid democracy like its neighbor, Barbados. In the late 1970s the opposition accused Prime Minister Gairy of being autocratic and corrupt, and in 1979, Maurice Bishop, the leader of the left-wing PRG (People's Revolutionary Government), led a bloodless coup. The constitution was suspended. During 1980 and 1981 there was an increase in repression and mounting fears by the PRG of an invasion by the United States. During 1982 Grenada was aligning itself with Cuba and the USSR. In 1983 the armed forces were put on alert out of fear of a U.S. invasion. Bishop tried to conciliate the United States, but was assassinated in a coup by more radical forces. The U.S. invasion occurred in October 1983. By December, most American troops had pulled out. There were preparations during 1984 for elections, which were held in December. Though there was tension over the trial of the coup leaders

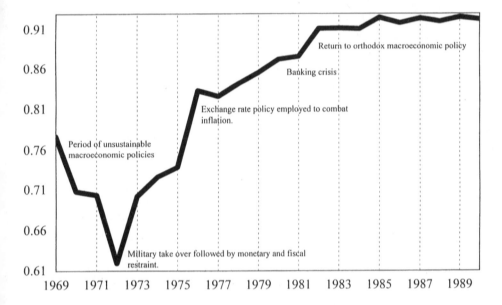

Fig. 4.3. Chile (CIM vs. Time)

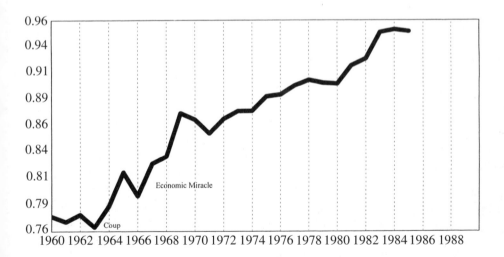

Fig. 4.4. Brazil (CIM vs. Time)

and restrictions on some left-wing politicians in 1988 and 1989, there was a return to democracy and relative stability.

Though there is a break in the data series for Grenada in 1983,[4] the year of the second coup and the U.S. intervention, the data are nonetheless instructive. From the mid-1970s to 1983, when political developments must have made contract and property rights less secure, there was a large decline in CIM. The new data-series starting in 1984 shows an increase in CIM along with the installation and gradual consolidation of a new democratic regime (fig. 4.5).

Turkey

The following summary paraphrases Haggard and Kaufman (1992, 289). The democratic government began losing control over the economy in the late 1970s. There was political fragmentation under proportional representation: government coalitions proved difficult to form, were hostage to the demands of small antisystem parties, and were pulled toward policy positions more radical than those of most of the electorate. In these circumstances it was difficult to cut government expenditure or adjust to the withdrawal of foreign lending. A stabilization program was announced in January 1980, but the government was quickly deadlocked over political issues and was ousted by the military in September. An economist, Ozal, became the leading economic policymaker under the military, and he won the (less-than-free) election held in 1983. In 1988, after democracy had been restored, he was reelected.

The data show a flat level of the CIM ratio from 1972 to 1975, followed by a decline to 1978. There was a slight recovery in 1979 and 1980, a jump in 1981, followed by a gradual rise to 1986, and then another mild decline in the late 1980s (fig. 4.6).

Indonesia

In the 1960s the country suffered serious macroeconomic and political instability. In 1965 an attempted communist takeover failed and was followed by a civil war in which millions were killed and the communists suppressed. In 1966 Western-trained economists gained Suharto's ear, and a stabilization program was carried out in the late 1960s. After 1970 Indonesia was ruled by a stable single-party government with an economic bureaucracy that was, because of the low level of independent interest-group mobilization and the absence of

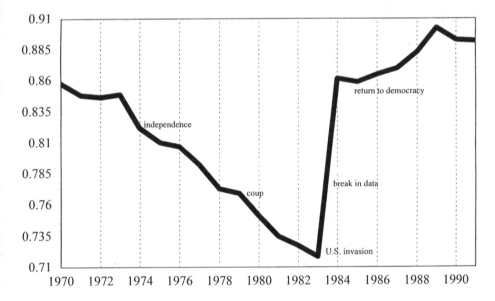

Fig. 4.5. Grenada (CIM vs. Time)

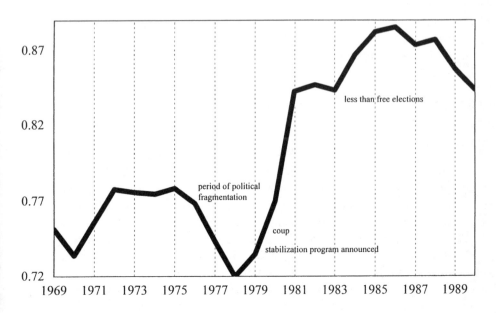

Fig. 4.6. Turkey (CIM vs. Time)

electoral pressures, relatively insulated and able to continue orthodox economic policies (see also Haggard and Kaufman 1992, 289).

The data show a fairly flat level of CIM in the early 1960s; there
are no data for 1963 and 1964. There is some rise from 1965 to 1968,
consistent with the end of the civil war, followed by a dramatic and
sustained rise from 1970 onward as the new regime showed evidence
of considerable staying power, predictable enforcement of contract
and property rights, and prudence in the management of economic
policy (fig. 4.7).

Most of the preceding countries fall into two main groups. In one
group of countries—Chile, Brazil, and Indonesia—weak governments with ill-chosen interventionist economic policies were replaced by strong military dictatorships in which economic tech-
nocrats had considerable influence. In all three cases, the CIM ratio
rose dramatically after the change in government and economic
policies. In the second group of countries—the Gambia, Grenada,
and Turkey—a democratic regime suffered a period of political uncertainty with an actual or threatened military coup, and then after
a time democratic stability was restored. During the period of turmoil there was a decline in the CIM ratio, but this ratio rose again
after the restoration of democracy. These patterns are consistent
with related work the authors have done (see chapter 6, this volume)
suggesting that the security of contract and property rights is greater
under strong and secure autocrats than under those of short tenure
or in transient democracies, and it reaches the highest levels in lasting democracies.

5. CIM and Complementary Measures of the Quality of Governance

The specific country examples offer reassurance that contract-intensive money mirrors real changes in politics, institutions, and economic
policies. In this section we provide evidence that it is also positively
correlated with independent measures of quality of governance and
institutions used in prior studies. These independent measures are
systematic subjective ratings generated by scholars, such as Gastil's
indexes of political freedoms and civil liberties (used, for example, in
Scully 1988), or produced by private firms that meet the market test
by selling their measures of political and institutional risk to investors, such as the ICRG, BERI, and BI ratings used by Knack and
Keefer (chapter 3, this volume), Mauro (1995), and many others.

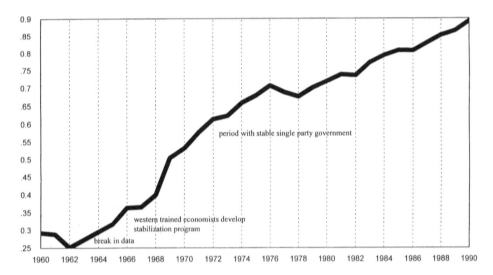

Fig. 4.7. Indonesia (CIM vs. Time)

There is a danger that these subjective measures may be influenced by outcomes—when economic performance is good, the
evaluators may be subtly induced to report that governance is also
good. The CIM ratio may also have some limitations; a study of the
period averages for individual countries suggests that some of the
cross-country variation in CIM may be idiosyncratic and have little to
do with differences in contract enforcement and security of property.[5] Fortunately, because the subjective measures and CIM—which
is an objective outcome of portfolio decisions by individuals and
firms in the countries at issue—are generated by different and independent processes, they almost certainly have no idiosyncrasies or biases in common. Thus it is a good sign for CIM, and for the subjective
measures, that CIM's correlations with these complementary measures of institutional quality are fairly high and remarkably consistent (at .62 or .63). Each type of measure adds credibility to the other.

Beyond its objectivity and precision as an indicator of property
rights security, CIM also has the virtue of being readily available on
a timely basis for a large number of countries (and for many of them
the data go back quite a number of years). Since CIM appears to be
both a credible and a useful new measure of the quality of a country's
institutions and economic policies, we proceed to test its relationship
to economic outcomes.

6. Governance and the Size of Finance and Other Contract-Dependent Sectors

The first hypothesis suggested by the foregoing discussion is that those sectors of the economy that are especially dependent on contract enforcement should be relatively larger in those countries with better contract enforcement and property rights. Levine (1998) provides evidence that subjective indicators of property rights are an important determinant of the extent of financial intermediation in a country and concludes that "countries that effectively enforce compliance with laws [governing the legal rights of creditors, among other things] tend to have better-developed banks than countries where enforcement is lax" (598). In this section, we expand on this theme by showing that CIM as well as the subjective measures are positively associated with the development of a wide range of contract-intensive activities.

The insurance industry, for example, is exceptionally dependent on contract enforcement, since those who pay premiums receive nothing on the spot and can benefit from insurance only if the policy contract is honored when there is a valid claim, often long after the contract has been signed. Accordingly, we obtained data on insurance premiums as a percent of gross national product up to 1994 from the International Insurance Council and tested whether CIM and other measures of institutional quality predicted average insurance premiums (from the five years 1990 through 1994) over GDP for the period. Since the demand for insurance may be related to income and wealth, we controlled for per capita GDP (1990). As table 4.1 shows, there is a statistically significant positive association between CIM (and ICRG and BERI) and the relative size of the insurance industry. Each 10-percentage-point rise in CIM is associated with a rise in the insurance share of GDP of about 1.2 percentage points—a sizable amount, since on average the insurance sector comprises 4 percent of GDP.

To obtain the broadest reasonable measure of the industries that are especially dependent on contract enforcement, we took the aggregate of the finance, insurance, real estate, and business services sectors as a percentage of GDP from the UN National Accounts data. This measure was available for more countries and years than were the insurance data, so we use the average of this variable over the 1980–90 decade as the dependent variable in equations 4, 5, and 6 in table 4.1. Again, all three of the measures of institutional quality are positively related to the size of the financial sector, holding per capita income (1980) constant, and all but one of the relationships are statistically significant.

7. CIM and the Level of Income and Wealth

The second hypothesis generated by our argument is that the better are institutions as measured by CIM, the greater the degree of specialization and the gains from trade and the higher the level of capital accumulation, productivity, and per capita income. We test this hypothesis using the specifications introduced by Hall and Jones (1996) in their study of the determinants of income per worker in 1988. Hall and Jones include the ICRG index of property rights along with several other independent variables (listed in the note to our table 4.2). We replicate their regressions for the countries in their sample for which CIM data are available, except that we replace ICRG with CIM in one case and add CIM in another (leaving ICRG as one of the Hall and Jones base regressors). Coefficients and standard errors for CIM and ICRG (but not for the other Hall-Jones regressors) are shown in table 4.2. Adjusted R^2-values in the first two rows of the top panel of table 4.2 show that CIM's explanatory power slightly ex-

TABLE 4.1.   Contract-Intensive Money and the Financial Sector

Dependent Variable	Insurance/GDP, 1990–94			Finance/GDP, 1980–90		
Equation	1	2	3	4	5	6
Constant	−17.060	−4.471	−8.137	−12.516	−12.006	−11.969
	(2.498)	(4.453)	(3.275)	(2.515)	(3.685)	(6.547)
Initial (log) GDP	1.679	0.385	0.534	1.822	2.295	2.535
per capita	(0.456)	(0.694)	(0.581)	(0.447)	(0.484)	(1.031)
Contract-	7.682			11.007		
intensive money	(2.765)			(2.686)		
ICRG		0.153			0.186	
		(0.048)			(0.062)	
BERI			1.132			0.392
			(0.308)			(0.445)
Adj. R^2	.47	.41	.55	.41	.34	.26
N	57	62	44	104	78	45
Mean, D.V.	3.90	4.07	4.31	10.7	10.3	12.1

Note: Standard errors (in parentheses) are computed using White's heteroskedastic-consistent variance/covariance matrix. Finance/GDP is the percentage of GDP accounted for by finance, insurance, real estate, and business services, from UN National Accounts data.

ceeds that of ICRG and that CIM is a significant determinant of income per worker even in the presence of ICRG.

Hall and Jones also estimate determinants of factor accumulation, first physical capital, then human capital. The second panel replicates their regressions of capital stock per worker, as estimated by them, on the same independent variables, with results broadly similar to those in the first panel. The third panel replicates the Hall-Jones human capital equation, in which they use the Barro-Lee (1993) educational attainment measure for 1985 as the dependent variable. Again, CIM (with or without ICRG in the model) is significantly related to factor accumulation. Finally, Hall and Jones estimated total factor productivity as a residual, regressing these estimates on the same set of independent variables. The bottom panel of table 4.2 shows that total

TABLE 4.2. CIM and Levels of Output, Factor Accumulation, and TFP Summaries of Regression Results

	CIM	ICRG	R^2
Log output/worker, 1988		1.938	
		(0.411)	.78
	1.852		
	(0.384)		.79
	1.393	1.274	
	(0.422)	(0.428)	.80
Log capital/worker, 1988		3.446	.69
		(0.685)	
	4.143		.74
	(0.569)		
	3.504	1.772	.75
	(0.656)	(0.735)	
Schooling/worker, 1985		8.356	.74
		(1.245)	
	5.736		.70
	(1.204)		
	3.290	6.787	.76
	(1.203)	(1.336)	
Log TFP, 1988		0.488	.66
		(0.299)	
	0.816		.68
	(0.312)		
	0.773	0.120	.67
	(0.339)	(0.319)	

Note: Cells of table report coefficients for CIM and ICRG. White-corrected standard errors are in parentheses. Other independent variables in every equation are: latitude (distance from the equator), percent English-speaking, percent speaking another "international language," dummies for "capitalist-statist" and "capitalist" systems ("statist" is reference category), and fraction of years from 1950–94 with open economy (from Sachs and Warner 1995). Sample size is 110.

factor productivity is significantly related to CIM. The correlation be-tween CIM and the level of economic development does not depend on the Hall-Jones specification; we obtained similar results with other specifications.

8. CIM, Investment, and Growth

In this section, we enter contract-intensive money into widely used cross-country investment and growth regressions. Variable defini-tions, data sources, and descriptive statistics used in these regressions are provided in the appendix. The independent variables we employ in addition to CIM are conventional in this literature (see Barro 1991; Levine and Renelt 1992). Higher initial GDP per capita should be associated with lower productivity of additional investment and lower subsequent growth. The relative price of investment goods as a percentage of the U.S. level should be negatively associated with in-vestment. Schooling attainment, measured as the mean years of com-pleted education for the population aged 25 and over, is a proxy for human capital.[6] Bruno and Easterly (1998) and others have found that inflation can have a negative effect on investment and growth. To ensure that inflation's effects on currency demand do not influence our results, we therefore add a measure of inflation to each regres-sion. This is the depreciation in the real value of money introduced by Cukierman and Webb (1995), that is, DEP = INF/(100 + INF), where INF is the rate of inflation in percent. (We consider inflation in more detail in section 10.)

The regression results on the determination of the ratio of invest-ment/GDP, averaged over the 1970–92 period for which CIM data are consistently available for a large sample, are shown in table 4.3. Equation 1 shows a strong, positive, and highly significant relation-ship between CIM and investment. Results for CIM are very similar for a subsample of developing (non-OECD) nations in equation 2, in-dicating that CIM is not merely capturing broad differences between the groups of developed and developing nations.

Standardized estimates of CIM's association with investment are large relative to those of other independent variables. A one-standard-deviation increase in CIM (i.e., an increase of .14) in equation 1 is as-sociated with an increase in investment as a proportion of GDP of one-third of a standard deviation, or about 3 percentage points. This effect exceeds the impact of a one-standard-deviation increase of any one of the other four independent variables.

TABLE 4.3. Contract-Intensive Money and Investment/GDP, 1970–92

Variation	Basic Model	Non-OECD	CIM 1969	CIM 1990	Robust Regression	Median Regression	M₂/GDP Added
Equation	1	2	3	4	5	6	7
Constant	-16.064	-9.882	-12.512	-12.698	-14.765	-11.852	-10.061
	(5.816)	(6.210)	(5.848)	(5.648)	(7.203)	(7.998)	(5.499)
Log 1970 GDP per capita	2.359	1.658	2.638	2.595	2.267	2.059	0.933
	(0.810)	(0.899)	(0.781)	(0.817)	(1.000)	(1.115)	(0.799)
Mean years of schooling, 1970	0.552	0.955	0.555	0.764	0.635	0.627	0.520
	(0.350)	(0.536)	(0.363)	(0.342)	(0.356)	(0.388)	(0.293)
Currency deprec. mean, 1969–90	-6.087	-6.618	-6.352	-4.082	-4.738	-3.116	18.672
	(4.190)	(5.571)	(4.371)	(4.275)	(5.157)	(5.661)	(4.990)
Price level inv. goods, 1970	-0.027	-0.025	-0.032	-0.029	-0.032	-0.039	-0.022
	(0.011)	(0.010)	(0.010)	(0.012)	(0.010)	(0.011)	(0.010)
Contract-intensive money, 1969–90	20.745	17.248	15.097	12.559	19.664	18.186	18.065
	(5.457)	(5.880)	(4.523)	(5.105)	(6.688)	(7.379)	(4.882)
M₂/GDP, 1969–90							9.649
							(2.924)
Adj. R^2	.61	.47	.60	.59	—	—	.68

Note: Sample size is 72 in equation 2, and 95 for all other equations. Standard errors (in parentheses) are computed using White's heteroskedastic-consistent variance/covariance matrix, except in equations 5 and 6. R^2 does not have its usual interpretation in equations 5 and 6. Mean of dependent variable is 16.9 for 95-country sample, and 14.2 for 72-country sample.

Since CIM and economic performance are measured contemporaneously in our analysis, our correlations conceivably capture effects of the latter on the former. Accordingly, in equations 3 and 4 respectively, we substitute the initial-year (1969) and end-year (1990) values of CIM for its 1969–90 average. The coefficient for initial CIM exceeds that for the end-of-period (1990) CIM value. When both are entered together in a regression (not shown), the coefficient for initial CIM is more than double that of the final CIM, and only initial CIM is statistically significant. Both results are contrary to what we would expect if our estimates using the 1969–90 average were biased upward by reverse causality.

To ensure that the association between CIM and investment in equation 1 is not sensitive to outliers, we report results of robust and median regressions in equations 5 and 6. The CIM coefficient is changed very little.

Adding other regressors such as the real interest rate, population growth, indicators of trade openness, and government size similarly leaves the CIM coefficient substantially unchanged.[7] Finally, we obtain similar results for CIM when the average of private investment/GDP for 1970–85 as constructed by Barro (1991) and the average of equipment investment/GDP for 1975–85 as estimated by DeLong and Summers (1991) are substituted for total investment.[8]

Growth equations are reported in table 4.4. The growth regressors are the same as those used for investment, expect that the price of investment goods is omitted. In equation 1, CIM is positively and significantly related to growth. Each standard deviation increase in CIM is associated with an increase in annual per capita growth of nearly one-half of a standard deviation, or nearly 1 percentage point. The association between CIM and growth is slightly weaker when developed nations are excluded, in equation 2. The growth regressors are the same as those used for investment except that the price of investment goods is omitted.

Equation 3 omits the school enrollment variables, which is arguably endogenous to CIM. Where contract and property rights are enforced, the returns to specialized education may rise and will also aid in the development of credit markets, which may make education beyond the primary level feasible for the poor (Galor and Zeira 1993). As expected, the CIM coefficient increases somewhat when schooling is omitted in equation 3.

The addition of investment/GDP as a regressor in equation 4 indicates that much of the impact of the contract enforcement and

TABLE 4.4. Contract-Intensive Money and Growth, 1970–92

Variation	Basic Model	Non-OECD	Schooling Omitted	Inv/GDP Added	Robust Regression	Median Regression	2SLS	M₂/GDP Added
Equation	1	2	3	4	5	6	7	8
Constant	-0.162	0.906	-1.849	2.960	-0.710	-0.788	-2.196	1.638
	(1.920)	(2.078)	(1.153)	(1.917)	(2.219)	(3.395)	(2.745)	(1.776)
Log 1970 GDP per capita	-0.477	-0.496	-0.286	-0.789	-0.558	-0.602	-0.726	-0.832
	(0.308)	(0.331)	(0.276)	(0.279)	(0.317)	(0.476)	(0.378)	(0.308)
Mean years of schooling, 1970	0.116	0.342		0.035	0.088	0.097	-0.009	0.108
	(0.099)	(0.133)		(0.090)	(0.114)	(0.176)	(0.149)	(0.083)
Currency deprec. mean, 1969–90	-4.028	-5.348	-4.100	-3.009	-3.220	-2.332	-4.201	-2.076
	(1.085)	(1.513)	(1.059)	(1.035)	(1.641)	(2.617)	(1.735)	(1.050)
Contract-intensive money, 1969–90	6.751	4.945	7.571	2.860	8.168	8.383	12.425	5.936
	(2.598)	(2.731)	(2.423)	(2.226)	(2.030)	(3.048)	(4.541)	(2.342)
Investment/GDP, 1969–90				0.147				
				(0.033)				
M₂/GDP, 1969–90								3.093
								(0.901)
Adj. R²	.21	.22	.60	.37	—	—	—	.29

Note: Sample size is 72 in equation 2, and 95 for all other equations. Standard errors (in parentheses) are computed using White's heteroskedastic-consistent variance/covariance matrix, except in equations 5–7. Instruments in 2SLS include a set of colonial heritage dummies and Sulivan's (1991) measure of ethnolinguistic homogeneity. R² does not have its usual interpretation in equations 5–7. Mean of dependent variable is 1.30 for 95-country sample, and 1.03 for 72-country sample.

governance as measured by CIM is through investment effects rather than through efficiency effects. The CIM coefficient in equation 4 is less than one-half its value in equations 1 through 3. This result is consistent with the conceptual framework outlined in section 2.

Results from robust and median regressions reported in equations 5 and 6 indicated that the association between CIM and growth is not sensitive to a few significant observations. The CIM coefficients in these tests are slightly larger than in equation 1. As in the case of investment, results also are little affected by adding other commonly used regressors such as population growth, trade intensity, and government size.

Unlike the case with CIM and investment, there is some evidence that the CIM-growth relationship may partially arise from reverse causality. The coefficient for end-of-period (1990) CIM exceeds that of initial (1969) CIM when these two variables are substituted for the period average of CIM (whether in separate regressions or together). Accordingly, we attempt in equation 6 to test the growth impact of the exogenous component of CIM using two-stage least squares.

The instruments for CIM include the other right-hand side variables (currency depreciation, initial income, and schooling), the percentage of a country's population belonging to the largest ethnic group, and a set of colonial heritage dummies, indicating whether a nation was colonized by the British, French, Spanish, Portuguese, or others (e.g., Dutch, Belgians, Italians, or Japanese), or was never colonized. The test of overidentifying restrictions fails to reject the null hypothesis that the instruments do not belong in the growth equation. Results in equation 7 indicate that the exogenous component of CIM is significantly correlated with growth.

The tests reported in tables 4.3 and 4.4 are all cross-sectional tests on country averages over the 1969–90 period. Our focus here is not as much on short-term policy changes as on continuing institutions for contract enforcement and property rights that, in stable environments, should not change much from year to year. We have not, in general, run tests treating each country-year in our sample as a separate observation. Nonetheless, we briefly summarize here severe tests of CIM's relationship to economic performance, focusing only on the idiosyncratic variations over time in CIM, investment, and income in each country. We do this using two-way fixed-effects models, with country and year fixed effects, both with the annual data and with decade averages. These tests should capture most connections CIM has with short- and medium-term changes in policy and with the less stable countries where there are major institutional changes in a given year or decade. We find that variations over time within countries in CIM are significantly correlated with changes in investment, but not with changes in growth.

9. Is CIM a Measure of the Contracting Environment or Financial Sector Development?

Significant research has identified a strong and causal relationship between financial development and growth (King and Levine 1993a; Levine 1998), leading one to reasonably ask whether contract-intensive money is simply an alternative measure of financial sector development. This is a difficult question since, as Levine (1998) has shown, financial sector development is itself very sensitive to subjective measures of the security of property and contract rights in a country. We offer several arguments in favor of the conclusion that CIM is properly regarded as a broad measure of the general security of contracts and property rights in all sectors of a country and not primarily those in the financial sector.

Measures of financial development reflect basic contractual features of a country, but they also track specific characteristics of the financial sector, such as the extent to which the sector facilitates diversification and the monitoring of managers (see Levine 1997). Conversely, measures of the security of property rights, including CIM, while indirectly related to the capacity of the financial sector to diversify risk, should more directly and strongly capture the overall security of transactions in a country, including not only financial sector transactions, but all contracts that put substantial resources at risk of contractual noncompliance (such as contracts between independent power producers and utilities). They should also capture not only the risk of government expropriation of financial assets (for example, through bank nationalization), but the expropriation through arbitrary regulation or outright confiscation of any type of fixed asset.

One piece of evidence that CIM is more appropriately categorized as a general indicator of contractual and property rights rather than as an indicator of financial development is its significant correlation with subjective measures of institutional quality, discussed earlier. A more rigorous test of the proposition is to conduct a factor analysis of many different measures of "quality of governance and institutions," on the one hand, and "financial development," on the other, using the four indicators of financial depth in King and Levine 1993a, CIM, and six different measures of institutions in the factor analysis. We allow the analysis to identify two factors. As table 4.5 shows, the institutional variables, including CIM, load most heavily on factor 1. The absolute value of the factor 1 loading of CIM is twice that of its factor 2 loading. The four indicators of financial development, PRIVY, M_2/GDP, PRIVATE, and BANK (described in the data appendix), all load more heavily onto the second factor. These are the results one would expect if CIM is predominantly an indicator of the security of contracts and property rather than of financial development.

A third piece of evidence that CIM is more of an institutional than a financial sector variable emerges from our country examples. These show that CIM tracks dramatic political developments that have little to do directly with the financial sector, although they may, simultaneously, also influence the usual measures of financial development.

Finally, CIM and indicators of financial development seem to capture different aspects of economic growth and investment. If we return to the growth and investment equations of the previous section, adding King and Levine's primary measure of financial depth (M_2/GDP) leaves the CIM coefficient essentially unchanged. This is evident in equations 7 of tables 4.3 and 4.4, where the CIM coefficient is only slightly less after the inclusion of the measure of financial depth than it is in the base sample. Financial depth is also significant, further reinforcing the notion that the variables capture different aspects of the institutional and economic environment in countries. CIM isolates the impact of improved contract enforcement and property rights security, which has a generalized effect that encompasses but is not exclusive to the financial sector. M_2/GDP

TABLE 4.5.   Factor Analysis of Governance and Financial Development Indicators
Rotated Factor Pattern (Varimax Rotation)

Variable	Factor 1 Loadings	Factor 2 Loadings
Gastil index	.89	−.25
Executive constraints	−.80	.25
Wright property rights index	.75	−.25
CIM	−.72	.36
ICRG property rights index	−.72	.54
Revolutions and coups frequency	.51	−.37
Kobrin expropriation frequency	.45	−.44
PRIVY	−.28	.85
M_2/GDP	−.18	.81
PRIVATE	−.44	.70
BANK	−.53	.66

captures the specific attributes of the financial sector that increase growth and investment, including the effect of the financial sector on the ability of economic agents to diversify risk and exert control over managers.

On the basis of these tests, we argue that CIM, even though it is derived from data in the money markets, is nevertheless most appropriately regarded as a more general measure of the quality of governance and institutions. There are policy implications of this conclusion. Countries with low CIM (or low scores on other, more subjective measures of property rights and contract security) would be advised to examine closely government policies related to enforcement of contracts between private economic actors and the due process guarantees that governments afford firms and individuals when they create and implement policies. Countries that exhibit low indicators of financial development need to address both the general contractual environment that inhibits growth of the financial sector and also examine specific policy issues that affect the sector, including the presence of discriminatory taxation (King and Levine 1993b), laws unfavorable to creditors, and poorly developed bankruptcy procedures.

10. Alternative Explanations for the CIM Findings

There are two possible problems that could arise in interpreting the foregoing results. The first is that CIM might be an artifact of inflation, interest rates, or monetary policies. CIM is related to inflation in two contrary ways. On the one hand, inflation reduces the value of money and raises nominal interest rates, and therefore provides an incentive to shift money from currency and non–interest-bearing accounts into interest-paying time deposits or into foreign currency accounts. This increases CIM. If changes in CIM were driven by changes in inflation in this way, it would be less likely that we would find positive associations between CIM and growth, investment, or other, subjective indicators of the security of property and contract rights.

On the other hand, with very high rates of inflation there is also greater uncertainty about the rate of inflation and even about the viability of the existing governmental and financial institutions. This makes deposits in financial institutions, and especially deposits with limits or penalties on timing of withdrawals, riskier, and it tends to reduce CIM. If this effect dominates, higher CIM would be associated with lower inflation; since lower inflation is likely to be associated with higher growth and investment, the possibility arises of a spurious positive relationship between CIM and these economic outcomes.

We have two pieces of evidence that our CIM results are not simply an artifact of inflation-related phenomena. First, all of our results are robust to the inclusion of inflation, as tables 4.3 and 4.4 demonstrate. Second, we find that only when the rate of inflation is very high—above about 60 percent per year—is it associated with lower CIM. Below this level, however, higher rates of inflation are associated with higher CIM, creating a bias for most of our observations against finding a positive relationship between CIM and growth and investment.

The second possible problem with interpretation arises if CIM is only a proxy for savings.[9] Countries with high savings rates (due, for example, to age profiles of their populations) might, because time deposits and other financial instruments are better vehicles for saving than currency, have high values of CIM. Since national savings rates are highly correlated with national investment rates, the association of CIM with investment might be a product of these influences. We examine this issue in two ways and find no support for the conclusion that CIM is simply a proxy for savings rates. First, in a fixed-effects regression of the annual observations of CIM on income and saving, with time and country dummies, we find that the coefficient of saving is extremely small. This result is robust to a variety of specifications. Second, we find that CIM is also a strong predictor of components of total investment—private investment and equipment investment—that are not forced, through accounting identities, to be as strongly associated with savings rates as is total investment.

11. Conclusions

This essay contributes to a growing literature that emphasizes the institutional or governmental foundations of well-functioning markets. While it is true that the markets for many self-enforcing transactions emerge spontaneously and bring some gains from trade everywhere, many of the markets that a society needs if it is to develop and achieve its economic potential are missing in most countries. In this essay we use our new measure of the security of contract enforcement and property rights, contract-intensive money, to support the claim that only countries where governments give private parties the capacity to make credible commitments that they could not otherwise make, and thereby achieve gains from trade that they could not otherwise obtain, achieve their economic potential.

We base the importance of CIM on the following three propositions: (1) the contract-intensive money ratio is a measure of the proportion of transactions that rely on third-party enforcement; (2) this proportion is a good indicator of the reliability of contract enforcement and the security of property rights in countries; and (3) contract enforcement reliability and property rights security are important for high levels of productivity and rapid economic growth.

While it is difficult to test these propositions one at a time, we have marshaled a good deal of evidence that is consistent with all three. In a series of case studies of dramatic change in politics and governance, CIM changed in ways consistent with these propositions. CIM is also correlated with other, subjective measures of the quality of governance and institutions that are now widely used in the literature.

Consistent with the theory, countries with relatively high values of CIM—and relatively high scores on other measures of quality of governance—have relatively more insurance and financial development. This is true even though we control for the level of per capita income. Governments that give their citizens the capacity to obtain more gains from trade and specialization also improve economic performance in other ways. The empirical evidence developed in the essay indicates that CIM is strongly associated with the size of the capital stock, the level of per capita income, and the total factor productivity of countries. We also find that countries with a high level of CIM tend to grow faster and to exhibit higher rates of investment.

The essay concludes by investigating three interpretations of these results that diverge from the one that we offer, that CIM is a measure of the security of property and contract rights, and that it is the insecurity of these rights that suppresses investment and growth. We present evidence, however, that is inconsistent with these three interpretations: differences across countries in levels of CIM are not predominantly due to differences with respect to financial sector development, inflation, or savings.

In sum, this essay introduces a measure of the security of economic rights that is available for many countries and for long periods, constituting, therefore, a valuable new resource for empirical studies. Because this measure is objective, and not based on subjective evaluations, we are also able in this essay to present the most persuasive evidence to date that economic growth and investment significantly accelerate when governments impartially protect and precisely define the rights of all participants in the economy.

Appendix: Variable Definitions and Sources

Growth, 1970–92 Average annual per capita GDP growth in percentage points, log method. *Source:* Summers and Heston 1991.

Investment/GDP, 1970–92 Investment as a percentage of GDP. *Source:* Summers and Heston 1991.

Log Initial GDP per capita, 1970 *Source:* Summers and Heston 1991.

Schooling, 1970 Average number of years of completed education, 25 and over population. *Source:* Barro and Lee 1993.

Price level of investment goods, 1970 As a percentage of the U.S. level. *Source:* Summers and Heston 1991.

Contract-intensive money (CIM), 1969–90 Ratio of noncurrency component of M_2 to total M_2. *Source:* International Financial Statistics (IFS).

Currency depreciation, 1969–90 Inflation rate/(100 + inflation rate). *Source:* IFS.

BANK Ratio of deposit money bank domestic assets to deposit money bank domestic assets plus central bank domestic assets, average from 1960–89. *Source:* King and Levine 1993a, as constructed from IFS.

PRIVATE Ratio of claims on the nonfinancial private sector to total domestic credit (excluding credit to money banks), average from 1960–89. *Source:* King and Levine 1993a, as constructed from IFS.

PRIVY Ratio of claims on the nonfinancial private sector to GDP, average from 1960–89. *Source:* King and Levine 1993a, as constructed from IFS.

M_2/GDP, 1969–90 *Source:* IFS.

Revolutions + Coups Average number per year, 1960–88.

Gastil Index Sum of political freedoms and civil liberties indexes, each scaled 1–7, averaged from 1973–86.

ICRG Index Sum of 5 subjective variables, each scaled 1–10: rule of law, quality of bureaucracy, corruption, risk of expropriation, and government repudiation of contracts.

BERI Index Sum of 4 subjective variables, each scaled 1–4: bureaucratic delays, contract enforceability, nationalization potential, and infrastructure quality.

Wright Property Rights Index Subjective 1–4 rating, with higher scores indicating worse protection of property rights.

Kobrin Expropriation 1–4 ordinal scale defined by frequency of expropriations or nationalizations in 1960–79 period, with higher values indicating greater frequency.

Executive Constraints 1–7 ordinal scale of constraints on power of the executive, with higher scores indicating more constraints.

Descriptive Statistics for 95-Country Sample Used in Tables 4.3 and 4.4

	Mean	Standard Deviation
Growth, 1970–92	1.30	1.96
Inv/GDP, 1970–92	16.9	8.4
Log per capita GDP, 1970	7.75	0.95
School attainment 1970	3.62	2.79
Currency depreciation 1969–90	0.13	0.11
Price of inv. goods, 1970	97.7	60.8
CIM, 1969–90	0.78	0.13
M_2/GDP, 1969–90	0.43	0.25

Notes

This chapter was previously published under the same title in the *Journal of Economic Growth* 4 (June 1999): 185–211. It is reprinted with permission from Kluwer Academic Publishers.

1. The importance of third-party enforcement of contracts has long been recognized. In 1651 Thomas Hobbes said that, in the absence of government, the party that "performs first has no assurance that the other will perform after, because the bonds of words are too weak to bridle men's ambition, avarice, anger, and other passions without the fear of some coercive power" (1958, 15). The distinction between self-enforcing transactions and those that require third-party enforcement are key to the arguments in North 1990. Olson (1992) analyzes the difficulties of the transition from communism in terms of this distinction.

2. For example, Knack and Keefer (chapter 10, this volume) find an association between the protection of property rights and levels of interpersonal trust in countries.

3. Currency comes from line 14a of International Financial Statistics, "currency outside deposit money banks." It does not include foreign currency in circulation, since there are no reliable measures of this, although foreign currency deposits in financial institutions, which are easily measured, are included in M_2. M_2 is defined by IFS as the sum of money and quasi money, or the sum of lines 14a (currency outside banks), 24 (demand deposits), 15 (time deposits), and 25 (time and savings deposits, including foreign currency deposits of resident sectors other than central government). We cannot control for variations in the mix of different types of money in M_2. For example, we would expect that where the incentives to hold currency increase, so also do incentives to substitute out of time deposits and into demand deposits. However, all components of M_2, including time and demand deposits, share the critical feature that they rely on economic actors to surrender control over their money to third parties for some period of time.

4. The Eastern Caribbean Central Bank was established in that year, and the currency figures become more precise starting in 1984. Prior to that year, the numbers of Eastern Caribbean dollars circulating in Grenada were based on estimates, while after that year, the ECCB placed a letter G on the EC dollars issued there and was therefore able to track the currency circulation precisely. This information was kindly supplied by Mr. Kawar of the IMF.

5. For example, South Africa has the third-highest value, while Malawi ranks above Belgium.

6. Pritchett (1996) finds that school enrollment is not a good proxy for the stock of educational capital and that increases in the stock of educational capital do not predict increases in output. The conventional specification may nonetheless be justified since school enrollment may be a proxy measure of

the desire and capability of a country's government to provide public goods that the market would otherwise underprovide.

7. A monetarist interpretation of CIM also suggests that real interest rates should be controlled for. Doing so only trivially affects the CIM coefficient and at a substantial cost in sample size due to gaps in the interest rate data. We therefore do not include the real interest rate in all regressions.

8. Results described in this paragraph are available on request. We use total investment from Summers and Heston 1991 as our primary investment variable because it is likely measured more accurately than are estimates of private or equipment investment.

9. We owe this suggestion to Brian Fikkert.

References

Barro, Robert J. 1991. "Economic Growth in a Cross Section of Countries." *Quarterly Journal of Economics* 106 (2): 407–43.

Barro, Robert J., and Jong-Wha Lee. 1993. "International Comparisons of Educational Attainment." *Journal of Monetary Economics* 32 (3): 363–94.

Borner, S., A. Brunetti, and B. Weder. 1995. *Political Credibility and Economic Development.* New York: St. Martin's Press.

Bruno, Michael, and William Easterly. 1998. "Inflation Crises and Long-Run Growth." *Journal of Monetary Economics* 41 (1): 3–26.

Cukierman, Alex, and Steven Webb. 1995. "Political Influence on the Central Bank: International Evidence." *World Bank Economic Review* 9 (3): 397–423.

DeLong, J. Bradford, and Larry Summers. 1991. "Equipment Investment and Economic Growth." *Quarterly Journal of Economics* 106 (2): 445–502.

The Europa World Yearbook (various years). London: Europa Publications.

Galor, Oded, and J. Zeira. 1993. "Income Distribution and Macroeconomics." *Review of Economic Studies* 60:35–52.

Grierson, P. J. H. 1904. *The Silent Trade.* Edinburgh: William Green and Sons.

Haggard, Stephan, and Robert R. Kaufman. 1992. *The Politics of Economic Adjustment: International Constraints, Distributive Conflicts, and the State.* Princeton: Princeton University Press.

Hall, Robert, and Charles Jones. 1996. "The Productivity of Nations." NBER Working Paper No. 5812.

Hayek, Friedrich A. 1948. "The Meaning of Competition." In *Individualism and Economic Order,* 92–106. Chicago: University of Chicago Press.

Hobbes, Thomas. 1958 [1651]. *Leviathan.* Indianapolis: Bobbs-Merrill.

International Monetary Fund. Various years. *International Financial Statistics Yearbook.*

King, Robert G., and Ross Levine. 1993a. "Finance and Growth: Schumpeter Might Be Right." *Quarterly Journal of Economics* 108 (3): 717–37.

———. 1993b. "Finance, Entrepreneurship and Growth." *Journal of Monetary Economics* 32:513–42.

La Porta, Rafael, Florencio Lopez-de-Silanes, Andrei Shleifer, and Robert W. Vishny. 1998. "Law and Finance." *Journal of Political Economy* 106: 1113–55.

Levine, Ross. 1997. "Financial Development and Economic Growth: Views and an Agenda." *Journal of Economic Literature* 35:688–726.

———. 1998. "The Legal Environment, Banks, and Long-Run Economic Growth." *Journal of Money, Credit and Banking* 30 (3): 596–613.

Levine, Ross, and David Renelt. 1992. "A Sensitivity Analysis of Cross-Country Growth Regression." *American Economic Review* 82 (4): 942–63.

Mauro, Paolo. 1995. "Corruption and Growth." *Quarterly Journal of Economics* 110 (3): 681–712.

North, Douglass C. 1990. *Institutions, Institutional Change, and Economic Performance.* Cambridge and New York: Cambridge University Press.

Olson, Mancur. 1992. "The Hidden Path to a Successful Economy." In *The Emergence of Market Economies in Eastern Europe,* ed. Christopher Clague and Gordon Rausser. Cambridge, MA: Blackwell.

Pritchett, Lant. 1996. "Where Has All the Education Gone?" World Bank Policy Research Working Paper No. 1581.

Rosenberg, Nathan, and L. E. Birdzell. 1986. *How the West Grew Rich: The Economic Transformation of the Industrial World.* New York: Basic Books.

Sachs, Jeffrey, and Andrew Warner, 1995. "Natural Resource Abundance and Economic Growth." HIID Development Discussion Paper No. 517a, Harvard University.

Scully, Gerald W. 1988. "The Institutional Framework and Economic Development." *Journal of Political Economy* 96 (3): 652–62.

Sullivan, Michael J. 1991. *Measuring Global Values.* New York: Greenwood.

Summers, Robert, and Alan Heston. 1991. "The Penn World Table (Mark V): An Expanded Set of International Comparisons, 1950–88." *Quarterly Journal of Economics* 106 (2): 327–68.

Townsend, Robert M. 1983. "Financial Structure and Economic Activity." *American Economic Review* 73 (5): 895–911.

Williamson, Oliver. 1983. "Credible Commitments: Using Hostages to Support Exchange." *American Economic Review* 73 (4): 519–40.

———. 1985. *The Economic Institutions of Capitalism.* New York: Free Press.

PART 2

Endogenizing Institutions

> If a covenant be made, wherein neither of the parties perform
> presently, but trust one another ... he that performeth first, has no as-
> surance the other will perform after; because the bonds of words are
> too weak to bridle men's ambition, avarice, anger, and other Passions,
> without the fear of some coercive Power ...
> — *Thomas Hobbes (Leviathan, 1651)*

"Dictatorship, Democracy, and Development" (chapter 5) was first
published in the *American Political Science Review* in September
1993. Mancur Olson applies his concept of "encompassing interest"[1]
to the question of the type of political regimes that is most likely to
protect the private sector from public and private predation. An individual or group has a more "encompassing" interest in a public
good—and is more likely to contribute to its provision—the greater
the share of the benefits from the public good that it receives. In
chapter 5, Olson in effect adds a time dimension to this concept. Autocrats with long time-horizons—those who expect to remain in
power for a long time—have a more encompassing interest in providing public order than do less secure autocrats. Less stable autocrats are akin to roving bandits: their benefits from plunder—
through outright confiscation, debt repudiation, and currency
debasement—are likely to exceed the costs of forgone tax revenue
from the resulting decrease in economic activity. For a secure autocrat, the long-run benefits to him in increased tax revenues may
justify the short-term cost of refraining from plunder. Among autocracies, dynastic succession can be conducive to growth, by length-
ening the autocrat's horizons. Because orderly successions can
never be taken for granted, however, even the most secure autocrats
cannot provide the level of certainty characteristic of stable democracies with a strong rule of law, independent judiciary, and respect
for individual rights. Thus, "it is no accident that the countries that
have reached the highest level of economic development and have

enjoyed good economic performance across generations are all stable democracies."

Christopher Clague, Philip Keefer, Stephen Knack, and Mancur Olson in chapter 6 elaborate on this important qualification of *stable* long-lasting democracy. This chapter, "Property and Contract Rights in Autocracies and Democracies," was first published in the *Journal of Economic Growth* in June 1996. This chapter argues that the same respect for law, independent judiciary, and other mechanisms that ensure that leaders are legally replaced in lasting democracies also ensure property and contract rights of the citizenry. These mechanisms severely limit the ability of leaders — no matter how self-interested, or how short their time horizons — to violate property and contract rights to their own benefit. New or transitory democracies in contrast often do not have an effective legal system enforcing the rule of law and can suffer from the same predatory policies as autocracies. The arguments from chapters 5 and 6 generate several testable predictions: (1) among autocracies, property and contract rights depend on the time horizons of the autocrat; (2) among democracies, these rights depend on the durability of the democratic system, not on the time horizons of leaders; (3) stable democracies will have the strongest property and contract rights, because time horizons are never indefinite even for the most secure autocratic regime. A variety of empirical tests in chapter 6 provide strong support for these hypotheses, using six alternative measures of property and contract rights, and using tenure of democratic regimes and of autocrats, respectively, as proxies for durability of democracy and of autocrats' time horizons. As predicted, property and contract rights increase with autocrats' time in power, and with the duration of democracy, but not with time in power of democratic leaders. Finally, results show that "long-lasting democracies offer better protection for property and contract rights than any other regime type of any duration."

Some observers have noted the apparent contradiction between Olson's (1982) earlier emphasis on the damaging effects of special interest groups that accumulate in stable democracies, and his emphasis in later work on the benefits of long-lasting democracy. Olson had actually addressed this issue in *The Rise and Decline of Nations*, in a passage on "the depressingly large number of less developed countries . . . that have been persistently unstable" (1982: 165). He argued there was no inconsistency in noting problems associated with both stability (accumulation of distributional coalitions) and instability (capital flight and distorted investment patterns): "On the whole, stable countries are more prosperous than unstable ones and this is no surprise. But, other things being equal, the most rapid growth will occur in societies that have lately experienced upheaval but are expected nonetheless to be stable for the foreseeable future" (165). Elaborating on these issues in his later work, Olson (2000: 99–100) notes that the interests of autocrats are more encompassing than those of special-interest groups, and that several countries have for a time experienced spectacular growth under autocrats with long planning horizons who often resist or repress special interest groups. Democracies will tend to perform better in the very long run, however, because "in any society with autocratic governments, an autocrat with the same incentives as a roving bandit is bound to appear sooner or later" (27).

Chapter 7 ("Does Inequality Harm Growth Only in Democracies?") was first published in the *American Journal of Political Science* in January 1997. This chapter critically examines a venerable political-economy hypothesis that conflicts with those in chapters 5 and 6. This alternative model suggests that the security of private property is incompatible with democracy. A certain amount of inequality in wealth and income is inevitable in any market system with private property. With majority-rule voting, the median voter will always support redistribution schemes favored by the poorer half of voters, keeping property rights in flux. Persson and Tabellini claim to provide support for this model in an influential article published in the *American Economic Review* in 1994. They do not directly examine property rights, but make inferences from growth performance. They find that greater income inequality is related to slower growth in per capita incomes in democracies, but not in autocracies, and argue that this result is consistent with the view that majority-rule voting makes property rights less secure. Stephen Knack and Philip Keefer argue— as do Clague et al. in section 2 of chapter 6—that autocrats' policies are not wholly insensitive to the preferences of some important constituencies (if not majorities); accordingly greater inequality could be associated with insecure property rights in autocracies (through political instability and violence for example) as well as in democracies. They show in chapter 7 that the empirical results of Persson and Tabellini are produced entirely by measurement error in income inequality and in their regime type indicator. Correcting for measurement error, the relationship between inequality and growth is equally strong in democracies and autocracies.

The causes of corruption are studied in chapter 8 ("Gender and Corruption" by Anand Swamy, Stephen Knack, Young Lee, and

Omar Azfar), published in the *Journal of Development Economics* in February 2001. The major finding is that countries with more women in positions of political authority have lower corruption levels.[2] This result is highly robust in the cross-sectional data and also shows up in time-series data: corruption levels fall more in countries where the share of women in parliament, and in high-level positions in the government bureaucracy, rises. Interestingly, Mexico City, Cuernavaca, and Lima have all at various times resolved to reduce bribe seeking among their police forces by increasing the number of policewomen. Enhanced participation by women in commerce and in government is often advocated by donor agencies and NGOs on gender-equity grounds. The findings in chapter 8, coupled with empirical links between corruption and economic performance discussed in chapter 1, suggest that raising the profile of women has efficiency as well as equity implications, potentially benefiting most men as well as women.

Notes

1. Olson introduced this term in *The Rise and Decline of Nations* (1982), but there are clear antecedents in his *Logic of Collective Action* (1965).

2. Lorenzetti's Renaissance-era frescoes known as "The Allegory of Bad Government" and "The Allegory of Good Government" suggest that a pair of pictures are worth several thousand words and several regressions: the characters representing bad government are mostly male, while the characters representing good government are disproportionately female.

Dictatorship, Democracy, and Development

Mancur Olson

In my student days, in reading Edward Banfield's account of the beliefs of the people in a poor village in southern Italy, I came upon a remarkable statement by a village monarchist. He said, "Monarchy is the best kind of government because the King is then owner of the country. Like the owner of a house, when the wiring is wrong, he fixes it" (1958, 26) The villager's argument jarred against my democratic convictions. I could not deny that the owner of a country would have an incentive to make his property productive. Could the germ of truth in the monarchist's argument be reconciled with the case for democracy?

It is only in recent years that I have arrived at an answer to this question. It turns out that for a satisfactory answer one needs a new theory of dictatorship and democracy and of how each of these types of government affects economic development. Once this new theory is understood, one can begin to see how autocracies and democracies first emerge. I shall set out this conception in a brief and informal way and use it to explain some of the most conspicuous features of historical experience.

The starting point for the theory is that no society can work satisfactorily if it does not have a peaceful order and usually other public goods as well. Obviously, anarchic violence cannot be rational for a society: the victims of violence and theft lose not only what is taken from them but also the incentive to produce any goods that would be taken by others. There is accordingly little or no production in the absence of a peaceful order. Thus there are colossal gains from providing domestic tranquillity and other basic public goods. These gains can be shared in ways that leave everyone in a society better off. Can we conclude that because everyone could gain from it, a peaceful order emerges by voluntary agreement?

From the logic of the matter, we should expect that in small groups a generally peaceful order will normally emerge by voluntary agreement but that in large populations it will not. The key to the matter is that each individual bears the full costs or risks of anything he or she does to help establish a peaceful order or to provide other public goods but receives only a share of the benefits. In a tiny group, such as a hunter-gatherer band, each person or family will obtain a significant share of the benefits of a peaceful order, and the net advantages of such an order are so great that even a single family's share of the gains can easily outweigh the sacrifices needed to obtain it. Moreover, when there are only a few, the welfare of each noticeably depends on whether each of the others acts in a group-oriented way. Thus each family, by making clear that cooperation by another will bring forth its cooperation but that noncooperation will not, can increase the likelihood that another will match its behavior, thereby increasing the incentive each has to act in the group interest. The theoretical prediction that sufficiently small groups can often organize for collective action is corroborated by countless observations (Olson 1965).

This prediction is also in accord with the anthropological observations of the most primitive societies. The simplest food-gathering and hunting societies are normally made up of bands that have, including the children, only about fifty or a hundred people. In other words, such a band will normally contain only a few families that need to cooperate. Anthropologists find that primitive tribes normally maintain peace and order by voluntary agreement, and that is to some extent what Tacitus, Caesar, and other classical writers observed among the less advanced Germanic tribes. The most primitive tribes tend to make all important collective decisions by consensus, and many of them do not even have chiefs. When a band becomes too large or disagreement is intense, the band may split, but the new bands normally also make decisions by unanimous consent. If a tribe is in the hunting-and-gathering stage, there is also little or no incentive for anyone to subjugate another tribe or to keep slaves, since captives cannot generate enough surplus above subsistence to justify the costs of guarding them.[1] Thus within the most primitive tribes of preagricultural history, the logical presumption that the great gains from a peaceful order can be achieved by voluntary agreement appears to hold true.

Once peoples learned how to raise crops effectively, production increased, population grew, and large populations needed governments. The same logic that shows why small groups can act consensually in their common interest tells us that when there is a large population, voluntary collective action *cannot* obtain the gains from a peaceful order or other public goods, even when the aggregate net gains from the provision of basic public goods are large.[2] The main reason is that the typical individual in a society with, say, a million people will get only about one-millionth of the gain from a collective good, but will bear the whole cost of whatever he or she does to help provide it, and therefore has little or no incentive to contribute to the provision of the collective good. There is by now a huge theoretical and empirical literature on this point, and the great preponderance of this literature agrees that, just as small groups can usually engage in spontaneous collective action, very large groups are not able to achieve collective goals through voluntary collective action.[3]

Thus we should not be surprised that while there have been lots of writings about the desirability of "social contracts" to obtain the benefits of law and order, no one has ever found a large society that obtained a peaceful order or other public goods through an agreement among the individuals in the society.

The First Blessing of the Invisible Hand

Why, then, have most populous societies throughout history normally avoided anarchy? An answer came to me by chance when reading about a Chinese warlord (see Sheridan 1966). In the 1920s China was in large part under the control of various warlords. They were men who led some armed band with which they conquered some territory and who then appointed themselves lords of that territory. They taxed the population heavily and pocketed much of the proceeds. The warlord Feng Yu-hsiang was noted for the exceptional extent to which he used his army for suppressing bandits and for his defeat of the relatively substantial army of the roving bandit, White Wolf. Apparently most people in Feng's domain found him much preferable to the roving bandits.

At first, this seems puzzling: why should warlords, who were stationary bandits continuously stealing from a given group of victims, be preferred, by those victims, to roving bandits who soon departed? The warlords had no claim to legitimacy, and their thefts were distinguished from those of roving bandits only because they took the form of continuing taxation rather than occasional plunder.

In fact, if a roving bandit rationally settles down and takes his theft in the form of regular taxation and at the same time maintains a monopoly on theft in his domain, then those from whom he exacts taxes will have an incentive to produce. The rational stationary bandit will take only a *part* of income in taxes, because he will be able to exact a larger total amount of income from his subjects if he leaves them with an incentive to generate income that he can tax.

If the stationary bandit successfully monopolizes the theft in his domain, then his victims do not need to worry about theft by others. If he steals only through regular taxation, then his subjects know that they can keep whatever proportion of their output is left after they have paid their taxes. Since all of the settled bandit's victims are for him a source of tax payments, he also has an incentive to prohibit the murder or maiming of his subjects. With the rational monopolization of theft—in contrast to uncoordinated competitive theft—the victims of the theft can expect to retain whatever capital they accumulate out of after-tax income and therefore also have an incentive to save and to invest, thereby increasing future income and tax receipts. The monopolization of theft and the protection of the tax-generating subjects thereby eliminates anarchy. Since the warlord takes a part of total production in the form of tax theft, it will also pay him to provide other public goods whenever the provision of these goods increases taxable income sufficiently.

In a world of roving banditry there is little or no incentive for anyone to produce or accumulate anything that may be stolen, and thus there is little for bandits to steal. Bandit rationality, accordingly, induces the bandit leader to seize a given domain, to make himself the ruler of that domain, and to provide a peaceful order and other public goods for its inhabitants, thereby obtaining more in tax theft than he could have obtained from migratory plunder. Thus we have "the first blessing of the invisible hand": the rational, self-interested leader of a band of roving bandits is led, as though by an invisible hand, to settle down, wear a crown, and replace anarchy with government. The gigantic increase in output that normally arises from the provision of a peaceful order and other public goods gives the stationary bandit a far larger take than he could obtain if he did not provide government.

Thus government for groups larger than tribes normally arises, not because of social contracts or voluntary transactions of any kind, but rather because of rational self-interest among those who can organize the greatest capacity for violence. These violent entrepreneurs naturally do not call themselves bandits but, on the contrary, give themselves and their descendants exalted titles. They sometimes even claim to rule by divine right. Since history is written by the winners, the origins of ruling dynasties are, of course, conventionally explained in terms of lofty motives rather than by self-interest. Autocrats of all kinds usually claim that their subjects want them to rule and thereby nourish the unhistorical assumption that government arose out of some kind of voluntary choice. (These claims have an echo in some literature in the "transaction costs" tradition that attempts to explain the emergence of various kinds of governments partly or wholly through voluntary contracts and the costs of the transactions associated with them. See Kiser and Barzel 1991; North 1981; North and Thomas 1973.)[4]

Any individual who has autocratic control over a country will provide public goods to that country because he has an "encompassing interest" in it.[5] The extent of the encompassing interest of an officeholder, political party, interest group, monarch, or any other partial or total "owner" of a society varies with the size of the stake in the society. The larger or more encompassing the stake an organization or individual has in a society, the greater the incentive the organization or individual has to take action to provide public goods for the society. If an autocrat received one-third of any increase in the income of his domain in increased tax collections, he would then get one-third of the benefits of the public goods he provided. He would then have an incentive to provide public goods up to the point where the national income rose by the reciprocal of one-third, or three, from his last unit of public good expenditure. Though the society's income and welfare would obviously be greater from a larger expenditure on public goods, the gain to society from the public goods that a rational self-interested autocrat provides are nonetheless often colossal. Consider, for example, the gains from replacing a violent anarchy with a minimal degree of public order.

From history, we know that the encompassing interest of the tax-collecting autocrat permits a considerable development of civilization. From not long after the first development of settled agriculture until, say, about the time of the French Revolution, the overwhelming majority of mankind was subject to autocracy and tax theft. History until relatively recent times has been mostly a story of the gradual progress of civilization under stationary bandits interrupted by occasional episodes of roving banditry. From about the time that Sargon's conquests created the empire of Akkad until the time of Louis XVI and Voltaire, there was an impressive development of civilization that occurred in large part under stationary banditry.[6]

The Grasping Hand

We can now begin to reconcile the village monarchist's insight and the foregoing argument with the case for democracy. Though the village monarchist was right in saying that the absolute ruler has as much incentive to fix what needs repair as the owner of a house, his analogy is nonetheless profoundly misleading. The autocrat is not in a position analogous to the owner of a single house or even to the owner of all housing, but rather to the owner of *all* wealth, both tangible and human, in a country. The autocrat does indeed have an incentive to maintain and increase the productivity of everything and everyone in his domain, and his subjects will gain from this. But he also has an incentive to charge a *monopoly* rent, and to levy this monopoly charge on *everything,* including human labor.

In other words, the autocratic ruler has an incentive to extract the maximum possible surplus from the whole society and to use it for his own purposes. Exactly the *same* rational self-interest that makes a roving bandit settle down and provide government for his subjects also makes him extract the maximum possible amount from the society for himself. He will use his monopoly of coercive power to obtain the maximum take in taxes and other exactions.

The consumption of an autocratic ruler is, moreover, not limited by his personal capacities to use food, shelter, or clothing. Though the pyramids, the palace of Versailles, the Taj Mahal, and even Imelda Marcos's 3,000 pairs of shoes were expensive, the social costs of autocratic leaders arise mostly out of their appetites for military power, international prestige, and larger domains. It took a large proportion of the total output of the Soviet Union, for example, to satisfy the preferences of its dictators.[7]

Some writers use the metaphor of the predatory state, but this is misleading, even for autocracies. As we saw earlier, a stationary bandit has an encompassing interest in the territory he controls and accordingly provides domestic order and other public goods. Thus he is not like the wolf that preys on the elk, but more like the rancher who makes sure that his cattle are protected and given water. The metaphor of predation obscures the great superiority of stationary banditry over anarchy and the advances of civilization that have resulted from it. No metaphor or model of even the autocratic state can therefore be correct unless it simultaneously takes account of the stationary bandit's incentive to provide public goods at the same time that he extracts the largest possible net surplus for himself.

Though the forms that stationary banditry has taken over the course of history are diverse, the essence of the matter can be seen by assuming that the autocrat gets all of his receipts in the form of explicit taxation. The rational autocrat will devote some of the resources he obtains through taxation to public goods, but will impose far higher tax rates than are needed to pay for the public goods since he also uses tax collections to maximize his net surplus. The higher the level of provision of public goods, given the tax rate, the higher the society's income and the yield from this tax rate. At the same time, the higher the tax rate, given the level of public good provision, the lower the income of society, since taxes distort incentives.

So what tax rate and what level of public good provision will the rational self-interested autocrat choose? Assume for the moment that the autocrat's level of public good expenditure is given. As Joseph Schumpeter (1991) lucidly pointed out, and Ibn Kalduhn (1967) sensed much earlier,[8] tax receipts will (if we start with low taxation) increase as tax rates increase, but after the revenue-maximizing rate is reached, higher tax rates distort incentives and reduce income so much that tax collections fall. The rational self-interested autocrat chooses the revenue-maximizing tax rate.

Though the amount collected at any tax rate will vary with the level of public good provision, the revenue-maximizing tax *rate* for the autocrat should not. This optimal tax rate determines exactly how encompassing the interest of the autocrat in the society is; that is, it determines what share of any increase in the national income he receives. He will then spend money on public goods up to the point where his last dollar of expenditure on public goods generates a dollar's increase in his *share* of the national income. At this point, the gain to society will, as we know, be the reciprocal of his share.

Though the subjects of the autocrat are better off than they would be under anarchy, they must endure taxes or other impositions so high that, if they were increased further, income would fall by so much that even the autocrat, who absorbs only a portion of the fall in income in the form of lower tax collections, would be worse off.

There is no lack of historical examples in which autocrats for their own political and military purposes collected as much revenue as they possibly could. Consider the largest autocratic jurisdictions in Western history. The Bourbon kings of France were (especially on the eve of the French Revolution) collecting all they could in taxes. The Hapsburg kings of Spain did the same. The Roman Empire ultimately pushed its tax rates at least to the revenue-maximizing level.

The Reach of Dictatorships and
Democracies Compared

How would government by a rational self-interested autocrat compare with a democracy? Democracies vary so much that no one conclusion can cover all cases. Nonetheless, many practical insights can be obtained by thinking first about one of the simplest democratic situations. This is a situation in which there are two candidates for a presidency or two well-disciplined parties seeking to form the government. This simplifying assumption will be favorable to democratic performance, for it gives the democracy an "encompassing" interest rather like the one that motivates the stationary bandit to provide some public goods. I shall make the opposite assumption later. But throughout, I shall avoid giving democracy an unfair advantage by assuming better motivation. I shall impartially assume that the democratic political leaders are just as self-interested as the stationary bandit and will use any expedient to obtain majority support.

Observation of two party democracies tells us that incumbents like to run on a "you-never-had-it-so-good" record. An incumbent obviously would not leave himself with such a record if, like the self-interested autocrat, he took for himself the largest possible net surplus from the society. But we are too favorable to democracy if we assume that the incumbent party or president will maximize his chances of reelection simply by making the electorate as a whole as well-off as possible.

A candidate needs only a majority to win, and he might be able to "buy" a majority by transferring income from the population at large to a prospective majority. The taxes needed for this transfer would impair incentives and reduce society's output just as an autocrat's redistribution to himself does. Would this competition to buy votes generate as much distortion of incentives through taxation as a rational autocracy does? That is, would a vote-buying democratic leader, like the rational autocrat, have an incentive to push tax rates to the revenue-maximizing level?

No. Though both the majority and the autocrat have an encompassing interest in the society because they control tax collections, the majority in addition earns a significant share of the market income of the society, and this gives it a more encompassing interest in the productivity of the society. The majority's interest in its market earnings induces it to redistribute less to itself than an autocrat redistributes to himself. This is evident from considering an option that a democratic majority would have if it were at the revenue-maximizing tax rate. At the revenue-maximizing tax rate, a minuscule change in the tax rates will not alter tax collections. A minuscule *increase* in the tax rate will reduce the national income by enough so that even though a larger percentage of income is taken in taxes, the amount collected remains unchanged, and a tiny *reduction* in the tax rate will increase the national income so much that even though a smaller percentage is taken in taxes, receipts are unchanged. This is the optimal tax rate for the autocrat because changes in the national income affect his income only by changing tax collections.

But a majority at the revenue-maximizing tax rate is bound to increase its income from a *reduction* in tax rates: when the national income goes up, it not only, like the autocrat, collects taxes on a larger national income but also earns more income in the market. So the optimal tax rate for it is bound to be lower than the autocrat's. The easiest arithmetic example comes from supposing that the revenue-maximizing tax rate is one-third and that the majority earns one-third of the national income in the marketplace. The rational autocrat will then find that the last dollar in taxes that he collects reduces the national income by three dollars. One-third of this loss is his loss, so he just breaks even on this last dollar of tax collection and is at his revenue-maximizing rate. But if a majority mistakenly chose this same tax rate, it would be hurting itself, for it would lose two dollars (the same dollar lost by the autocrat plus one dollar of market income) from the last dollar it collected in taxes. Thus a majority would maximize its total income with a lower tax rate and a smaller redistribution to itself than would be chosen by an autocrat.[9]

More generally, it pays a ruling interest (whether an autocrat, a majority, or any other) to stop redistributing income to itself when the national income falls by the reciprocal of the share of the national income it receives. If the revenue-maximizing tax rate were one-half, an autocrat would stop increasing taxes when the national income fell by two dollars from his last dollar of tax collection. A majority that, say, earned three-fifths of the national income in the market and found it optimal to take one-fifth of the national income to transfer to itself would necessarily be reducing the national income by five-fourths, or $1.25, from the last dollar that it redistributed to itself. Thus the more encompassing an interest—the larger the share of the national income it receives taking all sources together—the less the social losses from its redistributions to itself. Conversely, the narrower the interest, the less it will take account of the social costs of redistributions to itself.

This last consideration makes it clear why the assumption that the democracy is governed by an encompassing interest can lead to much-too-optimistic predictions about many real-world democracies. The small parties that often emerge under proportional representation, for example, may encompass only a tiny percentage of a society and therefore may have little or no incentive to consider the social cost of the steps they take on behalf of their narrow constituencies. The special interest groups that are the main determinant of what government policies prevail in the particular areas of interest to those interest groups have almost no incentive to consider the social costs of the redistributions they obtain. A typical lobby in the United States, for example, represents less than 1 percent of the income-earning capacity of the country. It follows from the reciprocal rule that such a group has an incentive to stop arranging further redistributions to its clients only when the social costs of the redistribution become at least a hundred times as great as the amount they win in redistributional struggle (Olson 1982).

It would therefore be wrong to conclude that democracies will necessarily redistribute less than dictatorships. Their redistributions will, however, be shared, often quite unequally, by the citizenry. Democratic political competition, even when it works very badly, does not give the leader of the government the incentive that an autocrat has to extract the maximum attainable social surplus from the society to achieve his personal objectives.

"Long Live the King"

We know that an economy will generate its maximum income only if there is a high rate of investment and that much of the return on long-term investments is received long after the investment is made. This means that an autocrat who is taking a long view will try to convince his subjects that their assets will be permanently protected not only from theft by others but also from expropriation by the autocrat himself. If his subjects fear expropriation, they will invest less, and in the long run his tax collections will be reduced. To reach the maximum income attainable at a given tax rate, a society will also need to enforce contracts, such as contracts for long-term loans, impartially; but the full gains are again reaped only in the long run. To obtain the full advantage from long-run contracts a country also needs a stable currency. A stationary bandit will therefore reap the maximum harvest in taxes—and his subjects will get the largest gain from his encompassing interest in the productivity of his domain—only if he is taking an indefinitely long view and only if his subjects have total confidence that their "rights" to private property and to impartial contract enforcement will be permanently respected and that the coin or currency will retain its full value.

Now suppose that an autocrat is only concerned about getting through the next year. He will then gain from expropriating any convenient capital asset whose *tax yield* over the year is less than its *total* value. He will also gain from forgetting about the enforcement of long-term contracts, from repudiating his debts, and from coining or printing new money that he can spend even though this ultimately brings inflation. At the limit, when an autocrat has no reason to consider the future output of the society at all, his incentives are those of a roving bandit, and that is what he becomes.[10]

To be sure, the rational autocrat will have an incentive, because of his interest in increasing the investment and trade of his subjects, to promise that he will never confiscate wealth or repudiate assets. But the promise of an autocrat is not enforceable by an independent judiciary or any other independent source of power, because autocratic power by definition implies that there cannot be any judges or other sources of power in the society that the autocrat cannot overrule. Because of this and the obvious possibility that any dictator could, because of an insecure hold on power or the absence of an heir, take a short-term view, the promises of an autocrat are never completely credible. Thus the model of the rational self-interested autocrat I have offered is, in fact, somewhat too sanguine about economic performance under such autocrats because it implicitly assumed that they have (and that their subjects believe that they have) an indefinitely long planning horizon.

Many autocrats, at least at times, have had short time-horizons: the examples of confiscations, repudiated loans, debased coinages, and inflated currencies perpetrated by monarchs and dictators over the course of history are almost beyond counting. Perhaps the most interesting evidence about the importance of a monarch's time horizon comes from the historical concern about the longevity of monarchs and from the once-widespread belief in the social desirability of dynasties. There are many ways to wish a king well; but the king's subjects, as the foregoing argument shows, have more reason to be sincere when they say "long live the king." If the king anticipates and values dynastic succession, that further lengthens the planning horizon and is good for his subjects.

The historical prevalence of dynastic succession, in spite of the near-zero probability that the son of a king is the most talented person for the job, probably also owes something to another neglected feature of absolutisms. Any ruler with absolute power cannot, by definition, also have an independent source of power within the society that will select the next ruler and impose its choice upon the society. An independent capacity to install a new ruler would imply that this capacity can be used to remove or constrain the present autocrat. Thus, as is evident from modern dictatorships in Africa and Latin America, most dictatorships are by their nature especially susceptible to succession crises and uncertainty about the future. These uncertainties add to the problem of short time-horizons that has just been described. In these circumstances, it may be advantageous to a society if a consensus emerges about who the next ruler will probably be, since this reduces the social losses arising from the absence in an autocracy of any independent power that could ensure a smooth succession. Given autocracy, then, dynastic succession can be socially desirable, both because it may reduce the likelihood of succession crises and because it may give monarchs more concern for the long run and the productivity of their societies.

Democracy, Individual Rights, and Economic Development

We have seen that whenever a dictator has a sufficiently short time-horizon, it is in his interest to confiscate the property of his subjects, to abrogate any contracts he has signed in borrowing money from them, and generally to ignore the long-run economic consequences of his choices. Even the ever-present possibility that an autocracy will come to be led by someone with a short time-horizon always reduces confidence in investments and in the enforcement of long-run contracts. What do the individuals in an economy need if they are to have the maximum confidence that any property they accumulate will be respected and that any contracts they sign will be impartially enforced?

They need a secure government that respects individual rights. But individual rights are normally an artifact of a special set of governmental institutions. There is no private property without government! In a world of roving bandits some individuals may have possessions, but no one has a claim to private property that is enforced by the society. There is typically no reliable contract enforcement unless there is an impartial court system that can call upon the coercive power of the state to require individuals to honor the contracts they have made.

But individuals need their property and their contract rights protected from violation not only by other individuals in the private sector but also by the entity that has the greatest power in the society, namely, the government itself. An economy will be able to reap all potential gains from investment and from long-term transactions only if it has a government that is believed to be strong enough to last and inhibited from violating individual rights to property and rights to contract enforcement. What does a society need in order to have a government that satisfies both of these conditions?

Interestingly, the conditions that are needed to have the individual rights needed for maximum economic development are exactly the same conditions that are needed to have a *lasting* democracy. Obviously, a democracy is not viable if individuals, including the leading rivals of the administration in power, lack the rights to free speech and to security for their property and contracts or if the rule of law is not followed even when it calls for the current administration to leave office. Thus the *same* court system, independent judiciary, and respect for law and individual rights that are needed for a lasting democracy are also required for security of property and contract rights.

As the foregoing reasoning suggests, the only societies where individual rights to property and contract are confidently expected to last across generations are the securely democratic societies. In an autocracy, the autocrat will often have a short time-horizon, and the absence of any independent power to assure an orderly legal succession means that there is always substantial uncertainty about what will happen when the current autocrat is gone. History provides not even a single example of a long and uninterrupted sequence of absolute rulers who continuously respected the property and contract-enforcement rights of their subjects. Admittedly, the terms, tenures, and time horizons of democratic political leaders are perhaps even shorter than those of the typical autocrat, and democracies lose a good deal of efficiency because of this. But in the secure democracy with predictable succession of power under the rule of law, the adjudication and enforcement of individual rights is not similarly short-sighted. Many individuals in the secure democracies confidently make even very-long-term contracts, establish trusts for great-grandchildren, and create foundations that they expect will last indefinitely and thereby reveal that they expect their legal rights are secure for the indefinite future.

Not surprisingly, then, capital often flees from countries with continuing or episodic dictatorships (even when these countries have relatively little capital) to the stable democracies, even though the latter are already relatively well supplied with capital and thus offer only modest rates of return. Similarly, the gains from contract-intensive activities such as banking, insurance, and capital markets are also mainly reaped by stable democracies like the United States, the United Kingdom, and Switzerland. Though experience shows that relatively poor countries can grow extraordinarily rapidly when they have a strong dictator who happens to have unusually good economic policies, such growth lasts only for the ruling span of one or two dictators. It is no accident that the countries that have reached the highest level of economic development and have enjoyed good economic performance across generations are all stable democracies. Democracies have also been about twice as likely to win wars as have dictatorships (Lake 1992).

The Improbable Transition

How do democracies emerge out of autocracies? It is relatively easy to see how autocratic government emerges and why it has been the predominant form of government since the development of settled agriculture: there is never a shortage of strong men who enjoy getting a fortune from tax receipts. It is much harder to see how democratic government can emerge out of autocracy.

It is a logical mistake to suppose that because the subjects of an autocrat suffer from his exactions, they will overthrow him. The same logic of collective action that ensures the absence of social contracts in the historical record whereby large groups agreed to obtain the advantages of government also implies that the masses will not overthrow an autocrat simply because they would be better off if they did so. Historical evidence from at least the first pharaohs through Saddam Hussein indicates that resolute autocrats can survive even when they impose heinous amounts of suffering upon their peoples. When they are replaced, it is for other reasons (e.g., succession crises) and often by another stationary bandit.[11] What special circumstances explain the cases where a more or less democratic[12] or at least pluralistic government emerges out of an autocracy?

One obvious special circumstance is that, partly for the reasons just set out, the richest countries are democracies, and democracies have usually prevailed in the competitions with their major autocratic competitors, whether fascist or communist. The triumphant democracies have sometimes encouraged or subsidized transitions to democracy in other countries. In some cases, such as Germany, Japan, and Italy after World War II, the victorious democracies more or less demanded democratic institutions as a price for giving independence to the vanquished nations. The theoretical challenge is not to explain these transitions but rather those that are entirely internal and spontaneous.

Easy as it would be to argue that the initially or spontaneously democratic countries were blessed with democratic cultures or selfless leaders, this would be an ad hoc evasion. The obligation here is to explain the spontaneous transitions to democracy from the same parsimonious theory that has been used in the rest of this essay.

The theory suggests that the key to an explanation of the spontaneous emergence of democracy is the *absence* of the commonplace conditions that generate autocracy. The task is to explain why a leader who organized the overthrow of an autocrat would not make himself the next dictator or why any group of conspirators who overthrew an autocrat would not form a governing junta. We have seen that autocracy is a most profitable occupation and that the authors of most coups and upheavals have appointed themselves dictators. So the theory here predicts that democracy would be most likely to emerge spontaneously when the individual or individuals or group leaders who orchestrated the overthrow of an autocracy could not establish another autocracy, much as they would gain from doing so. We can deduce from the theory offered here that autocracy is prevented and democracy permitted by the accidents of history that leave a balance of power or stalemate—a dispersion of force and resources that makes it impossible for any one leader or group to overpower all of the others.

But this deduction does *not* give us any *original* conclusion: rather, it points directly toward one of the major inductive findings in some of the literature in history and in political science on the emergence of democracy. If the theory here is right, there must be a considerable element of truth in the famous Whig interpretation of British history and in the explanations of democracy offered by political scientists such as Robert Dahl (1971) and, especially, Tatu Vanhanen (1989). If the theory offered here is right, the literature that argues that the emergence of democracy is due to historical conditions and dispersions of resources that make it impossible for any one leader or group to assume all power is also right.

Yet it is also necessary to go back again to the theory for a crucial detail. Even when there is a balance of power that keeps any one leader or group from assuming total control of a large area or jurisdiction, the leader of each group may be able to establish himself as an autocrat of a small domain. A dispersion of power and resources over a large area can result in a set of small-scale autocracies but no democracy. If, however, the different contending groups are scrambled together over a wide and well-delineated domain, then small autocracies also are not feasible. They may not be feasible also if each of the leaders capable of forming a small-scale autocracy believes that a domain of that small scale would not be viable, whether because of aggression by other autocrats or for any reason.

If scrambled constituencies or any other factor rules out division of a domain into miniautocracies, then the best attainable option for the leader of each group when there is a balance of power is power sharing. If no one leader can subdue the others or segregate his followers into a separate domain, then the only alternatives are to engage in fruitless fighting or to work out a truce with mutual toleration. The provision of a peaceful order and other public goods will, in these circumstances, be advantageous for all of the groups; thus, the leaders of the different groups have an incentive to work out mutually satisfactory arrangements for the provision of such goods. Given peaceful conditions, there are great gains to leaders and other individuals in each group from being able to make mutually advantageous contracts with others and thereby a common interest in establishing a disinterested and independent judiciary. With several groups, it is not certain in advance how elections will turn out, yet each group can, by allying with other groups, ensure that no one other group will continually dominate elections. Thus elections as well as consensual agreements among the leaders of the different groups can be consistent with the interest of the leaders and members of each group.

Though there are a fair number of democracies, there have not been many spontaneous and entirely autonomous transitions from autocracy to democracy. Most of the democracies in the English-speaking world owed a good deal to the pluralism and democracy that emerged in late-seventeenth-century Britain, and thus they usually do not offer a completely independent test of the argument about the transition to democracy offered here.

Happily, the initial emergence of democracy with the Glorious Revolution of 1689 in England (and its very gradual transition from a democracy with a highly restricted franchise to universal suffrage) nicely fits the logic of the democratic transition predicted by the present theory. There were no lasting winners in the English civil wars. The different tendencies in British Protestantism and the economic and social forces with which they were linked were more or less evenly matched. There had been a lot of costly fighting, and, certainly after Cromwell, no one had the power to defeat all of the others. The restored Stuart kings might have been able to do this, but their many mistakes and the choices that ultimately united almost all of the normally conflicting Protestant and other political tendencies against them finally led to their total defeat.

None of the victorious leaders, groups, or tendencies was then strong enough to impose its will upon all of the others or to create a new autocracy. None had any incentive to give William and Mary the power to establish one either. The best option available to each of the leaders and groups with power was to agree upon the ascendancy of a parliament that included them all and to take out some insurance against the power of the others through an independent judiciary and a bill of rights. (The spread of the franchise is too long a story to tell here. But it is not difficult to see how, once the society was definitely nonautocratic and safely pluralist, additional groups could parlay the profitable interactions that particular enfranchised interests had with them—and the costs of suppression that they could force the enfranchised to bear—into a wider suffrage.)

With a carefully constrained monarchy, an independent judiciary, and a bill of rights, people in England in due course came to have a relatively high degree of confidence that any contracts they entered into would be impartially enforced and that private property rights, even for critics of the government, were relatively secure. Individual rights to property and contract enforcement were probably more secure in Britain after 1689 than anywhere else, and it was in Britain, not very long after the Glorious Revolution, that the Industrial Revolution began.[13]

Though the emergence of a democratic national government in the United States (and in some other areas of British settlement, such as Australia and Canada) was partly due to the example or influence of Great Britain, it also was due in part to the absence of any one group or colonial government that was capable of suppressing the others. The thirteen colonies were different from one another even on such important matters as slavery and religion, and none of them had the power to control the others. The separate colonies had, in general, experienced a considerable degree of internal democracy under British rule, and many of the colonies were, because of the different religious and economic groups they contained, also internally diverse. Many of the authors of the U.S. Constitution were, of course, also profoundly aware of the importance of retaining a dispersion of power (checks and balances) that would prevent autocracy.

The Different Sources of Progress in Autocracies and Democracies

Since human nature is profoundly complex, and individuals rarely act out of unmixed motives, the assumption of rational self-interest that I have been using to develop this theory is obviously much too simple to do justice to reality. But the caricature assumption that I have been using has not only simplified a forbiddingly complex reality but also introduced an element of impartiality: the same motivation was assumed in all regimes. The results are probably also robust enough to hold under richer and more realistic behavioral assumptions. The use of the same motivational assumption and the same theory to treat both autocracy and democracy also illuminates the main difference in the sources of economic growth and the obstacles to progress under autocracy and under democracy. In an autocracy, the source of order and the provision of other public goods and likewise the source of the social progress that these public goods make possible is the encompassing interest of the autocrat. The main obstacle to long-run progress in autocracies is that individual rights, even such relatively unpolitical or economic matters as property and contracts, can never be secure, at least over the long run.

Although democracies can also obtain great advantages from encompassing offices and political parties, this is by no means always understood (Olson 1982, 1986); nor are the awesome difficulties in keeping narrow special interests from dominating economic policymaking in the long-stable democracy. On the other hand, democracies have the great advantage of preventing significant extraction of social surplus by their leaders. They also have the extraordinary virtue that the same emphasis on individual rights that is necessary to lasting democracy is also necessary for secure rights to both property and the enforcement of contracts. The moral appeal of democracy is now almost universally appreciated, but its economic advantages are scarcely understood.

Notes

This chapter was previously published under the same title in the *American Political Science Review* 87 (3) (September 1993): 567–76. It is reprinted with permission from the American Political Science Association.

1. There is quantitative evidence from an exhaustive survey of ethnographic accounts showing that references to slaves are virtually absent in the accounts of the very most primitive peoples but rather common in more advanced agricultural societies (Hobhouse, Wheeler, and Ginsberg 1965). Slavery is unprofitable in hunting-gathering societies (Olson 1967).

2. Small tribes can sometimes form federations and thereby increase the number who can obtain collective goods through voluntary action (Olson 1965, 62–63). Some of the very earliest agricultural societies may have been of this character. But when the number of small groups itself becomes very large, the large-number problem is evident again, and voluntary collective action is infeasible.

3. For citations to much of the best literature extending and testing the argument in *The Logic of Collective Action,* as well as for valuable new analyses, see Hardin 1982 and Sandler 1992.

4. This literature is most constructive and interesting, but to the extent that it tries to explain government in terms of voluntary transactions, it is not convincing. North, while emphasizing transaction costs and contracts, also uses the notion of the predatory state and the logic of collective action in his account of the state, so his approach must be distinguished from that of Kiser and Barzel.

5. For the definition of an encompassing interest and evidence of its importance, see Olson 1982. The logical structure of the theory that encompassing interests will be concerned with the outcome for society whereas narrow groups will not is identical with the logic that shows that small groups can engage in voluntary collective action when large groups cannot.

6. Many of the more remarkable advances in civilization even in historic times took place in somewhat democratic or nondictatorial societies such as ancient Athens, the Roman Republic, the North Italian city-states, the Netherlands in the seventeenth century, and (at least after 1689) Great Britain. The explanation for the disproportionate representation of nonautocratic jurisdictions in human progress is presented later in the article.

7. The theory offered here applies to communist autocracies as much as to other types, though the theory needs to be elaborated to take account of the "implicit tax-price discrimination" pioneered by Joseph Stalin. This innovation enabled Stalinist regimes to obtain a larger proportion of social output for their own purposes than any other regimes had been able to do. This explained Stalin's success in making the Soviet Union a superpower and the great military capacity of many communist regimes. It also generated a unique dependence of the system on its management cadre, which ultimately proved

fatal. For how the theory applies to communist autocracies and societies in transition, see Clague and Rausser 1992, preface and chapter 4; Murrell and Olson 1991 [and Olson 2000, published after the author's death —ed.].

8. Schumpeter's analysis is in his "The Crisis of the Tax State," written in the highly taxed Austria-Hungarian Empire late in World War I; Ibn Kalduhn's is in his classic *The Mugaddimah.*

9. A mathematical and geometrical proof of this conclusion and an analysis of many other technical questions raised by the present theory are available on request.

10. When war erodes confidence about what the boundaries of an autocrat's domain will be, an autocrat's time horizon with respect to his possession of any given territory shortens—even if he believes he will remain in control of some territory somewhere. In the limit, complete uncertainty about what territory an autocrat will control implies roving banditry. The advantages of stationary banditry over roving banditry are obviously greatest when there are natural and militarily defensible frontiers. Interestingly, the earliest states in history emerged mainly in what one anthropologist calls "environmentally circumscribed" areas, that is, areas of arable land surrounded by deserts, mountains, or coasts (see Carneiro 1970). The environmental circumscription not only provides militarily viable frontiers but also limits the opportunity for defeated tribes to flee to other areas in which they could support themselves (as Carneiro points out). This in turn means that the consensual democracy characteristic of the earliest stages of social evolution is, in these geographical conditions, replaced by autocratic states earlier than in other conditions.

11. For more examples of other types of reasons, see Olson 1990.

12. In the interest of brevity, democracy is here defined as competitive elections, social pluralism, and the absence of autocracy, rather than in terms of universal suffrage. Although how a narrower suffrage turns into a wider suffrage can be explained by straightforward extensions of the logic of the theory offered here, developing these extensions and testing them against the historical evidence would not be a small undertaking.

13. For striking evidence on how the growth of cities was much greater in medieval and early modern Europe in democratic or less autocratic regimes, see DeLong and Shleifer 1993. In effect, the DeLong and Shleifer essay is a test of the advantages of democracy that I put forward.

References

Banfield, Edward. 1958. *The Moral Basis of a Backward Society.* Glencoe, IL: Free Press.

Carneiro, Robert L. 1970. "A Theory of the Origin of the State." *Science* 169:733–38.

Clague, Christopher, and Gordon Rausser, eds. 1992. *The Emergence of Market Economies in Eastern Europe.* Cambridge, MA: Basil Blackwell.

Dahl, Robert. 1971. *Polyarchy, Participation, and Opposition.* New Haven: Yale University Press.

DeLong, J. Bradford, and Andrei Shleifer. 1993. "Princes and Merchants: European City Growth before the Industrial Revolution." *Journal of Law and Economics* 36:671–702.

Hardin, Russell. 1982. *Collective Action.* Baltimore: Johns Hopkins University Press.

Hobhouse, L. T., G. C. Wheeler, and M. Ginsberg. 1965. *The Material Culture and Social Institutions of Simpler Peoples.* London: Routledge and Kegan Paul.

Kalduhn, Ibn. 1967. *The Mugaddimah.* Trans. Franz Rosenthal. Princeton: Princeton University Press.

Kiser, Edgar, and Yoram Barzel. 1991. "Origins of Democracy in England." *Journal of Rationality and Society* 3:396.

Lake, David A. 1992. "Powerful Pacifists: Democratic States and War." *American Political Science Review* 86:24–37.

Murrell, Peter, and Mancur Olson. 1991. "The Devolution of Centrally Planned Economies." *Journal of Comparative Economics* 15:239–65.

North, Douglass. 1981. *Growth and Structural Change.* New York: Norton.

North, Douglass, and Robert Thomas. 1973. *The Rise of the West.* Cambridge: Cambridge University Press.

Olson, Mancur. 1965. *The Logic of Collective Action.* Cambridge: Harvard University Press.

———. 1967. "Some Historic Variation in Property Institutions." Princeton University. Mimeo.

———. 1982. *The Rise and Decline of Nations.* New Haven: Yale University Press.

———. 1986. "A Theory of the Incentives Facing Political Organizations: Neo-corporatism and the Hegemonic State." *International Political Science Review* 7:165–89.

———. 1990. "The Logic of Collective Action in Soviet-Type Societies." *Journal of Soviet Nationalities* 1 (2): 8–33.

———. 2000. *Power and Prosperity: Outgrowing Communist and Capitalist Dictatorships.* New York: Basic Books.

Sandler, Todd. 1992. *Collective Action: Theory and Applications.* Ann Arbor: University of Michigan Press.

Schumpeter, Joseph. 1991. "The Crisis of the Tax State." In *Joseph A. Schumpeter: The Economics and Sociology of Capitalism,* ed. Richard Swedberg. Princeton: Princeton University Press.

Sheridan, James E. 1966. *Chinese Warlord: The Career of Feng Yu-hsiang.* Stanford: Stanford University Press.

Vanhanen, Tatu. 1989. "The Level of Democratization Related to Socioeconomic Variables in 147 States in 1980–85." *Scandinavian Political Studies* 12:95–127.

CHAPTER 6

Property and Contract Rights in Autocracies and Democracies

Christopher Clague, Philip Keefer,
Stephen Knack, and Mancur Olson

1. Introduction

What types of governments are most likely to have economic policies and institutions that generate good economic performance? There are examples of good—and of bad—economic performance under both autocratic and democratic governments. Many empirical studies have compared the economic performance of autocracies and democracies, but their conclusions are remarkably varied and inconclusive. We shall show here that it is naive to suppose that one of these types of political systems will regularly have better economic performance than the other.

The quality of economic policies and institutions depends partly on the incentives and constraints that face those who make governmental and legal decisions. These incentives and constraints vary from one autocracy to another and from one democracy to another. We contend that they vary so much within these two types of regimes that any empirical tests that merely distinguish governments as autocratic or democratic are bound to be misspecified. We show that, when appropriate distinctions are drawn within each of these two types of governments, clear and robust empirical findings emerge.

The importance of incentives within different types of governments becomes immediately evident when we think about the sometimes hoped-for benevolent dictator who understands (or who is guided by economic advisers who understand) the advantages of markets and uses them effectively to elicit economic growth through the rational self-interest behavior of his subjects. A moment's reflection reveals a methodological inconsistency: if the autocrat's subjects are supposed to be self-interested, we should impartially assume that the autocrat will also take his own interests into account. If he does, then whenever insecurity about his hold on power or anything else gives him a short time-horizon, he will gain from expropriating any assets of his subjects whose tax-yield to him over the short time-horizon is less than their capital value. He will typically also gain resources by printing money to spend on his own purposes, thereby taxing real money balances through inflation, and by repudiating his debts. Such measures increase the resources he can use to attempt to hold on to his power or to serve his interests in other ways. There are countless examples throughout history of autocrats who have taken such measures. In such cases, the rational self-interest of an autocrat is inconsistent with the private property rights that are necessary for an effective market economy.

By contrast, a similarly rational and self-interested autocrat expecting to rule for a long time (especially one with dynastic expectations) would gain from respecting—and even protecting—the property of his subjects. This would increase investment and future productivity and thus also his long-run tax collections. There are many historical examples of autocrats who have served their long-run interests in this way.

Thus autocrats with different time horizons face dramatically different incentives. This means that we cannot correctly estimate the impact of autocratic government on economic performance without taking the time horizons of the individual autocrats into account. The empirical results in this essay suggest that this is a matter of some importance.

Consider now the factors that can endanger property and contract rights in a beginning democracy. Suppose the democratic debut involves nothing more than an election that gives victory to some political leader or optimizing party. When an elected leader has such power, it brings him benefits, so we cannot take it for granted that democratic leaders will be indifferent to whether or not they continue in power or that they will exercise their power without regard to their own interests. The elected leadership might maximize its chances of reelection by confiscating the assets of unpopular minorities or of the rich and distributing the proceeds among those from whom it hopes to obtain a majority in the next election. It might sometimes also improve its chances of staying in power by seizing opposing media of communication, or the assets of political opponents, or any firms or fortunes that are linked to its opponents.

Such measures terminate or at least endanger the democracy (and often are a sign that the current elected leader is on the way to becoming a dictator). They could not even be implemented if the democracy has courts that rigorously enforce the rule of law. But an initial election (however fair) does not by itself guarantee that there is an effective legal system enforcing the rule of law. Thus transitory democracies can easily suffer from expropriations that have the same harmful effects on property rights as the predations of an autocrat. If a government does not have (or respect) the legal mechanisms that constrain usurpations of individual rights, it cannot be a lasting democracy, but some democracies do not last long.

The situation in a lasting democracy is utterly different not only from transitory democracies but also from autocratic governments. Though lasting democracies suffer from sclerotic accumulations of special-interest lobbying and (like all other types of governments) often have economically inefficient policies, they *necessarily* hold elections under law, and the governmental leaders or parties that are defeated surrender power in accord with the law. There cannot be genuine elections unless even the leading opponents of the party in power have not only political rights but also the economic rights needed to obtain a livelihood. If even those who are the main competitors of the existing leaders of government have these rights, they should normally be available to others as well. (This is true of any lasting representative government, whether it has universal adult suffrage, such as is typical now, or a more restrictive suffrage, such as was characteristic of representative governments in the nineteenth century and earlier. Thus our argument applies to all representative governments, but since the representative governments in our data base are overwhelmingly universal-suffrage democracies, we use the familiar word *democracy* to cover all representative governments.)

Moreover, the independent judiciary, the courts, the respect for law, or whatever other mechanisms ensure that a democracy abides by competitive elections held according to law necessarily also ensure that the citizenry has the freedom to do whatever is permitted under the law. This freedom by definition provides some individual rights: individuals have the socially protected *right* to do whatever is not prohibited by law. Property rights are simply the individual rights that relate to things that may be bought and sold. As James Madison put it, just "as a man is said to have a right to his property, he may equally be said to have a property in his rights."[1] Property and contract rights are protected by the same institutions that protect other individual rights. Societies are therefore constrained in their choices: they cannot prohibit all types of private property and freedom of contract and also have a lasting democracy. A stable democracy without any property and contract rights is not feasible. All lasting representative governments that have been observed, however wise or unwise their laws may be, always have some extensive property and contract rights.

Whereas in an autocracy it is the leader's interest in his future tax returns (and thus in the future income of his domain) that is the source of any property and contract rights, in any lasting democracy it is the very mechanisms that ensure that a leader can *not* unilaterally extend his hold on power that are the source of property and contract rights. Though some democracies suffer from excessive turnover of leadership, the legal replacement of democratic leaders is in general a sign of the effective rule of law, and thus of the property and contract rights of the citizenry.

Property and contract rights in a democracy rest mainly on the need, if the democracy is to last, to leave decisions about whether the law is being followed to relatively *disinterested* parties. Political leaders have an incentive to interpret the law in whatever way best furthers their own interests, so a democracy will not last if they can interpret the law as they please. The rule of law needed for a lasting democracy will prevail only if disputes under the law are adjudicated mainly by individuals who have no stake in the dispute. This in turn requires institutions that, by social design, have a very special structure of incentives and constraints: one in which those who make decisions do not share in the losses or gains of any party to the dispute and in which a knowledge of the law and a reputation for fairness increase the chances for advancement. To last, a democracy must maintain and abide by such institutions, notably courts with an independent judiciary.

We hypothesize that the dependence of any lasting democracy on legal institutions with this special structure of incentives and constraints is the main source of property and contract rights in democracies. In an autocracy, on the other hand, the autocrat is by definition the source of law and thus above the law and able to override any of his courts. Thus his motive for providing property and contract rights, even if they are provided through courts, is rather mainly his interest in the income and taxable capacity of his domain. The structures of incentives and constraints that give rise to property and contract rights in democracies and autocracies are, therefore, dramatically different.

The preceding logic leads us to hypothesize that in autocracies it is the time horizon of the *individual autocrat* (or, occasionally, the ruling clique) that is the main determinant of property and contract rights, whereas in democracies these rights depend upon whether the *democratic system* is durable.

Many democracies are transitory, and such property and contract rights as they provide can be quite inferior to those provided by some secure autocrats. An autocrat has, however, the capacity to seize any assets in the country that he rules, whereas no single individual in a continuing democracy can unilaterally seize the assets of others or abrogate their rights under contracts. Any autocratic society will sooner or later come to have rulers with short time-horizons due to succession crises or other causes. We therefore hypothesize that democracies that have lasted for some time and are expected to last much longer provide better property and contract rights than any other type of regime. The societies that are consistently havens for capital flight and that have experienced steady capital accumulation across generations are all lasting democracies.[2]

In this essay we test empirically the theory that has just been described. Section 2 shows how the theory lends itself to relatively straightforward empirical tests, both because here past experience is a relatively good guide to the future, and also because the tests are not likely to be subject to any severe endogeneity problems. Section 3 describes our data on regime type, regime duration, and property rights. Section 4 reports empirical findings on property rights and regime type, while section 5 presents findings on property rights and regime duration. Sections 6, 7, and 8 test the robustness of our results and show that they are not an artifact of reverse causation, sample selection, measurement error, or heteroskedasticity. We conclude with section 9.

2. Empirical Tractability

However long a political regime has survived, the incentive structure changes drastically if that regime is expected to collapse soon. This expectation will not only change behavior in the political system, but will also alter behavior in the market. Even if property or contract rights are good at the moment, it will usually not pay to make long-term contracts or investments if one expects that contracts will not be enforced or property rights protected a year from now. Therefore, the institutions and policies that determine contract and property rights, like monetary and macroeconomic policies, affect reality not only directly but also through their impact on the expectations of the participants in the economy.

It might seem that, because expectations about the future are important, yet not directly measurable, this theory would be difficult to test. In fact, there are some important and interesting reasons that make empirical testing relatively straightforward. The idea that the past is prologue is especially relevant in this area.

Consider democratic systems first. The length of time that a legal system has been operating is a major determinant of how well property and contract rights are defined and delineated. It is beyond the wit of man to think of all possible contingencies that might lead to disputes about contracts or property. Thus legal systems that have litigated a great many cases and have accumulated a vast store of precedents offer better defined and delineated contract and property rights than otherwise similar systems that have just started. Some new political systems have sometimes dealt with this problem by adopting wholesale the commercial codes and court precedents of other countries. Though in some cases, such as in the continued use of English common law precedents in the United States after it achieved independence, this is relatively easy, there are often substantial problems arising from differences in technology, customs, language, and experience between the country with the new political system and the country whose legal codes and precedents are being adopted. Thus the length of time a legal system has been operating affects the way it works, quite apart from the way that its age affects its viability.

The impact of age on viability is nicely illustrated by elections in the United States. Though there are substantial industries that do economic and political forecasting, one virtually never sees forecasts about whether, say, the 1998 congressional elections will take place. In large part because elections in the United States have been held as scheduled for more than 200 years, it is simply taken for granted that they will be held as scheduled. Similarly, the fact that the British court system has protected property and contract rights with continuity for more than 300 years means that certain property and contract rights in Britain are not the object of explicit forecasts, but are unthinkingly taken for granted. Such tacit assumptions about the institutional reality are, in turn, part of the institutional reality: what everyone expects—and especially what everyone takes for granted—is more likely to happen precisely because of these explicit or tacit expectations.

New democracies not only usually lack the security that comes from such expectations, but they are often also set up in extremely fluid—and sometimes nearly anarchic—situations. When the flag of a new democracy is raised, it may not even be clear how many will salute: there is not only uncertainty about how long the new democracy will last, but sometimes it is not even clear that the new democracy has the power needed to protect property and contract rights. Thus we conclude that the age of a democratic political system is not only directly pertinent to the property and contract rights in a democracy, but also a reasonable proxy measure of both the likelihood and the popular expectation that a given democratic system and the rights it provides will last for the foreseeable future.

Now let us consider autocracy. It is instructive to start with Mao's maxim that political power grows out of the barrel of a gun. Accepting this maxim does not imply, however, that an autocrat is the best marksman in the country, much less that he personally could outgun any large number of his subjects. The power of an autocrat when he is powerful grows mainly out of the belief that his subordinates will use their guns in the service of the autocrat, thereby making it exceedingly costly for other subjects to rebel. But who guards the guards? What explains why a given officer in the autocrat's army or police will obey the autocrat's orders, when they do, in fact, obey? If any officer *expects* that all or almost all of the other officers will follow the autocrat's orders, then he has no choice but to follow these orders also. What each of the other officers does also depends on what they, in turn, expect their colleagues to do. If almost everyone expects that almost all of the officers will follow the autocrat's orders, the autocrat is securely in control and likely to remain in control for some time. What it is rational to do depends on what average opinion expects average opinion to be. When someone has appointed himself the new autocrat, it is usually not clear what each officer will expect, or expect that his colleagues will expect. So autocrats who have not consolidated their power do not, in fact, necessarily have much power.

Thus the power of an autocrat is in large part the outcome of a co-ordination game. Just as it is irrational to drive on a different side of the road than other people going the same direction expect to use, so it is irrational to ignore the expectations of others in assessing an autocrat's power. This means that usually the longer an autocrat exercises power, the more people will take for granted that his orders will be followed, and the more power he has.

One check on the validity of the preceding arguments is the correlation between duration and the likelihood of a coup. We calculated the probability of a coup for all regimes for all years from the data for 1948 through 1982 as a ratio of two numbers. The numerator is the sum of all autocrats who were deposed by a coup in year t of their tenure. The denominator is the sum of all autocrats with tenure greater than or equal to $t - 1$. The probabilities of both successful and unsuccessful coup attempts are quite high in the first five years of autocrat tenure, but decline dramatically as tenure increases. The probability of a coup attempt (including successful coups) is 32 percent in the first year, 20 percent in the second year, and below 10 percent for most years beyond the sixth. This pattern suggests that the duration of an autocrat's rule is a reasonable approximation of regime stability and expected remaining duration. This pattern is also consistent with our use of the log of duration in all empirical specifications, so that increases from, say, 0 to 3 years in the elapsed duration of an autocrat's rule are weighted much more heavily than increases from 10 to 13 years. A similar calculation was made for democracies. Again, the probabilities of successful and unsuccessful coups tend to decline as the elapsed duration of democracy within a country increases.

It might be thought that the expected remaining duration of an autocrat's regime would be inversely related to the age of the autocrat, since human life is finite and this sets a maximum value on the expected remaining duration of an autocrat's regime. Age and duration increase together, making duration to date a suspect proxy for the expected remaining time in power. However, the prospects of natural death constrain the time horizons of even very old leaders less than one might expect. The probability of death from natural causes in a particular year is not high even at advanced ages. From the life tables of the United States, average remaining years of life exceeds five years even for an eighty-year-old male. Furthermore, our use of the log of duration ensures that minimal weight is given to further increases in tenure for aging autocrats of long standing included in our sample, such as Banda of Malawi and Franco of Spain. In any event, the expectation of natural death will have less impact on an autocrat's incentives than the expectation of exiting via a coup. An autocrat may spend substantial amounts of a country's resources attempting to stave off a coup—or preparing for a luxurious exile—but there are limits to what he can usefully spend to stave off natural death. A proxy measure that declined in value when autocrats reached advanced ages thus might be a less accurate measure of incentives to protect property rights than the one used here. Thus we take the elapsed duration of an autocrat's (or an autocratic group's) rule and the current age of a democratic system life as proxies for its expected remaining life: what has survived for a long time is expected to be more likely to last than that which is new.

There is another reason why testing the implications of the foregoing theory is relatively straightforward. The key causal variables are the age of a democratic *system* and the duration of an *individual* autocrat's rule. As Grossman and Noh (1990) have shown, the time in office of a democratic leader in a political system with free entry is likely to be quite sensitive to the policies chosen by that leader. A leader or political party with a rapacious policy is much less likely to be able to win support for continuation in office than one that has followed a policy that favors the welfare of the citizenry. To determine the relationship between the tenure in office of an individual democratic leader and his impact on property and contract rights, one would have to measure not only the effect of leaders' time horizons on the policies they chose, but also the impact of the policies chosen on the probability of reelection. There would presumably be strong causal connections going in both directions, and this would complicate empirical testing. By contrast, when the age of a democratic *system* — or the length of a *single autocrat's* rule — is at issue, the situation is relatively straightforward.

In a secure democracy in which the continuation of representative government is taken for granted, the incumbent leader may not even give any thought to the implications of his policies for the life of the political system. Moreover, the property and contract rights at issue are more often the province of the courts and the legal system than of the elected officials. In a democracy that is quite insecure the courts may be much weaker, and the incumbent leader obviously may take an interest in the question of how long the democracy will last, since his position as leader may be affected. But it would be wrong to conclude that he is necessarily motivated by a desire to prolong the life of the democracy: he could, for the reasons set out previously, also be motivated by a desire to become a dictator who does not have to continue to answer to the electorate. Thus, just as he might choose policies that are intended to increase the life of the democracy, so he might choose policies with the opposite objective. While our theoretical framework suggests that there should be a strong tendency for lasting democracies to have better individual rights than those that have not yet been securely established, it does not suggest that there should be any strong and regular tendency for democratic leaders to choose policies about property and contract rights that are intended to change the duration of the democratic system. Accordingly, our theory implies that the age of a democratic system is not directly influenced by policy choices. Policy choices may influence the survival probability of a democratic system through their impact on economic performance, but we control for per capita GDP levels and growth rates, and this should capture much of the effect of any endogenous policy choices. We shall later see that our statistical examination of this issue offers further reassurance.

In the case of autocracy, there can be no doubt that an autocrat has an incentive to choose policies that will extend his tenure. Though this effect can indeed lead to bias in our estimates, the bias runs against our hypothesis. We assume autocrats optimize, so that an autocrat with a low survival probability *increases* his exactions and reduces his expenditures on the legal infrastructure. One reason he does this is because he has little reason to take account of the reduction in future tax receipts that this brings about. Another reason is that he rationally gives a relatively higher value to resources that he can obtain now to shore up his hold on power by strengthening his instruments of social control and by subsidizing pivotal allies. Though a government whose survival depends on popularity with an electorate may gain from lowering taxes, an autocrat's tenure does not depend on any electorate. It typically depends instead on the power and loyalty of his military and police forces and on the support of his allies.[3] He needs resources to obtain this power, loyalty, and support. If most autocrats tried to increase their tenures by improving the welfare of their subjects, much of the effects of this will in any event be captured by per capita GDP levels and growth rates, which we control for.

Thus in our model an autocrat's incentive to increase taxes and reduce expenditures on legal infrastructure *improves* his survival probabilities. Higher taxes still have an opportunity cost for an autocrat, however: higher taxes (and insecure property and contract rights) reduce future GDP levels. At a sufficiently high probability of survival, the costs of forgone future tax revenues from reducing GDP outstrip the benefits from using current tax revenues to extend one's tenure, particularly if one makes the reasonable assumption that survival probabilities increase at a diminishing rate as expenditures on repressive forces and pivotal allies increase.

Accordingly, optimization by insecure autocrats assures that they adjust their economic policies to make their tenure less short or in-secure than it would otherwise be. They do this by increasing their ex-actions or confiscations to obtain more resources for protecting their hold on power. To the extent that autocrats who would otherwise have a short tenure succeed in extending their hold on power, our co-efficients on the tenure of autocrats tend to be biased downward: those insecure autocrats whose expedient expropriations have en-abled them to cling to power for extended periods reduce the gener-ally positive association between the elapsed duration of an auto-crat's rule and the security of property and contract rights. We nonetheless later report the results of tests that correct for the possi-bility our coefficients are biased upward by a feedback from im-proved policies to lengthened tenure.

3. Regime Types, Regime Duration, and Property Rights: The Data

This section describes the variables we use to assess regime types, regime duration, and property and contract rights. Since both the regime type and regime duration variables have been newly con-structed for this essay and should ultimately also prove useful to other investigators, we must describe them fully. But the rest of the essay should be comprehensible even to those readers who have skipped this section.

Defining Regime Types

Most recent empirical studies of democracy and economic perfor-mance make use of Gastil's (1989) measures of political rights and/or civil liberties. The Gastil measures include some rights that are more nearly outcomes of political and economic processes than defining features or requisites of a democratic political system.[4] Given that our interest is in assessing the impact of regime type on property rights, the outcomes-based nature of the Gastil indices makes them inappropriate indicators of democracy. In addition, they do not cover part of our sample period.

Our definition of democracy is procedural. In a democratic regime the chief executive and the legislature are both elected in competitive elections, and the legislature is effective, in the sense that it has con-siderable autonomy. In this definition both presidential and parlia-mentary systems can be fully democratic. A regime falls short of full democracy if the elections are not fully competitive or if the executive's power is so predominant that the legislature does not provide an effective check on that power.

Our definition of democracy is procedural, but the existence of competitive democratic procedures implies the existence of certain rights. It is obviously impossible for a society to have continuing and truly competitive elections unless certain freedoms are maintained. Thus continuing representative government implies free speech, the right to campaign freely, the right to form political parties, the right of peaceful demonstration, and freedom from arbitrary arrest. It also implies that at least some opponents of the party in power must be able to survive economically and thus have at least enough property and contract rights to remain viable. The only fully competitive elections are those in which even the opponents of the party in power have the rights they need to compete and to survive.

A full-fledged dictatorship, on the other hand, is a regime in which neither the chief executive nor the legislature (if one exists) is chosen in a competitive election, or one in which a competitively elected legislature is rendered ineffective by a nonelected (or not competitively elected) executive.[5]

We classify regimes by relying as much as possible on the judgments made by other observers, although in a few situations we draw our own inferences in resolving ambiguities. These instances are explained below. Our basic sources for data on selection of the chief executive and effectiveness of the legislature are Gurr's *Polity II* (1990) and Banks (1979). Our classification assigns a number from I to V to each country in each year, where these numbers have the following meanings:

I. Dictatorship
II. Almost Dictatorship
III. Intermediate Category
IV. Almost Democracy
V. Democracy

These classifications are based on the variables executive competitiveness (XRCOMP) from Gurr and executive selection (EXSELEC) and legislative effectiveness (LEGEF) from Banks. Gurr and Banks provide two alternative judgments about the selection of the chief executive. Gurr's XRCOMP classifies countries into one of three categories with respect to how the chief executive is selected. These may be loosely described as (1) no elections or rigged elections; (2) dual/transitional, where there are two executives or there is a transition between selection and election; and (3) competitive election. Banks's EXSELEC provides essentially a two-way classification: the chief executive is either elected or not. Banks's LEGEF classifies countries into one of three categories with respect to the legislature: (1) no legislature or one that is rendered completely ineffective by domestic turmoil or by the actions of the chief executive; (2) a partially effective legislature; (3) an effective legislature, elected under competitive conditions.

Five categories (I–V) are derived from these variables in the following way. A full-fledged Democracy (V) is in the top category on all three variables, while a full-fledged Dictatorship (I) is in the bottom category on XRCOMP and LEGEF. An Almost Democracy (IV) falls short of the top rating on either XRCOMP or LEGEF, while an Almost Dictatorship (II) is in the intermediate category on LEGEF. The other cases are classified in the Intermediate Category (III), or are inconsistent (for example, because Gurr and Banks rate the chief executive differently, or because the legislature is rated as fully effective yet the chief executive was selected rather than elected).[6] In our empirical tests, we treat countries in categories IV or V as democracies, and countries in categories I and II as autocracies. The small number of country-year observations in category III are omitted. The Gurr and Banks data are available only through 1986. Our research assistant Suzanne Gleason updated regimes codings through 1990, relying primarily on the *Europa Yearbook*. Only seven countries were judged to have changed classification between 1986 and 1990.[7]

Empirically, the differences between our procedural definition and the Gastil outcomes-based measures turn out to be relatively minor.[8] A crucial advantage of our measure for present purposes is that the data it is based on are available well before the 1973 beginning date for Gastil's indices.

Measurement of Regime Duration

For democracies, we create two duration measures: DEMDUR refers to the number of consecutive years that a country has been a democracy[9] (i.e., regime type IV or V), while DEXDUR is the number of years that the chief executive has been in office in a democracy. Thus, DEMDUR is reset to one in any year in which the country lapses from democratic status (i.e., drops to category III or below), while DEXDUR is reset to one in any year in which the chief executive changes.

For autocracies, the variable AUTDUR is defined as the number of consecutive years that the chief executive in an autocratic nation has been in power. The value of AUTDUR thus increases by one for each year that the autocrat remains in power and the regime remains in either of the categories I and II. The variable is reset to one in any year in which the chief executive changes. This proxy for the time horizons of decision makers in autocracies fits the simplest and most common type of modern autocracy: one-man rule with no established procedures for succession.

There are, however, some cases for which this proxy for autocratic time horizons does not apply. Though autocracies are much less likely to be institutionalized than democracies, some relatively autocratic or at least nondemocratic regimes have achieved a degree of institutionalization. For these regimes, the tenure of the chief executive will be a somewhat noisy measure. In exceptional cases, such as Mexico in the heyday of the PRI, where institutionalization reaches levels that are not normally found outside of the advanced democracies, the expected remaining duration of the president's rule is never more than his institutionally given single term of six years, but the time horizon of the PRI's oligarchic establishment has been far longer. In the more general case of undemocratic and entrenched ruling parties,[10] the chief executive may be removed by the party's ruling council or Politburo while the dictatorial rule of the party continues. As in Saudi Arabia, the monarch often attains and maintains power only with the backing of other members of the royal family. For a chief executive who intends to have his son succeed him in power, the autocratic planning horizon is so long that any confiscation that reduces investment and thus future income and tax collections will not be advantageous. What is common to all of these cases is the presence of a "ruling group," a family or party with an indefinitely long life-span and thus a longer-run interest in the nation's long-term economic performance than an individualistic autocrat would have. Autocratic ruling groups usually also impose some constraints on the unilateral decisions of their leaders.[11]

These considerations lead us to adopt a second measure of tenure for autocracies, the duration of the ruling group (AUTGROUP). Whenever one autocrat is succeeded by another autocrat belonging to the same "group," the counter variable AUTGROUP continues, rather than restarting at one, as AUTDUR does. As with AUTDUR and DEMDUR, we hypothesize that farsighted policies regarding property rights will be associated with higher values of AUTGROUP, our measure of stability of the ruling group. In defining groups, our primary criterion is the peaceful transfer of power. Except in rare circumstances (such as an overthrow within a ruling family, as in Oman in 1970), exit via a coup is regarded as a change in group. Information from *Europa Yearbook* and other sources was used in judging the extent to which a new leader represented a sharp break with his predecessor. Monarchical succession and transfers of power within strong ruling parties (or revolutionary councils) were coded as occurring within a given group. In all, about 30 percent of transfers were judged to be intragroup.

Property Rights Measures

There are many ways in which governments can violate—or fail to protect against private theft and usurpation—the property and contract rights of its citizens and subjects: direct expropriation of assets, defaulting on public debt, debasing the currency, prohibiting any transactions other than those at officially established prices, and failing to provide a legal infrastructure that impartially enforces contracts and adjudicates disputes about property rights. No one measure can capture all of these aspects of property and contract rights, so we use six separate variables: the amount of "contract-intensive money," indices from two firms evaluating risks to foreign investors, a subjective measure of default risk, currency depreciation, and the black market exchange premium.

Contract-intensive money (CIM) is defined as $(M_2 - C)/M_2$, where M_2 is a broad definition of money and C is currency outside banks. In environments in which third-party enforcement of contracts is reliable and where property rights facilitate pledging of assets as security for loans, banks and other financial intermediaries will profit from providing retail banking services at low cost, and sometimes even from paying interest on bank deposits, in order to obtain money that they can lend at higher rates. If the public can rely on institutional stability and third-party enforcement of contracts, they can be confident that the banks or government will not confiscate their deposits. Thus the rationale for this measure is that those forms of money, such as currency, that rely least on the fulfillment of contractual obligations by others will be preferred when property and contractual rights are insecure, whereas other forms of money are more advantageous for most purposes in environments with secure contract-enforcement and property rights. Since the noncurrency components of M_2 are, by definition, held in banks or other financial institutions, poor contract-enforcement and property rights imply that any advantages of using money in the form of deposits in financial institutions are small and that there is also the risk that sums deposited will not be recovered. Thus the poorer the contract-enforcement and other institutions in a society, the smaller the proportion of contract-intensive money individuals will hold. We have found the proportion of contract-intensive money to be a useful and reliable measure in other contexts as well.[12]

For two other measures of property rights, we employ ratings compiled by two private firms for potential foreign investors. Though these ratings are subjective, the firms that produced them for sale had an incentive to make them as accurate as possible, and the fact that they were purchased by investors who would lose from wrong information also adds something to their credibility. The International Country Risk Guide (ICRG), published since 1982, covers more than 100 countries. Business Environmental Risk Intelligence (BERI) has provided ratings for about 50 countries beginning in 1972.

From five variables contained in one of these sources and four scored by the other, we create the two simple additive indices, "ICRG" and "BERI."[13] The five variables comprising the ICRG index are "Expropriation Risk," "Risk of Contract Repudiation by the Government," "Quality of the Bureaucracy," "Corruption in Government," and "Rule of Law."[14] Variables entering the BERI index include "Contract Enforceability," "Nationalization Risk," "Bureaucratic Delays," and "Infrastructure Quality."[15]

"Contract Enforceability" by BERI and "Risk of Repudiation of Contracts by Government" by ICRG are measures of how well contracts are enforced. "Rule of Law" scores reflect the strength of the court system and the degree to which citizens accept the lawmaking powers and dispute resolution mechanisms of legal institutions, rather than depending on force or other illegal means to settle claims.[16] Definitions of "Corruption in Government," "Quality of the Bureaucracy," "Bureaucratic Delays," and "Transportation and Communication Quality" justify their use as measures of the general efficiency of provision of government services as well as the extent of rent-seeking behavior of government officials.[17]

Our fourth measure of property and contract rights is a subjective rating of the risk of default on sovereign debt. This credit-rating variable (CREDIT) can range from 0 to 100 (higher values indicate a lower risk of default, but values are not interpretable as probabilities). This measure is an average of evaluations by a panel of international bankers published semiannually by *Institutional Investor*.[18]

Our fifth measure is the debasement of the currency as measured by the rate of currency depreciation (DEPREC), which is equal to (100 + inflation rate)/100. Inflation (as well as default on the sovereign debt) can be viewed as an indirect method of expropriation, an alternative to directly expropriating assets.

Our final measure is the (log of the) black market premium on currency exchange (PREMIUM). A high black market premium suggests that there are exchange controls and severe imports restrictions. These controls and restrictions not only limit the types of contracts and the uses of property that are permissible in a country, but also give government officials a wide range of discretionary power through the granting or withholding of licenses and other permissions. Each of the preceding measures has its own idiosyncrasies, but to the extent they are uncorrelated, they can be viewed as complementary. Our empirical findings are not dependent on the use of any one of these measures.

Control Variables

Given the dearth of empirical literature on the determinants of property rights, there are no well-established precedents on model specification. We include only (the log of) per capita income and time variables as regressors accompanying regime type and duration indicators in the regressions reported in the tables.

Theoretical accounts of property rights claim that more is spent to define and protect property rights when the rights themselves become more valuable. Growth could make them more valuable (Eggertsson 1990). Rosenberg and Birdzell (1985, 115–17) have noted that formal arrangements for protecting property rights, such as judicial systems based on precedent, are not instituted until there is a sufficient volume of transactions to make them practicable. We can imperfectly control for these effects by including per capita income and aggregate GDP as proxies for the value of assets and volume of transactions.[19] One might alternatively posit a threshold effect, whereby (for example) a legal system is instituted when the value of assets and volume of transactions imply that the social benefits of setting up courts exceed the social costs. Casual observation does not support such a view—even in very small developing countries, increased expenditures on courts would surely pass such a cost-benefit test[20]—and we do not test for threshold effects.

The close historical connection between the emergence of democratic political institutions and the development of property and contract rights poses problems for testing the causal effects of one upon the other. A consensus is forming on the view that secure property and contract rights are important facilitators of economic growth. Thus a high level of income in a society today suggests that there were good property and contract rights in the past. Given the persistence of the institutions that sustain property and contract rights, income is also a good predictor of these institutions. Moreover, there are many aspects of a political regime that influence growth and hence, over time, the level of income. These include bureaucratic competence, political legitimacy, and rule obedience, on the one hand, and susceptibilities to political violence and extreme inequalities, on the other. These characteristics also tend to persist. Thus a high level of income in a society today usually means that there was a well-functioning political regime in the past, and, because of persistence of these characteristics, it also increases the probability that the current political regime also has the same attributes.

What makes our empirical analysis of the effects of political regimes possible is that there are some independent forces producing changes in political regime. In particular there have been wars won by democracies, after which democracies were set up in countries that had lacked them. More important for our sample, massive decolonization has occurred, as well as other historical factors that have altered many countries' political institutions.

But it remains true that current-period income contains much information about the current state of property rights and political regime. Since our analysis controls for current income and necessarily employs relatively crude measures of political regimes to investigate the impact of political conditions on property rights, our tests are quite demanding.

There are some secular and exogenous developments that may also affect the security of property and contract rights. The proportion of contract-intensive money may be sensitive to advances in banking technology that lower the costs of intermediation. For subjective measures that have ceilings on the maximum possible scores, each country might be rated with reference to other countries at a given point in time: mean scores for the world could then remain constant even with a general improvement over time in the security of property and contract rights around the world. To avoid spuriously associating such changes, or nonchanges, with regime type and duration, time (equal to the current year minus 1969) is included as an explanatory variable.[21]

The proportion of contract-intensive money might seem likely to be greatly influenced by inflation and interest rates (see chapter 4, this volume). In fact, the inclusion of these variables has only a minute impact on the coefficients for regime type and duration in CIM equations. They are accordingly not included in the results reported here.

Inequalities in income and wealth and other social cleavages based on ethnicity, religion, or region may generate social conflict endangering individual rights. Similarly, culture, religion, and colonial heritage may influence property and contractual rights. We do not include measures of these as regressors, however. For our sample, the coverage of available data over time and across countries on inequality and other social cleavages is inadequate. Existing theories do not account for the differences in the apparent effects of cultural variables across regions or over time. Why did British influences lead to strong property rights regimes only in some former colonies? Why was Confucianism until relatively recently thought to be unfavorable to economic development? Also, since others have used cultural and heritage indicators to explain political freedoms (Bhalla 1994; Abrams and Lewis 1993), inclusion of these variables as regressors along with regime type would potentially confound tests of the latter's impact on property rights. In any event, to the extent that inequality, other social cleavages, culture, and colonial heritage remain constant over time, their effects are captured by country intercepts in our fixed-effects tests.

4. Property and Contract Rights in Different Types of Regimes

Some recent and sophisticated statistical studies on postwar data have supported Lipset's (1959) thesis that high incomes are conducive to the emergence and survival of democracy (Barro 1996; Burkhart and Lewis-Beck 1994; Helliwell 1994). By contrast, there is no clear tendency that has yet emerged from studies of the effects of democracy on economic performance. The three studies just cited conclude that democracy has either no influence or a negative influence on subsequent growth. A recent study by Bhalla (1994), by contrast, finds a positive effect of political rights on growth.[22] Consistent with Bhalla's results is evidence from earlier periods of history suggesting that representative or at least nonabsolutist government is favorable to economic performance (e.g., DeLong and Shleifer 1993).

We focus here on one of the proposed links between regime type and economic performance: the hypothesis that more democratic regimes will better protect property and contract rights. We have elsewhere documented the impact of property and contract rights on investment and growth rates (chapters 3 and 4, this volume).

The effects of regime type—and of regime duration—were first tested with pooled time-series cross-sectional regressions, using country-years as units of analysis. Results of these tests were very supportive of the hypotheses.[23] Errors from these regressions, however, were highly autocorrelated, indicating that it is inappropriate to treat yearly observations of a country as independent.

In a purely cross-sectional design, on the other hand, difficulties arise in assigning values for regime type for countries moving across categories one or more times over the period. Averaging the different regime types—that is, treating a country shifting from type II to type IV halfway through the period identically to one remaining a category III over the entire period—would unjustifiably impose cardinality on our regime-type index as well as fail to make use of important variations in the data.

We adopted two alternative solutions. First, we created an observation for each country-regime, that is, for each spell of democracy (for regressions with DEMDUR), and for each period that a particular autocrat rules (for AUTDUR).[24] With country-regime units of analysis, we retained some over-time variation across regime types within countries, but suffered far less serious autocorrelation problems (as confirmed by Durbin-Watson statistics). Second, we retained country-year units of analysis but incorporated fixed country and/or regime effects, thereby arguably removing the most important sources of possible autocorrelation and heteroskedasticity.

Table 6.1 presents cross-sectional regressions, using country-regime units of analysis, examining the effects of regime type on property rights (mean values over the period), controlling for mean per capita income and mean time over the period the country-regime lasts.[25] In each case we find democracies outperforming autocracies, even controlling for the higher per capita incomes prevailing in most democracies. The Autocracy coefficient has the expected sign in all six cases: negative for CIM, ICRG, BERI, and CREDIT, and positive for

DEPREC and PREMIUM. These coefficients are highly significant for two of these property rights variables. Higher incomes are associated with significantly better scores on each of the dependent variables with the exception of DEPREC. The latter, along with PREMIUM and CIM, all significantly increase with time, controlling for income and regime type. The time trend in CIM probably reflects secular improvements in banking technology. Negative coefficients for time on CREDIT and (in some specifications) BERI suggest that scores for these variables reflect only the relative positions of countries at a single point in time.

The finding that democracies as a group outperform autocracies in protecting property and contractual rights does not, if the arguments at the beginning of this article are right, necessarily imply that the short- or medium-term effects of shifting from autocracy to democracy will improve performance. To explore this issue, we switch to country-year units of analysis, to exploit the time-series variation in the data, and control for fixed country-specific effects. The autocracy coefficient under this approach is influenced only by over-time variation in regime type and property rights. Given the length of our sample period (9 to 22 years, depending on the dependent variable), this test is designed to reveal short- or medium-term effects of changes in regime type on our property rights variables. Estimates from country-regime regressions in table 6.1 are heavily influenced

TABLE 6.1. Regime Type and Property Rights Country-Regimes Cross-Sectional Regressions

Independent Variable	Dependent Variable					
	CIM	ICRG Index	BERI Index	Credit Risk	Currency Depreciation	Black Market Premium
Intercept	−0.057	−25.154	−7.023	−84.239	−0.011	1.119
	(0.067)	(9.255)	(2.245)	(17.422)	(0.096)	(0.258)
Log (income)	0.101*	5.567*	1.950*	19.772*	0.012	−0.136*
	(0.008)	(0.779)	(0.198)	(1.569)	(0.011)	(0.048)
Time	.0047*	0.610	−0.022	−1.849*	.0049*	0.019*
	(.0013)	(0.353)	(0.053)	(0.424)	(.0021)	(0.006)
Autocracy	−0.051*	−5.995*	−0.446	−5.687	0.020	0.063
	(0.015)	(1.652)	(0.505)	(3.340)	(0.025)	(0.071)
Adj. R^2	.50	.57	.50	.71	.02	.09
N	240	137	93	133	223	217

Note: Autocracy dummy = 1 for regime types I and II; 0 for regime types IV and V. Table entries are regression coefficients, with White-corrected standard errors in parentheses.
*$p < .05$ (two-tailed test).

by democracies of long standing, in Western Europe and among the English-speaking nations. No nation remaining a democracy (or an autocracy) over the entire sample period influences the autocracy coefficients in table 6.2; those estimates are based solely on over-time variation within countries. Results for the autocracy dummy in table 6.2 are thus the product of a relatively small number of countries with interregime shifts during the sample period.[26]

The results summarized in table 6.2 strongly indicate that new democracies tend to face many of the difficulties outlined earlier that can render property rights less secure than in a country ruled by a secure autocrat. Autocracy is associated with significantly higher CIM and BERI values and significantly lower inflation (coefficients on the other three variables are not significant). Many of the benefits of democracy seem to accrue only over a substantial period of time, which may exceed the duration of most new democracies installed in our sample period. Most important, long-standing democracies, unlike all other regimes, have a predictable succession of power. They also tend to have more effective checks on executive power, in the form of independent legislatures, central banks, and judiciaries, and this makes it more difficult for any leader to abridge property or contract rights.[27] In new democracies such as Argentina, Nigeria (abortively), and Pakistan, by contrast, individuals cannot enter into long-term contracts secure in the knowledge that successions will be orderly and legal, and that a chief executive cannot preempt the powers of other branches of government.

In addition to the uncertainty and instability pervading new democracies generally, other factors potentially contribute to the positive

TABLE 6.2.   Regime Type and Property Rights Fixed-Effects Regressions

Independent Variable	Dependent Variable					
	CIM	ICRG Index	BERI Index	CREDIT	DEPREC	PREMIUM
Log	0.089*	0.922	1.815*	35.054	−0.188*	−0.522*
(income)	(0.008)	(0.960)	(0.217)	(1.760)	(0.017)	(0.070)
Autocracy	0.015*	0.173	0.446*	−0.148	−0.047*	−0.069
	(0.005)	(0.508)	(0.114)	(1.015)	(0.011)	(0.045)
R^2	.92	.97	.93	.97	.62	.53
N	1,977	768	812	951	1,828	1,612

Note: Autocracy dummy = 1 for regime types I and II; 0 for regime types IV and V. Additional regressors include year and country dummies.
*$p < .05$.

Autocracy coefficients in table 6.2. First, new democracies in recent years are hardly a random sample of all democracies. These "marginal" democracies exhibit a substantially worse income distribution, more ethnic tensions, and more political violence than exhibited by countries remaining democracies throughout the 1970s and 1980s. Prevailing social conditions often subject these new democracies to extraordinary populist pressures, which autocrats in these same countries were (sometimes) better able to resist.[28] Second, democracies are more likely to replace successful autocracies. Autocracies almost never replace democracies unless the latter are performing poorly—when their legitimacy in the eyes of the public is especially low. Conversely, with the exception of Argentina, autocrats giving way to new democratic regimes during our sample period apparently chose to do so when the economic climate was favorable for a smooth transition to democracy (as in Chile, Uruguay, and Turkey). Given these selection processes, the autocracy coefficient in fixed-effects tests is conceivably capturing a regression-to-the-mean effect: autocrats succeeding democracies have more opportunity to improve the policy climate than do leaders of democracies succeeding autocrats.

5. Property Rights and Regime Duration

For the reasons set out at the beginning of this essay, we hypothesize that the length of time a democratic system has survived and the time horizons of each autocrat are important determinants of the effects of regime type on property and contract rights. If these temporal considerations are as important as we expect them to be, any comparisons of economic performance under autocracy and democracy that leave them out are likely to be misspecified. The same is true for the comparisons of property and contract rights under differing regime types in the preceding section.

In this section, we test our hypotheses about how duration of regime affects the security of property and contract rights in each type of regime. That is, we test our hypothesis that autocrats with longer duration will be associated with better property and contract rights than short-term autocrats, and our hypothesis that the longer a democratic system has lasted the better these rights will be.

The regressions in table 6.3 test for the impact of regime duration on the security of property rights. As with table 6.1, cross-sectional regressions using country-regime units are reported in table 6.3. Control variables include mean income and time. Autocracies and democracies

TABLE 6.3. Regime Duration and Property Rights Summary of Country-Regimes Cross-Sectional Regressions

Sample (Duration Variable)	Autocrats (AUTDUR) B (SE)	Autocrats (AUTDUR) Adj. R^2 N	Autocrat Groups (AUTGROUP) B (SE)	Autocrat Groups (AUTGROUP) Adj. R^2 N	Democratic Regimes (DEMDUR) B (SE)	Democratic Regimes (DEMDUR) Adj. R^2 N	Democratic Leaders (DEXDUR) B (SE)	Democratic Leaders (DEXDUR) Adj. R^2 N
Contract-intensive money (CIM)	0.007 (0.008)	.34 174	0.010 (0.009)	.30 131	0.018 (0.011)	.58 66	.0087 (.0045)	.54 248
International Country Risk Guide Index (ICRG)	1.351* (0.524)	.10 84	2.398* (0.433)	.21 71	5.303* (1.142)	.81 53	0.764 (0.850)	.69 111
Business Environmental Risk Intelligence Index	0.240 (0.154)	.31 53	0.486* (0.165)	.36 34	0.854* (0.269)	.69 40	0.416* (0.154)	.59 157
Institutional Investor credit rating	2.446* (1.122)	.61 83	3.939* (1.014)	.64 65	1.503 (4.636)	.70 50	1.310 (1.583)	.63 147
Currency depreciation	−0.025* (0.010)	.05 155	−0.018 (0.011)	.01 117	−0.047* (0.022)	.12 68	−0.026* (0.010)	.08 244
Black market currency exchange premium	−0.054 (0.038)	.12 169	−0.026 (0.039)	.07 126	−0.073 (0.072)	.08 48	0.004 (0.022)	.03 141

Note: Table entries show coefficients and (White-corrected) standard errors for duration variables. The duration variable is the log of the number of years the regime lasts, where the regime is defined in terms of the chief executive's tenure in the "autocracy" and "democratic leader" samples, and in terms of the number of continuous years which democracy has been in place in the "democratic regimes" sample. Independent variables in addition to regime duration include the log of per capita income and time (= year − 1969).

are separated for these tests, as duration is defined differently for each group.

The coefficient for duration of autocrats (AUTDUR)—specifically, the log of duration the year the regime ends—has the expected sign in every case in table 6.3, with three of these statistically significant at .05 or better. Results are similar for AUTGROUP, with better policies associated with higher duration of the ruling group in every case, and significant associations in three cases.

Coefficients for the duration of democratic regimes (DEMDUR) are all in the expected direction, with three significant at the .05 level. These generally favorable results on DEMDUR are consistent with the view that new democracies cannot offer investors the same predictability (of succession) and credibility (of policy) offered by the long-standing democracies.

This emphasis on the importance of the duration of democratic systems does not apply to the tenure of particular *leaders* of democracies. While policy-making in democracies is not immune to the short-term needs of chief executives with limited time horizons, there are far more powerful checks on the ability of chief executives in democracies, compared to autocrats, to expropriate assets, to renege on debts, and to print money.

The results in table 6.3 support the view that the duration of democracy itself matters more than the time in power of chief executives in democracies. For these tests, we define democratic leader regimes similarly to autocratic regimes: each unit of analysis corresponds to the time in power of a chief executive. For all six dependent variables, the effect of a one-year increase in the duration of a democratic leader (DEXDUR) has a smaller impact (see fourth panel of table 6.3) than an identical increase in the duration of democracy (see third panel).

Our theory also suggests that the impact of DEXDUR should be weaker than the impact of AUTDUR—the duration of autocratic leaders. The estimated impacts of leader duration are nonetheless similar for autocrats and for democratic chief executives in the cross-sectional tests reported in table 6.3. The results from fixed-effects models reported later, however, are supportive of our theory.

Table 6.4 illustrates the economic significance of the results in table 6.3 by substituting values for time, income, and duration into the regressions to determine the predicted values of property rights indicators. The values in each cell correspond to predicted values of the property rights variables, with time = 11 (i.e., 1980) and per capita income of $2,500. Within each row, duration increases from 2 to 10 to 25. For each dependent variable, there are four rows, corresponding to autocratic leaders, autocrat "groups," democratic leaders, and democratic regimes. The most dramatic improvements associated with increasing duration occur for the democratic regimes, particularly for ICRG, DEPREC, and PREMIUM. Focusing on the column for which duration = 2, new autocrats have "better" values than new democracies on four of the six dependent variables. However, democratic regimes lasting 25 years outscore autocrats of 25 years duration on four out of six measures. While many democracies surpass 25 years in duration, there is an upper limit to how long an individual autocrat can last. These results are consistent with the theory that long-standing democracies provide the most secure property rights.

We further explore the effects of duration variables using fixed-effects regressions. With the cross-sectional design of table 6.3 regressions, we cannot rule out unobserved country-specific variables that may be responsible for both high rates of leadership turnover and insecure property and contractual rights. By including country dummies in regressions using the full time-series available, we can examine the influence of variations in the duration of leaders over time, within countries, on the property rights variables.[29]

In five out of six cases (all except CREDIT), increases in autocratic duration (AUTDUR) are associated with highly significant improvements in our property and contract rights measures within countries (table 6.5, first panel). By contrast, increases in the duration of the chief executive's leadership in democracies (DEXDUR) are associated with significant improvement in only 1 of the 6 (CREDIT), with DEXDUR's coefficient taking on the wrong sign in four cases (see third panel of table 6.5). Table 6.6 presents marginal effects for duration values as estimated from table 6.5 regressions, for changes in duration from 2 to 10 years, and from 10 to 25 years.[30]

By pooling the autocratic and democratic observations, and constructing an interaction term equal to the autocracy dummy multiplied by the duration of the chief executive, we can test whether differences between autocracies and democracies in the impact of leader duration on property rights are statistically significant. Coefficients on these interaction terms indicate that more time in power for an autocrat improves property and contract rights more than does a longer time in office for a democratic leader; the interactions are highly significant for CIM and the BERI index, and significant at .05 or .06 levels for ICRG, DEPREC, and PREMIUM.[31] These results

TABLE 6.4. Predicted Values of Property Rights Variables (from table 6.3 regressions)

Dependent Variable	Regime Type	Duration and Income Values								
		2			10			25		
		500	2,500	5,000	500	2,500	5,000	500	2,500	5,000
CIM	Aut (L)	.553	.734	.812	.564	.745	.823	.570	.751	.830
	Aut (G)	.555	.720	.791	.572	.736	.807	.581	.746	.817
	Dem (L)	.689	.804	.853	.703	.818	.867	.711	.826	.875
	Dem (R)	.672	.766	.806	.701	.795	.835	.718	.812	.852
ICRG Index	Aut (L)	13.51	16.67	18.03	15.68	18.84	20.21	16.92	20.08	21.44
	Aut (G)	11.64	13.94	14.93	15.50	17.80	18.79	17.69	20.00	20.99
	Dem (L)	7.66	24.85	32.26	8.89	26.08	33.49	9.59	26.78	34.19
	Dem (R)	-4.74	6.30	11.05	3.80	14.83	19.58	8.66	19.69	24.44
BERI Index	Aut (L)	5.35	7.37	8.23	5.74	7.75	8.62	5.96	7.97	8.84
	Aut (G)	5.37	6.57	7.08	6.16	7.35	7.86	6.60	7.79	8.31
	Dem (L)	3.46	7.51	9.26	4.13	8.18	9.93	4.51	8.56	10.31
	Dem (R)	1.56	5.12	6.65	2.94	6.49	8.02	3.72	7.27	8.80

Credit risk	Aut (L)	10.31	37.74	49.55	14.25	41.68	53.49	16.49	43.92	55.73
	Aut (G)	8.80	31.77	41.67	15.14	38.11	48.01	18.75	41.72	51.62
	Dem (L)	4.46	43.57	60.41	6.57	45.68	62.52	7.77	46.88	63.72
	Dem (R)	23.24	58.52	73.72	25.66	60.94	76.14	27.04	62.32	77.52
Currency depreciation	Aut (L)	.151	.188	.204	.111	.148	.164	.088	.125	.141
	Aut (G)	.145	.178	.192	.116	.149	.164	.100	.133	.147
	Dem (L)	.236	.175	.149	.194	.133	.107	.170	.110	.084
	Dem (R)	.214	.236	.245	.139	.161	.170	.096	.118	.127
Black market premium	Aut (L)	.608	.389	.295	.521	.303	.209	.472	.253	.159
	Aut (G)	.514	.377	.319	.473	.336	.277	.449	.313	.254
	Dem (L)	.373	.238	.180	.379	.244	.186	.382	.248	.190
	Dem (R)	.528	.402	.347	.410	.283	.229	.343	.216	.162

Note: Aut (L) = Autocratic Leader; Aut (G) = Autocratic Group; Dem (R) = Democratic Regime; Dem (L) = Democratic Leader.

strongly support the theory that the duration of leaders affects property and contract rights in autocracies but not in democracies.

Our theory would also predict that the time in power of "almost" autocrats—category II in our classification—would matter less than the duration of less-constrained autocrats (in most cases, the presence of a partially effective legislature is what differentiates the category I from category II leaders). Results from tests using table 6.5 specifications, but with autocrats and almost autocrats separated, strongly support this prediction. For the sample of relatively unconstrained autocrats, the AUTDUR coefficient is significant in all five cases in which it was significant in the first panel of table 6.5; in most cases the coefficient is larger in absolute value (see table 6.7). For the relatively constrained autocrats, coefficients attain the right sign only in CIM, BERI, and PREMIUM equations, with only CIM significant.

Property rights appear to deteriorate with increasing life of democratic systems (table 6.5, fourth panel). The unexpected results here

TABLE 6.5.   Regime Duration and Property Rights Fixed-Effects Models

Dependent Variable	Autocrats B (SE)	Autocrats R^2 N	Autocrat Groups B (SE)	Autocrat Groups R^2 N	Democratic Leaders B (SE)	Democratic Leaders R^2 N	Democratic Regimes B (SE)	Democratic Regimes R^2 N
Contract-intensive money (CIM)	0.013* (0.002)	.89 1,082	0.014* (0.003)	.89 1,082	−.0012 (.0015)	.86 895	−0.016* (0.002)	.86 895
International Country Risk Guide Index (ICRG)	0.499* (0.162)	.93 394	0.818* (0.215)	.93 394	0.112 (0.169)	.98 374	0.430 (0.481)	.98 374
Business Environmental Risk Intelligence Index	0.574* (0.076)	.82 275	0.992* (0.100)	.84 275	−0.017 (0.038)	.96 537	−0.366* (0.061)	.96 537
Institutional Investor credit rating	0.553 (0.387)	.93 440	1.721* (0.550)	.93 440	0.689* (0.280)	.98 511	0.906 (0.677)	.98 511
Currency depreciation	−0.015* (0.005)	.58 943	−0.009 (0.005)	.57 943	.0043 (.0037)	.77 885	0.014* (0.006)	.77 885
Black market currency exchange premium	−0.057* (0.018)	.56 1,099	−0.077* (0.020)	.56 1,099	.0064 (.0166)	.42 513	0.078* (0.020)	.44 513

Note: Independent variables in addition to regime duration include per capita income, year dummies, and country dummies.

*$p < .05$

on the duration of democracy are largely the product of a few long-lasting democracies that were replaced by reform-minded autocracies, but then returned to democracy during our sample period. Chile, Uruguay, and Turkey are the most notable examples of this phenomenon. For each of these countries, a few high DEMDUR values are coupled with poor property rights at the outset of our sample period, and a few very low DEMDUR values are coupled with much improved property rights at the end of the period. In these cases, the improvements in property rights and policies over the period are primarily attributable to the reform-minded autocratic regimes. These countries heavily influence the coefficient for DEMDUR for the sample as a whole, despite the fact that the inverse correlation between DEMDUR and property rights measures within these countries is produced by an interruption of democracy by autocratic rule.

TABLE 6.6. Marginal Effects of Duration on Property Rights Variables (from table 6.5 regressions)

Dependent Variable	Regime Type	Duration Values		
		2	10	25
CIM	Aut (L)	0	.021	.034
	Aut (G)	0	.023	.035
	Dem (L)	0	−.001	−.001
	Dem (R)	0	−.011	−.016
ICRG	Aut (L)	0	0.80	1.26
	Aut (G)	0	1.31	2.06
	Dem (L)	0	0.08	0.13
	Dem (R)	0	0.30	0.47
BERI	Aut (L)	0	0.92	1.45
	Aut (G)	0	1.60	2.51
	Dem (L)	0	−0.01	−0.02
	Dem (R)	0	−0.26	−0.40
CREDIT	Aut (L)	0	0.89	1.39
	Aut (G)	0	2.77	4.34
	Dem (L)	0	0.49	0.76
	Dem (R)	0	0.63	0.99
DEPREC	Aut (L)	0	−.023	−.037
	Aut (G)	0	−.015	−.024
	Dem (L)	0	.003	.004
	Dem (R)	0	.011	.016
PREMIUM	Aut (L)	0	−.092	−.145
	Aut (G)	0	−.124	−.194
	Dem (L)	0	.004	.006
	Dem (R)	0	.054	.086

Note: Aut (L) = Autocratic Leader; Aut (G) = Autocratic Group; Dem (L) = Democratic Leader; Dem (R) = Democratic Regime.

Deleting these three regime-switching countries dramatically weakens the perverse findings for DEMDUR in the CIM and BERI equations in table 6.5. A similar weakening of those findings is obtained by using a fixed-effects test that substitutes regime dummies for country dummies.[32] The table 6.5 coefficients on DEMDUR, therefore, do not reflect an actual deterioration in property and contract rights when a given democratic regime lasts longer.

6. Endogeneity of Regime Duration

The time in power of autocrats is conceivably endogenous to economic performance. Previous studies have found coup probabilities to be negatively related to recent growth rates (Alesina et al. 1996; Londregan and Poole 1992)[33] and income levels (Londregan and Poole 1992). The coefficient of AUTDUR could be biased upward if property rights improve economic performance, which in turn improves an autocrat's survival probability and thereby increases AUTDUR. Another possibility is that increases in income add to autocrat duration and improve property rights, creating a spurious association between the latter two variables. Our regressions control for current

TABLE 6.7.   Regime Duration and Property Rights Fixed-Effects Models for
Autocrats and Near-Autocrats

Dependent Variable	Autocrats (Regime Type I)		Near-Autocrats (Regime Type II)	
	B (SE)	R^2 N	B (SE)	R^2 N
Contract-intensive money (CIM)	0.013* (0.003)	.88 883	0.012* (0.004)	.94 199
International Country Risk Guide Index (ICRG)	0.784* (0.187)	.92 319	−0.119 (0.420)	.95 75
Business Environmental Risk Intelligence Index	0.790* (0.110)	.80 182	0.077 (0.090)	.93 93
Institutional Investor credit rating	−0.023 (0.462)	.93 344	−0.218 (0.670)	.96 96
Currency depreciation	−0.013* (0.005)	.61 757	−0.006 (0.009)	.71 186
Black market currency exchange premium	−0.064* (0.021)	.55 903	0.022 (0.023)	.84 196

Note: Independent variables in addition to regime duration include per capita income, year dummies, and country dummies.
*$p < .05$

income levels, however. In specifications not reported in our tables, AUTDUR coefficients are found to be unaffected by the inclusion of growth over the previous year as an additional regressor.[34]

If autocratic leaders behave in the same way as do governmental leaders in the Grossman and Noh model, property rights could influence AUTDUR independent of the impact of property rights on economic performance. Though in our model higher rent extraction by an autocrat provides more resources to maintain his hold on power, on the alternative interpretation a lower extraction of rent from the populace would improve an autocrat's survival probability directly and thus generate a reverse causation from property rights to duration.

If such reverse causation were driving our results, we would expect duration in the previous period to predict current property rights better than duration in the following period. We introduced one-year lags and, alternatively, one-year leads of duration into our fixed-effects regressions of property rights on autocrat duration. Neither leads nor lags performed as well as contemporaneous duration, although differences were not dramatic. Neither lags nor leads clearly performed better than the other one, either. These findings offer no support for the view that our results are primarily capturing reverse causation.

A second piece of evidence against reverse causality is that the coefficient on AUTDUR in most cases exceeds the coefficient on DEXDUR, the duration of democratic leaders. A plausible assumption is that the time in power of chief executives in democracies, as compared to autocracies, is more sensitive to their choice of policies: indeed, this sensitivity to short-term electoral pressures is commonly cited as a disadvantage of democracy. Thus, the endogeneity objection outlined previously should apply as strongly, or more strongly, to the time in office of democratic leaders. Therefore, if reverse causality from property rights to time in power were the primary force driving our results, coefficients for DEXDUR should exceed those for AUTDUR. For five of the six dependent variables in table 6.5, however, coefficients for DEXDUR and AUTDUR indicate a stronger link between duration and property rights for autocratic leaders than for democratic leaders, as reported in more detail previously. Again, no evidence for reverse causation is found.

Finally, we also attempted to correct for endogeneity by instrumenting for AUTDUR, despite our skepticism concerning the appropriateness of available instruments. The two instruments used were age of the autocrat at the time of accession[35] and completed duration of the previous autocrat.[36] As neither of these instruments varies by year, we use them only in the country-regime regressions of property rights on AUTDUR. Results using instrumented values of AUTDUR were mixed. Recall that in table 6.3 AUTDUR had the predicted sign in all six regressions. Coefficients for instrumented values of AUTDUR are greater in absolute value in four of these six cases, including each of the three cases (ICRG, CREDIT, and DEPREC) in which AUTDUR was significant in table 6.3. Only in the case of DEPREC—and of CIM, which reverses sign—is the instrumented value of AUTDUR statistically significant, however. In all six cases, standard errors are several times higher than in table 6.3, due in part to reductions in sample size attributable to missing data on the instruments, but primarily to the relatively poor explanatory power of the instruments.

7. Heterogeneity of Autocrats

Our results on AUTDUR are conceivably an artifact of omitted-variable bias associated with heterogeneity (sample selection) of autocrats. As a simple example, suppose that autocrats attaining power come in two types, skilled and unskilled, with equal numbers in each group. Assume further that for each group, there is a constant hazard of deposition by coup in each period, and that this constant rate is substantially higher for the unskilled group, as depicted by the two horizontal lines of figure 6.1. Autocrats know which group they are in and perceive a constant low or high hazard-rate over time, depending on whether they are skilled or unskilled. The overall hazard rate for any given value of duration will be a weighted average of the rates for the two separate groups. In $t = 1$, the overall hazard will be exactly halfway between that for each of the two groups, since they are represented in equal numbers at $t = 1$. After that time, however, as higher attrition in the unskilled group implies that the ratio of skilled to unskilled leaders rises, in each subsequent year the weighted average rate of hazard will be increasingly close to the lower hazard rate of the skilled group.

In observing only the overall hazard rate, we attribute increasing horizons to leaders that survive longer in power and hypothesize an improvement in property rights. Yet, each autocrat perceives only one of the two constant hazard rates and thus does not feel more secure in power as his time in power lengthens. A consequence of heterogeneity is that it potentially makes tenure to date an inappropri-

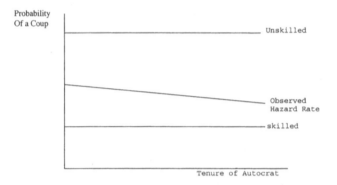

Fig. 6.1. Hazard rates and the tenure of autocrat

ate proxy for time horizons. Any correlation between time in power
and property rights may be spurious if duration has little or no relationship to the "true" time horizons perceived by autocrats.

We believe the decline in hazard rates as the time in power of an
autocrat lengthens is more than an artifact of sample selection. First,
the concept of consolidation of power is difficult to argue against.
Second, skill is only one of many factors determining who stays in
power.[37] Third, some of the most important possible sources of unobserved heterogeneity may cancel each other out: hereditary succession may enhance a leader's legitimacy, yet his other skills may
be inferior to those of a leader rising to power on his own. Note it is
not necessarily true that unobserved heterogeneity would bias the
coefficient of AUTDUR upward. Charisma may help a leader to
stay in office, but if that charisma is based in part on an ideology an-
tagonistic to markets, increases in an autocrat's time in power will
be associated with deteriorating property rights. In any event, we
correct for this potential problem of heterogeneity, finding that the
positive impact of autocrat duration on property rights is robust to
these corrections.

Our test is borrowed from the Abraham and Farber (1987) study
of the impact of seniority on wages. The long duration and favorable
property-rights policies of some autocrats are conceivably both products of some omitted autocrat-specific characteristic such as superior
skills. In principle, we could include autocrat dummies in our fixed-
effects tests. Collinearity of duration with time and income made
these very demanding tests, however.

Abraham and Farber faced a similar problem in attempting to

control for unobserved worker skills and worker-job match in time-series cross-sectional regressions of wages on seniority and experience. They could not estimate job-specific effects because changes in seniority and experience over time were perfectly collinear within a given job. As an alternative, they included as an additional regressor completed job duration, as a proxy of these unobserved characteristics.

Analogously, we include terminal duration in a time-series cross-section model without country- or autocrat-specific intercepts. For each country-year observation, TERMDUR equals the (log of) duration of the autocrat in his final year in power. Unmeasured skills of autocrats formerly captured by AUTDUR are hence captured by TERMDUR instead.

The addition of TERMDUR has relatively little effect on the results for AUTDUR (see table 6.8, where column 1 equations do not contain TERMDUR but column 2 equations do). TERMDUR has the positive sign implied by the sample selection objection in only four of six cases and is never significant. AUTDUR retains the expected sign in five of six cases (all but ICRG), with the coefficient rising substantially in two cases (CIM and BERI). Property rights are generally found to improve with autocrat duration, independent of autocrat skills, as measured by differences in terminal duration.

TABLE 6.8. Regime Duration and Property Rights Terminal Duration of Autocrats in Time-Series Cross-Section Tests

Independent Variable	Equation 1	Equation 2	
	AUTDUR	AUTDUR	TERMDUR
	B	B	B
Dependent Variable	(SE)	(SE)	(SE)
Contract-intensive money	0.011*	0.019*	−0.013
(CIM)	(0.004)	(0.007)	(0.008)
International Country	0.481	−0.646	1.571
Risk Guide Index (ICRG)	(0.307)	(0.775)	(0.992)
Business Environmental	0.340*	0.487*	−0.214
Risk Intelligence Index	(0.101)	(0.175)	(0.207)
Institutional investor	2.238*	1.199	1.499
credit rating	(0.565)	(1.178)	(1.482)
Currency depreciation	−0.023*	−0.013	−0.014
	(0.004)	(0.008)	(0.010)
Black market currency	−0.073*	−0.066*	−0.011
exchange premium	(0.018)	(0.033)	(0.040)

Note: Independent variables in addition to regime duration variables include per capita income, and year dummies.

*p < .05

8. Additional Robustness Tests

The ranges of several of the dependent variables—both objective and subjective—are limited. Most notably, CIM is bounded by 0 and 1, while CREDIT is bounded by 0 and 100. Using OLS on these variables could lead to predicted values outside these bounds. In fact, very few predicted values violated these bounds. Reestimating all CIM and CREDIT equations using logistic transformations of CIM and of CREDIT/100, constraining the predicted values to the 0–1 interval, yielded results very similar to those reported in the tables.

Each fixed-effects regression was rerun using corrections for autocorrelation. All duration effects that were statistically significant in the tables reported here remained significant. Random-effects specifications were also run. In these tests, duration of autocrat leader significantly improved values on all six dependent variables; AUTDUR was not a significant predictor of CREDIT in the fixed-effects results of table 6.5. A Hausman test rejects the random-effects specification in favor of the fixed-effects specification, however.

The country-regime units cover widely varying periods: some last less than one year while others cover thirty or more years. Accordingly, we reran all country-regime tests reported in tables 6.1 and 6.3 weighting observations by the (square root of) duration of the regime. Results on the regime type and duration variables vary somewhat from OLS, but not in a consistent direction, and lead to similar conclusions. Furthermore, the error variance of the unweighted regressions is generally uncorrelated with regime duration. We therefore report OLS rather than WLS results in our tables. All standard errors reported in tables are White-corrected (1980).

9. Conclusions

We began with a theory of the incentives and constraints that explain property and contract rights in autocracies and in democracies. We argued that a secure autocrat with a long time-horizon has an incentive to respect and protect property and contract rights in his domain because this increases the future income of his domain and thus also his tax collections. By contrast, an autocrat who, because of an insecure hold on power or for any other reason, has a sufficiently short time-horizon will find that the tax yield from any asset over that short time-horizon is less than the value of the capital good, so that he is rational to seize any easily confiscable assets.

In democracies, we argued, property and contract rights arise from a dramatically different set of incentives and constraints. There is no reason why the election that initiates a democracy should bring good property and contract rights. Democracies often emerge in unsettled and sometimes even somewhat anarchic conditions that are unfavorable to the protection of property rights, and the new democracies may not be strong enough to protect these rights. Even if the leadership of the new elected government is powerful, there is no assurance that property rights will be secure, for this democratic government may not last long, and one of the prominent possibilities is that the democratically elected leader will become a dictator.

By contrast, it is not feasible for a long-lasting democracy to prohibit all forms of private property and contracting: the same adherence to the rule-of-law and protections for individual freedoms that are needed to maintain free elections in which any defeated incumbents step down entail that there are some property rights—the individuals in a free society have what James Madison called "a property in their rights." Thus we hypothesized that long-lasting democracies generally provide better property and contract rights than either transient democracies or autocracies.

Our empirical evidence supports our hypotheses. We found that autocrats who had been in power longer and who by our argument had reason to have longer time-horizons were associated with better property and contract rights than autocrats who were in power only for a shorter time. We also found that, in general, democracies provide greater security of property and contractual rights than autocracies. But these benefits of democracy did *not* appear quickly: the property and contract rights were often poor in democracies that lasted only a short time. Among the relatively small group of countries within our sample that moved from one regime type to another, the security of property and contract rights was *greater* while they were autocracies than while they were democracies. We found, by contrast, that long-lasting democracies offer better protection for property and contract rights than any other regime type of any duration.

Our results also show that, as our theory predicted, the duration of democratic *systems* matters much more than the duration of democratic *leaders* for property and contract rights. Moreover, we found that, after controlling for country effects, the security of property rights is more sensitive to changes in autocratic leaders' time in power than to democratic leaders' time in office.

We conclude that statistical tests of economic performance under autocracies and democracies that leave out the hypotheses that we have developed and tested are misspecified. It is only natural, given our theory and our empirical results, that the comparisons of economic performance under autocracies and democracies have been so varied and inconclusive. It is, we argue, just as important in the analysis of government and politics as in the analysis of market behavior to analyze the incentives and constraints that face the individuals involved. Such an analysis suggests that property and contract rights in democracies and autocracies have utterly different sources, and our empirical results are consistent with this hypothesis.

Appendix: The Gurr-Banks Annual Scheme

BASIC VARIABLES

2.2 XRCOMP (from Gurr)
- 00. This unnamed category applies to situations in which power transfers are coded "unregulated" in variable 2.1 or involve a transition to/from unregulated.
- 1. Selection of chief exec. [hereditary succession, or rigged elections, or by coups, or by military designation, or repeated incumbent selection of successors]
- 2. Dual/transitional [Dual means there are two executives, one chosen by hereditary succession, the other by competitive election. Also used for transitional arrangements between selection and election.]
- 3. Election of chief exec [competitive election]

9.7 EXSELEC (from Banks)
- 1. Direct election
- 2. Indirect election
- 3. Nonelective

9.12 LEGEF, Legislative Effectiveness (Banks)
- 0. None
- 1. Ineffective: either rubber stamp, or domestic turmoil makes the implementation of legislation impossible, or the effective executive prevents the legislature from meeting or substantially impedes the exercise of its function.

2. Partially effective. A situation in which the effective executive's power substantially outweighs but does not completely dominate that of the legislature.
3. Effective. Possession of significant governmental autonomy by the legislature.

Classifications are:
1. Dictator (DI)
2. Almost Dictator (AD)
3. Intermediate category (I)
4. Almost Democracy (AD)
5. Democracy (DE)

EMPTY = category predicted to be empty (EM)

INTERMEDIATE REGIMES

There are 18 logically possible combinations of XRCOMP, EXSELEC, and LEGEF as displayed in the table.

The intermediate combinations are five in number. Three of them (cases 4, 13, and 16) involve a totally ineffective legislature with a chief

Classification of Regime Types

#	XRCOMP 01	2	3	EXSELEC 1,2	3	LEGEF 01	2	3	DI	AD	I	EM	AD	DE
1	X			X		X			1					
2	X			X			X			1				
3	X			X				X				N		
4		X		X		X					I			
5		X		X			X				I			
6		X		X				X				N		
7			X	X		X						N		
8			X	X			X					N		
9			X	X				X				N		
10	X				X	X			1					
11	X				X		X			1				
12	X				X			X				N		
13		X			X	X			1					
14		X			X		X				I			
15		X			X			X					1	
16			X		X	X					I			
17			X		X		X						1	
18			X		X			X						1

executive that is either competitively elected or a dual/transitional case. The other two (cases 5 and 14) involve a partially effective legislature and dual/transitional executive. All of these cases seem to be correctly classified as intermediate between almost democracy and almost dictatorship.

There are six cases in the EMPTY column. These are the ones that seem inconsistent. Four of the six cases (cases 3, 6, 9, and 12) involve a highly effective legislature combined with a chief executive that is not competitively elected or not elected at all. One (case 7) has a competitively elected chief executive and a totally ineffective legislature, and one (case 8) has a competitively elected chief executive in XRCOMP and a nonelected chief executive in EXSELEC.

UPDATING GURR-BANKS. The data run through 1986. The annual data were extended to 1990 on the basis of the information in the *Europa Yearbook*. The following countries were judged by Suzanne Gleason to have changed category from 1986 to 1990.

Country	Year in which regime changed
Lesotho	1990
Sierra Leone	1990
Pakistan	1988
Philippines	1986
Suriname	1988
Fiji	1987
Vanuatu	1989

Notes

This chapter was originally published under the same title in the *Journal of Economic Growth* 1 (June 1996): 243–76. It is reprinted with permission from Kluwer Academic Publishers.

  1. In the *National Gazette* for March 27, 1792 (Madison Papers 1983).

  2. The preceding theory is set out more fully in chapter 5 and in McGuire and Olson 1996.

  3. See Olson 1965 on the logic behind this conclusion and Lichbach 1995 for a most thorough survey of the literature on this subject. See also Svensson 1998 for a broadly similar model in which investments in legal infrastructure in period 1 are negatively related to the current government's prospects of remaining in power in period 2. Unlike our results reported below, Svensson's empirical tests utilize only country-level averages of instability, property rights, and investment, and do not differentiate democracies from autocracies.

4. The civil liberties checklist includes "personal social rights, including those to property, internal and external travel, choice of residence, marriage, and family," "freedom from gross social inequality," "freedom from gross government indifference or corruption," and "socio-economic rights: including freedom from dependency on landlords, bosses, union leaders, or bureaucrats." The political rights checklist includes "recent shifts in power through elections," "significant opposition vote," and "informal consensus: de facto opposition power."

5. The definitions of democracy and dictatorship refer exclusively to the characteristics of the national government. We do not attempt to characterize the selection of officials at the subnational levels.

6. Our conception of democracy is fundamentally consistent with the conceptions of Bollen (1990) and other political scientists who have adopted a procedural definition of democracy. There is a conceptual difference, though, between our scheme and those that add up the scores on different indicators. Such a methodology assumes that the contribution of a characteristic to the democratic nature of a regime is independent of the level of other characteristics. However, the marginal productivity of an input (in this case, in producing democracy) usually depends on the level of other inputs. A dictator who tolerates freedom of the press during periods in which he feels secure in his position does not on that account become a more democratic ruler. Similarly, the fact that the ballots are counted honestly does not make a regime more democratic if important political alternatives are prevented from participating in the elections. As can be seen in the appendix, our classification does not yield a ranking identical to one obtained from a mechanical adding up of the scores on each of the three indicators.

7. Further details on our classification are in the appendix.

8. The simple Spearman rank-order correlations between our 5-category political regime indicator and the 7-point Gastil measures are quite high: 0.87 for political rights and 0.82 for civil liberties. Changes in Gastil ratings of countries over time are highly correlated with changes in our classification. Correlations of each with property rights indicators differ very little.

9. Our data on property rights go back no further than 1969. In measuring duration of regimes, we begin counting in 1930. Since we use the log of duration in regressions, neglecting to identify an earlier starting date for democracy in the United States, Britain, etc., affects our estimates for DEM-DUR's impact only trivially.

10. In addition to Mexico, prominent examples include Taiwan and most communist countries (which are not in our sample).

11. The chief of such a dictatorial party usually has little chance of success if he attempts to use society's resources to maintain power in the face of widespread opposition within his party. The costs of losing power are also usually lower where autocracy is institutionalized, as the party can offer a deposed leader credible guarantees of a safe, comfortable retirement.

12. For a more extensive description of and justification for CIM, and evidence on its relationship to economic performance, see chapter 4, this volume.

13. These simple additive scales were found to be highly correlated ($r >$ .99) with alternative scales weighted by factor scores generated from factor analyses.

14. The latter 3 measures are scored on a 0–6 scale. We multiply them by 10/6 to put them on the same 0–10 scale as the former 2 variables. The resulting additive index has a potential range of 0–50.

15. Each variable is scored 0–4, with fractional values possible. BERI scores are averages from a permanent panel of experts, while ICRG ratings are evaluated by the staff of Political Risk Services.

16. High scores for "Rule of Law" also indicate "provisions for an orderly succession of power," raising the possibility that correlations with regime type might be tautological. Deleting "Rule of Law" from our ICRG index does not change any results, however, as this alternative index is correlated with the one we use at .998.

17. See chapter 3 for more detailed definitions and discussion of the ICRG and BERI variables. Some of these variables may be taken as empirical proxies for Clague's concept of "rule obedience" (chapter 9, this volume).

18. We use the mean of the two scores assigned each year (in March and September) to a country as the country's value for that year.

19. Aggregate GDP is generally not a significant determinant of our property rights measures and has virtually no impact on coefficients for regime type and duration variables. Thus, regressions reported in the following tables do not include this variable.

20. In Egypt, many courts do not operate much during the summer months due to a simple lack of air conditioning (*Washington Post,* March 13, 1995).

21. Results using the log of time were very similar. In fixed effects regressions, we use year dummies instead of time.

22. The difference in results between Bhalla and the other three studies appears to relate mainly to the choice of other independent variables and instruments for democracy. We focus on these four studies because they make use of the most recent data on a large number of countries and because they pay careful attention to endogeneity problems, mainly through the use of instrumental and lagged variables. The earlier literature is also thoroughly inconclusive regarding the effects of democracy on growth. See, for examples, the review in Brunetti and Weder 1993.

23. Results available on request from authors.

24. Thus, Egypt in 1954–69, 1970–80, and 1981–90 (1990 is the last year for our regimes and income data) counts as three separate observations in table 6.1 and in the AUTDUR panel of table 6.3. In the AUTGROUP panel of table 6.3, Egypt 1954–90 is one observation as Nasser, Sadat, and Mubarak are all judged to be of the same "group."

25. "Time" = year − 1969. Where there is missing data on a dependent variable for some years within a country-regime, we delete time and income data for the corresponding years. Calculating mean time and mean income for Franco's regime using all available data from the 1930s onward would yield means far below those that actually apply to (for example) the 1972–90 period covered by BERI. Then, income and time would underpredict BERI, and positive BERI residuals would be spuriously associated with a high duration value.

26. During our sample period eight countries shifted from autocracy to democracy, two shifted in the other direction, and eleven more experienced multiple shifts (e.g., Chile).

27. In the United States, the role of the Supreme Court as a check on unconstitutional actions of the Congress was not established, nor recognized, until *Marbury v. Madison,* decided during Jefferson's presidency.

28. Keefer and Knack (2002) find that income distribution is a more important determinant of property rights in democracies than in autocracies. Persson and Tabellini (1994) find that inequality is harmful to growth, particularly in democracies. One could alternatively interpret a significant interaction between democracy and inequality in growth equations as implying that democracy is beneficial to growth where and only where there exists a suitably egalitarian distribution of income.

29. Results on the log of autocrat duration are generally weaker when regime dummies are substituted for country dummies. Regime effects are highly correlated within countries and add very little explanatory power over the country intercepts. The major difference between the two models is that within a regime (as opposed to a country) over time, duration always increases—when a new autocrat comes into power, duration re-starts at 1. As time and (usually) income also increase each year, there are potentially serious multicollinearity problems using regime dummies. (Using time, as opposed to year dummies, and duration, as opposed to its log, would in fact result in perfect collinearity.)

30. We do not calculate predicted values because of the differing country intercepts.

31. Results are not shown in tables, but are available on request.

32. Recall that within a democratic regime, DEMDUR always increases: DEMDUR reverts to a value of 1 only when a new democratic regime replaces a nondemocratic regime. Interruptions in democracy by spells of autocratic rule thus cannot influence the DEMDUR coefficient when regime intercepts are included.

33. Alesina et al. (1996) find, however, that the probability of government changes and of "major" government changes (both of which include coups as one type of government change) is unaffected by recent economic performance.

34. Growth in most cases is not a significant predictor of property rights. These results are available on request.

35. Age is a highly imperfect measure of the time horizons relevant to policy choices by autocrats, for reasons discussed earlier in the essay.

36. Where there was no previous autocrat, as in the newly independent African nations, we used the average of completed duration for the initial autocrats of similar countries. For example, we used the average completed duration of all other initial autocrats in formerly British African colonies as the instrument for AUTDUR for Uganda's first autocrat. Age was highly significant ($t = 4.70$) but previous duration only marginally significant ($t = 1.64$) in explaining AUTDUR. The R^2 was only .12.

37. "Examples abound of leaders who were considered 'smart' or 'skilled' but who did not hold power very long, such as Kofi Busia in Ghana and Sylvanus Olympio in Togo" (Bienen and van de Walle 1991, 6).

References

Abraham, Katharine G., and Henry S. Farber. 1987. "Job Duration, Seniority, and Earnings." *American Economic Review* 77 (3): 278–97.

Abrams, Burton A., and Kenneth A. Lewis. 1993. "Cultural and Institutional Determinants of Economic Growth: A Cross-Section Analysis." Presented at the 1993 Public Choice annual meetings, New Orleans.

Alesina, Alberto, Sule Ozler, Nouriel Roubini, and Philip Swagel. 1996. "Political Instability and Economic Growth." *Journal of Economic Growth* 1:189–211.

Banks, Arthur S. 1979. "Cross-National Time Series Data Archive." Center for Social Analysis, State University of New York at Binghamton (updated).

Barro, Robert. 1996. "Democracy and Growth." *Journal of Economic Growth* 1 (1): 1–28.

Bhalla, Surjit. 1994. "Freedom and Economic Growth: A Virtuous Circle?" Paper presented at Nobel Symposium, "Democracy's Victory and Crisis," Uppsala University, Sweden, August 27–30.

Bienen, Henry, and Nicolas van de Walle. 1991. *Of Time and Power: Leadership Duration in the Modern World.* Stanford: Stanford University Press.

Bollen, Kenneth A. 1990. "Political Democracy: Conceptual and Measurement Traps." *Studies in Comparative International Development* 45 (1): 7–24.

Brunetti, Aymo, and Beatrice Weder. 1993. "Political Sources of Growth: The Need for New Measurement." WWZ Discussion Paper no. 9313, University of Basel, Switzerland.

Burkhart, Ross, and Michael Lewis-Beck. 1994. "Comparative Democracy: The Economic Development Thesis." *American Political Science Review* 88 (4): 903–10.

DeLong, J. Bradford, and Andre Shleifer. 1993. "Princes and Merchants: European City Growth before the Industrial Revolution." *Journal of Law and Economics* 36:671–702.

Eggertsson, Thrain. 1990. *Economic Behavior and Institutions.* Cambridge: Cambridge University Press.

Gastil, Raymond D. 1989. *Freedom in the World.* New York: Freedom House.

Grossman, Herschel I., and Suk Jae Noh. 1990. "A Theory of Kleptocracy with Probabilistic Survival and Reputation." *Economics and Politics* 2 (2): 157–71.

Gurr, Ted Robert. 1990. *Polity II: Political Structures and Regime Change, 1800–1986.* First ICPSR Edition, Inter-University Consortium for Political and Social Research, P.O. Box 1248, Ann Arbor, Michigan.

Helliwell, John. 1994. "Empirical Linkages between Democracy and Growth." *British Journal of Political Science* 24:225–48.

Keefer, Philip, and Stephen Knack. 2002. "Polarization, Politics and Property Rights: Links between Inequality and Growth." *Public Choice* 111 (1–2): 127–54.

Lichbach, Mark Irving. 1995. *The Rebel's Dilemma.* Ann Arbor: University of Michigan Press.

Lipset, Seymour Martin. 1959. "Some Social Requisites of Democracy: Economic Development and Political Legitimacy." *American Political Science Review* 53:69–105.

Londregan, John, and Keith T. Poole. 1992. "The Seizure of Executive Power and Economic Growth: Some Additional Evidence." In *Political Economy, Growth, and Business Cycles,* ed. Alex Cukierman, Zvi Hercowitz, and Leonardo Leiderman. Cambridge: MIT Press.

McGuire, Martin, and Mancur Olson. 1996. "The Economics of Autocracy and Majority Rule: The Invisible Hand and the Use of Force." *Journal of Economic Literature* 34:72–96.

Olson, Mancur. 1965. *The Logic of Collective Action.* Cambridge: Cambridge University Press.

Persson, Torsten, and Guido Tabellini. 1994. "Is Inequality Harmful for Growth?" *American Economic Review* 84 (3): 600–621.

Rosenberg, Nathan, and L. E. Birdzell. 1985. *How the West Grew Rich: The Economic Transformation of the Industrial World.* New York: Basic Books.

Svensson, Jakob. 1998. "Investment, Property Rights, and Political Instability: Theory and Evidence." *European Economic Review* 42 (7): 1317–42.

White, Hal. 1980. "A Heteroskedasticity-Consistent Covariance Matrix Estimator and a Direct Test for Heteroskedasticity." *Econometrica* 48:817–38.

CHAPTER 7

Does Inequality Harm Growth Only in Democracies? A Replication and Extension

Stephen Knack and Philip Keefer

Late-eighteenth-century and nineteenth-century political theorists viewed democracy as incompatible with the security of private property necessary for investment and economic growth to occur. Their intuition can easily be phrased in terms familiar to modern-day theorists of political economy. With a rightward-skewed distribution of income and wealth, the median income in society will fall short of the mean income. Under majority-rule voting on redistributional issues, the median-income voter will have an incentive to ally with the poorer half of voters to transfer income and wealth from the richer half.

In "Federalist #10," Madison argued that "the most common and durable source of factions has been the various and unequal distribution of property. Those who hold and those who are without property have ever formed distinct interests in society." In the absence of sufficient checks and balances on popular majorities, "democracies . . . have ever been found incompatible with personal security or the rights of property; and have in general been as short in their lives as they have been violent in their deaths." In a letter to Jefferson, John Adams predicted: "Democracy will envy all, contend with all, endeavor to pull down all." Similarly, universal suffrage was deemed to be incompatible with property rights by David Ricardo, J. S. Mill, Thomas Macaulay, Karl Marx, and Daniel Webster, among others.

Modern-day theorists have formalized such thinking in models of political redistribution in democracies. For example, Meltzer and Richard (1981) develop a model in which the income tax rate chosen by the median voter is higher when income inequality is higher.

Persson and Tabellini (1994) add this political redistribution mechanism to an overlapping-generations model with an intertemporal externality permitting endogenous growth, generating the prediction that investment and growth are decreasing functions of inequality in democracies. For nondemocracies, they argue, the predicted relationship between inequality, on the one hand, and investment and growth, on the other, is ambiguous. The median voter is not decisive in those polities, as decisions are not made through majority-rule voting. The redistributive policy favored by the decisive individual or group, they claim, may have very little to do with the distribution of income and wealth in nondemocracies.

Persson and Tabellini test their hypotheses using cross-national data. They find, as predicted, a negative relationship between government transfers as proportion of GDP (averaged over 1960 through 1981) and the share of national income accruing to the middle quintile of income earners (as measured circa 1960). With only 13 observations, this relationship is not statistically significant, however.[1] They similarly find a negative but insignificant effect of transfers on growth.

Given this weak evidence on the direct links between inequality and transfers, and between transfers and growth, Persson and Tabellini turn to indirect tests examining the impact of inequality on economic performance. Using time-series cross-sectional data for nine developed nations going back to 1830, they find inequality is significantly associated with lower growth rates. They report, however, that the strength of inequality's dampening effect on growth does not increase with the enfranchised proportion of the population—as one would expect if democracy impairs growth through politically driven redistribution. Additionally, they report that when time dummies are added, inequality no longer is significantly associated with growth. In other words, at a given point in time, there is little cross-country correlation between the two variables.

Empirical evidence in favor of the Persson and Tabellini model thus rests crucially on their analysis of a postwar cross-section of 49 nations, in which they conclude that a significant and negative correlation exists between inequality and growth only within their subsample of 29 democracies. If inequality influenced growth through channels other than the political distribution mechanisms they posit, one would expect a similar correlation between inequality and growth in their subsample of 20 nondemocracies. They claim to show there is no such correlation within these nondemocracies. The fact that "this relation is only present in democracies" is cited by Persson and Tabellini (1994, 600) as the key piece of empirical evidence in favor of their theory.

Table 7.1, equations 1 and 2 replicate these key results from Persson and Tabellini (1994, 612). The dependent variable is average annual growth in per capita incomes over the 1960–85 period. Independent variables standard in the growth literature[2] include per capita GDP levels in 1960, as a measure of catch-up growth opportunities, and the percentage of the relevant age group enrolled in primary school in 1960, as a measure of human capital. The income distribution variable is the percentage of national income received by the middle quintile of the population. The higher this value, the more egalitarian is the distribution of income.

Our initial attempts at replication failed, although the discrepancy in results was not dramatic. We obtained from Persson a printout of values for all of his variables except per capita GDP. His values for income distribution perfectly matched those contained in Paukert 1973, the source cited by Persson and Tabellini. Values for primary schooling for nine countries differed from those contained in the data set used (and widely distributed) by Barro (1991), and which we used in our initial replication attempt. Values in Persson's printout turned out to correspond exactly with those printed in the 1984 *World Development Report,* cited by Persson and Tabellini as their source.[3] We were then able to perfectly replicate the results for the democracy sample.

Among the nondemocracies, Persson's value for growth in per capita income for Brazil of 4.79 percent differed substantially from Barro's 3.52 percent, despite being derived from a common source (Summers and Heston 1988); all other values for growth matched.[4] Minor differences in results remained after substituting Persson's growth value for Barro's. By process of elimination, we concluded these differences were attributable to discrepancies in one or more values of per capita income for 1960—a variable not reported in Persson's printout.

Summers and Heston report only per capita GDP levels; researchers compute their own growth rates from these levels. A possible source, then, of the discrepancy in growth values for Brazil was different values for per capita income in 1960. By using the value for 1985 per capita GDP contained in Barro, and Persson's value for growth, we computed an implied value for Brazil's 1960 per capita GDP which differed from that contained in Barro by several hundred dollars. After substituting this implied value for Brazil in place of Barro's, we were able to replicate the Persson and Tabellini nondemocracy findings sufficiently closely that the trivial remaining differences could be attributed to rounding.[5]

TABLE 7.1. Inequality and Economic Growth , 1960–85 (by Regime Type)

Equation	1	2	3	4	5	6
Regimes sample	Democracies	Autocracies	Autocracies	Democracies	Autocracies	Autocracies
Regimes definition	Persson-Tabellini	Persson-Tabellini	Persson-Tabellini	Gurr	Gurr	Gurr
Bad inequality observations deleted	No	No	Yes	No	No	Yes
Constant	-5.159	0.952	0.010	-4.635	-0.843	-2.498
	(-3.362)	(0.528)	(0.005)	(-1.646)	(-0.541)	(-1.509)
Per capita GDP, 1960	-0.587	-1.725	-1.349	-0.574	-1.369	-0.897
	(-3.578)	(-2.980)	(-2.189)	(-2.672)	(-2.685)	(-1.763)
Primary school enrollment, 1960	4.868	5.669	3.954	4.992	5.136	3.306
	(3.627)	(3.126)	(1.858)	(2.433)	(3.665)	(2.038)
Income equality	0.326	-0.072	0.070	0.279	0.060	0.256
	(3.234)	(-0.558)	(0.440)	(2.010)	(0.517)	(1.860)
Adj. R^2	.46	.31	.19	.22	.31	.36
N	29	20	13	22	27	20
SEE	1.26	1.46	1.31	1.31	1.58	1.42
Mean, D.V.	2.40	1.34	1.49	2.58	1.46	1.61

Note: t-values are shown in parentheses.

Two simple checks on these Persson and Tabellini results strongly suggest that the differential impact of inequality on growth in democracies and nondemocracies is entirely an artifact of measurement error. We conclude that the hypothesis that inequality harms growth as much in nondemocracies as in democracies cannot be rejected.

The first correction for measurement error deletes the seven observations—all autocracies—on inequality that Paukert (1973, 125), the sole source of inequality data for Persson and Tabellini, warns are of "rather doubtful value."[6] If autocracies tend to be poor, and poverty and closed political systems generate less reliable data, we are less likely to detect a "true" relationship between inequality and growth among nondemocracies than among democracies. The fact the seven observations Paukert questions are all autocracies is consistent with this conjecture.

Deleting these seven suspect observations in fact increases the coefficient on income equality somewhat for the autocracies (table 7.1, equation 3). Given the resulting small sample size, a more informative test employs the combined sample of democracies and autocracies, in which income equality is interacted with a democracy dummy. The coefficient on this interaction term drops substantially upon deletion of these seven autocracies (table 7.2, compare coefficients on equality × democracy in equations 1 and 2), and the difference in the impact of income equality across the two regime types is no longer statistically significant.

The second correction concerns the highly dubious regime-type classifications of Persson and Tabellini, who include El Salvador, South Korea, Madagascar, Mexico, Panama, the Philippines, and Senegal among their democracies. Gurr's (1990) *Polity II* data set indicates whether the chief executive of countries is elected competitively and whether the legislature is an effective check on the executive. Of these seven dubious democracies, only the Philippines ever had an effective legislature (for 12 years, out of 26) in the 1960–85 period in question. Only El Salvador, Korea, the Philippines, and Senegal ever chose their chief executive through competitive elections during the period, and only for 10, 10, 12, and 2 years, respectively. Many nations classified as autocracies by Persson and Tabellini actually have more effective legislatures and electorates than these "democracies." Argentina (12 years), Chile (13), Ecuador (12), and Sierra Leone (12) all chose their chief executives through competitive elections during about half of the period. Argentina (3 years), Brazil (3), Chile (12), Nigeria (4), and Peru (5) sometimes had an effective legislature.[7]

Reclassifying these seven authoritarian regimes as nondemocracies (while retaining the seven poor-data-quality observations previously identified) substantially alters the coefficients on income equality for the two subsamples (compare equations 4 and 5 in table 7.1 to equations 1 and 2 respectively). In the combined sample, the coefficient for the interaction of income equality and democracy drops by nearly one-half and again is no longer significantly different from zero (table 7.2; compare equation 3 to equation 1).

Differences between democracies and nondemocracies in inequality's growth effects disappear entirely when the two corrections are made together, that is, when regimes are reclassified and the seven suspect observations on income equality are dropped. The coefficients and *t*-statistics on income equality are nearly identical for the two samples (equations 4 and 6 in table 7.1). The coefficient for the interaction term drops precipitously when the two corrections are made together (table 7.2, equation 4): the positive and significant coefficient for income equality in the interaction specification indicates

TABLE 7.2. Inequality, Regime Type, and Economic Growth, 1960–85 Interaction Specifications

Equation	1	2	3	4	5	6
Regimes definition	Persson-Tabellini	Persson-Tabellini	Gurr	Gurr	Gastil	Gastil
Bad inequality observations deleted	No	Yes	No	Yes	No	Yes
Constant	0.535	−1.184	−1.423	−3.121	−5.933	−4.464
	(0.331)	(1.900)	(−1.007)	(−2.094)	(−1.892)	(−1.368)
Per capita GDP, 1960	−0.673	−0.619	−0.679	−0.563	−0.846	−0.689
	(−3.917)	(−3.749)	(−3.310)	(−2.902)	(−3.714)	(−2.917)
Primary school enrollment, 1960	3.942	3.493	4.191	3.256	4.091	3.517
	(4.009)	(3.348)	(4.145)	(2.897)	(3.990)	(2.972)
Income equality	−0.054	0.110	0.094	0.276	−0.201	0.098
	(−0.441)	(0.707)	(0.872)	(2.230)	(−0.897)	(0.355)
Democracy	−5.481	−3.387	−2.801	0.070	−0.502	−0.198
	(−2.468)	(−1.458)	(−1.089)	(0.027)	(1.452)	(0.531)
Equality × Democracy	0.443	0.271	0.236	0.012	0.046	0.020
	(2.680)	(1.438)	(1.250)	(0.060)	(1.789)	(0.689)
Adj. R^2	.39	.38	.32	.35	.35	.36
N	49	42	49	42	49	42
SEE	1.40	1.32	1.49	1.36	1.45	1.35
Mean, D.V.	1.97	2.12	1.97	2.12	1.97	2.12

Note: t-values are shown in parentheses.

that income equality enhances growth in nondemocracies as well as in democracies.

Any dichotomous classification of regime type is admittedly too simple. As an alternative to the Persson-Tabellini- and Gurr-based dichotomies, we used an index based on Gastil in equations 5 and 6 of table 7.2. Beginning in 1973, Gastil (1987) assigned a rating of 1 to 7 for each of two variables, political freedoms and civil liberties, with higher scores indicating less freedom. We averaged these variables over the period 1973–85, summed the two averages, and finally reversed the scores so that higher values indicate greater democracy.[8] For the full sample of 49 countries, the interaction of income equality and democracy is only marginally significant (table 7.2, equation 5). When the seven most suspect inequality observations are deleted, the coefficient drops by more than half and no longer approaches significance (equation 6).

Employing a common method of correcting for possible measurement error, Persson and Tabellini report results of two-stage least-squares estimates, using as instruments for income equality the share of the labor force in agriculture, male life expectancy, and secondary school enrollment (all measured in 1960). The coefficient for income equality remains much higher in their democracy sample than in their autocracy sample. This result proves to be highly dependent on their use of secondary enrollment—perhaps the most inappropriate possible instrument. Secondary enrollment is strongly correlated with the error term of growth equations and is in fact a standard regressor in growth equations (e.g., Barro 1991). The most widely cited theory of education's impact on growth does not posit inequality as a channel through which secondary education influences growth (Nelson and Phelps 1966). In some theoretical models (e.g., Saint-Paul and Verdier 1993), education is even endogenous to inequality.

Persson and Tabellini note evidence of heteroskedasticity in their test, finding that their regression residuals are larger in absolute value for countries with smaller per capita incomes—consistent with the view that measurement error is greater in poorer countries. They reestimate their model, weighting each observation by per capita income, and report obtaining results very similar to their OLS results. Our test confirmed that weighting by income does not materially affect their results, nor ours reported in tables 7.1 and 7.2. Neither any of their results nor ours are altered by using heteroskedastic-consistent standard errors as estimated by White's (1980) method.

Despite the elegance of median voter theories, the finding presented here—that inequality's impact on growth does not differ significantly by regime type—is likely to surprise few observers of world politics. Even where autocrats or bureaucrats, rather than elected representatives, choose tax policies, their choices can be influenced by the need to maintain popular support, or at least acquiescence. Additionally, even where leaders' choices of taxation and redistribution policies are not highly sensitive to inequality, growth may be harmed by political violence furthered by inequalities in income and wealth. Theories on possible links between inequality and political violence date to Aristotle, and numerous recent empirical studies have investigated these links, albeit not conclusively.[9] Barro (1991) and others have shown that political violence is detrimental to growth. The types of political violence most strongly predictive of slow growth—revolutions and coups—are far more common in autocracies than in democracies.

Notes

This chapter was originally published under the same title in the *American Journal of Political Science* 41 (1) (January 1997): 323–32. It is reprinted with permission from the University of Wisconsin Press.

1. They use only data on OECD nations, on the grounds that data on transfers are poor for other countries. If larger samples are used, egalitarian income distributions are generally positively associated with transfers, counter to the Persson and Tabellini thesis (Keefer and Knack 2002).

2. See, for example, Barro 1991.

3. The 1984 WDR, in turn, cited various years of the UNESCO Yearbook as its source for enrollment data. Barro cites UNESCO Yearbook and an International Labor Organization publication.

4. Summers and Heston periodically revise their estimates of per capita GDP. Brazil's annual growth rate for 1960–85 as calculated using a recent update (version 5.5 of their data set) is only 3.24 percent. Neither the original Persson-Tabellini results nor our extensions here are sensitive to correcting the (apparently) mistaken values for per capita GDP in 1960 and growth they use for Brazil.

5. Growth rates in Barro are reported out to two fewer decimal places than in Persson's printout. Given the error with which income levels across countries are surely measured, little if anything is lost by rounding to two decimal places.

For easier interpretation of coefficient values, we use per capita GDP in thousands of dollars and define primary education enrollment as a proportion; Persson and Tabellini used dollars and percentages, respectively.

6. The seven countries are Burma, Chad, Morocco, Niger, Nigeria, Sudan, and Tunisia.

7. Persson and Tabellini cite Banks 1987 and Taylor and Jodice 1983 as their sources for classification of regime types, with no further details. The nearest Taylor and Jodice come to such a classification is a table listing Gastil's ratings of civil liberties and political freedoms for the 1970s. These ratings conform much more closely to our Gurr-based classification than to Persson and Tabellini's, however. Banks does not classify regime types. The recent histories of various countries described therein do not appear to support the Persson-Tabellini classifications—South Korea's entry, for instance, is a long narrative of authoritarianism.

8. Numerous other studies (e.g., Burkhart and Lewis-Beck 1994) have used an additive index of Gastil ratings as a measure of democracy.

9. See Wang et al. 1993 for a sample of this research.

References

Banks, Arthur. 1987. *A Political Handbook of the World.* Binghamton, NY: CSA Publication, SUNY-Binghamton.

Barro, Robert J. 1991. "Economic Growth in a Cross Section of Countries." *Quarterly Journal of Economics* 106:407–43.

Burkhart, Ross E., and Michael Lewis-Beck. 1994. "Comparative Democracy: The Economic Development Thesis." *American Political Science Review* 88:903–10.

Gastil, Raymond D. 1987. *Freedom in the World.* Westport, CT: Greenwood.

Gurr, Ted Robert. 1990. *Polity II: Political Structure and Regime Change, 1800–1986.* First ICPSR edition, Inter-university Consortium for Political and Social Research, Ann Arbor, MI.

Keefer, Philip, and Stephen Knack. 2002. "Polarization, Politics and Property Rights: Links between Inequality and Growth." *Public Choice* 111 (1–2): 127–54.

Madison, James, Alexander Hamilton, and John Jay. 1961. "Federalist #10." In *The Federalist Papers,* ed. Clinton Rossiter. New York: New American Library.

Meltzer, Allan H., and Scott F. Richard. 1981. "A Rational Theory of the Size of Government." *Journal of Political Economy* 89:914–27.

Nelson, Richard R., and Edmund S. Phelps. 1966. "Investment in Humans, Technological Diffusion, and Economic Growth." *American Economic Review* 56:69–75.

Paukert, Felix. 1973. "Income Distribution at Different Levels of Development: A Survey of the Evidence." *International Labor Review* 108:97–125.

Persson, Torsten, and Guido Tabellini. 1994. "Is Inequality Harmful for Growth?" *American Economic Review* 84:600–621.

Saint-Paul, Gilles, and Thierry Verdier. 1993. "Education, Democracy and Growth." *Journal of Development Economics* 42:399–407.

Summers, Robert, and Alan Heston. 1988. "A New Set of International Comparisons of Real Product and Price Levels: Estimates for 130 Countries, 1950–85." *Review of Income and Wealth* 34:1–25.

Taylor, Charles, and David Jodice. 1983. *World Handbook of Political and Social Indicators.* New Haven: Yale University Press.

Wang, T. Y., William J. Dixon, Edward N. Muller, and Mitchell A. Seligson. 1993. "Inequality and Political Violence Revisited." *American Political Science Review* 87:979–93.

White, Hal. 1980. "A Heteroskedasticity-Consistent Covariance Matrix Estimator and a Direct Test for Heteroskedasticity." *Econometrica* 48:817–38.

World Bank. 1984. *World Development Report, 1984.* Washington, DC: World Bank.

CHAPTER 8

Gender and Corruption

Anand Swamy, Stephen Knack, Young Lee,
and Omar Azfar

1. Introduction

In recent years there has been a concerted effort, by various national governments and international organizations, to increase the representation of women in public life. A prominent example is recent legislation in France requiring all parties to field equal numbers of male and female candidates in all party-list elections, and equal numbers within an error margin of 2 percent in constituency-based elections (*Economist* 2000). Proponents of these reforms suggest that women may make different policy choices than men, and indeed there is some evidence supporting this proposition.[1] Recently, however, an even more provocative claim has been made: in several different locations influential public officials have advocated increasing representation of women on the grounds that this will lower the extent of corruption. In Mexico City the police chief has taken away ticket-writing authority from the city's 900 male traffic policemen and created a new force consisting exclusively of women, hoping to reduce corruption (Moore 1999). A similar policy has also been introduced in Lima, Peru, where it is claimed there has been a fall in corruption after the introduction of women (McDermott 1999). This essay evaluates the plausibility of such claims, using a variety of independent data sources.[2]

We present evidence that (a) in hypothetical situations women are less likely to condone corruption, (b) women managers are less involved in bribery, and (c) countries that have greater representation of women in government or in market work have lower levels of corruption. This evidence, taken together, provides some support for the idea that, at least in the short or medium term, increased presence of women in public life will reduce levels of corruption.

Claims about gender differences can easily be misinterpreted. It is therefore important for us to clarify that we do *not* claim to have discovered some essential, permanent, or biologically determined differences between men and women. Indeed the gender differences we observe may be attributable to socialization, or to differences in access to networks of corruption or in knowledge of how to engage in corrupt practices, or to other factors. We do not attempt to identify these underlying factors, but rather to document several statistically robust relationships that point toward a gender differential in the incidence of corruption. We discuss some theories about the origin of this differential in section 5, but do not take a position on this question.

Our evidence is organized as follows. We first present data from the World Values Survey, in which men and women in a large number of developed and developing countries were asked a series of questions regarding their attitudes in hypothetical situations in which there was room for dishonest or opportunistic behavior. We show that men were more likely to choose options that are equivalent to the "defect" option in a Prisoner's Dilemma game. After showing gender differences in a range of attitudes, we present more detailed multivariate evidence on gender differentials in the attitude to bribery. We then present evidence of behavior in actual as opposed to hypothetical situations. Using a survey of enterprise owners and managers in Georgia (formerly part of the Soviet Union) we show that officials in firms owned or managed by men are significantly more likely to be involved in bribe-giving.[3]

One concern in these analyses is that corruption is self-reported. Because of this, it is conceivable that our results reflect gender differentials in *acknowledgment* of corruption, rather than in *incidence* of corruption. Data on corruption that are not self-reported are available only at the national level. Using corruption indices developed by Kaufmann et al. (1999), Transparency International, and Political Risk Services, we find that greater participation by women in market work and government is associated with lower levels of corruption. This result is of value not only because national-level corruption data are not self-reported, but also because it shows that gender differentials have macrolevel impacts. These findings are consistent with arguments that, at least in the short run, policies designed to increase the role of women in commerce and politics, commonly justified on grounds of gender equity and poverty alleviation, may also have an efficiency payoff, by lowering corruption.[4]

2. Microevidence: The World Values Survey

The World Values Survey are a set of surveys carried out in dozens of developed and developing countries in the early 1980s and the early 1990s. The purpose of these surveys was to collect information on the attitudes and values of the peoples of various societies around the world. An effort was made to ensure that in each case the sample was nationally representative.[5] We are able to use data from 18 surveys in 1981 and 43 surveys in 1990–91.

In addition to hundreds of other items, these surveys inquire about the acceptability of various dishonest or illegal behaviors. For each behavior respondents are asked to place themselves on a 1–10 scale, where 1 indicates that the behavior can "never be justified" and 10 indicates it can "always be justified." For most items in most countries the natural cutoff point is at the value 1, as a majority of respondents typically assert (fortunately) that the behavior can never be justified. Aggregating over all countries in the surveys, the gender gap consistently favors women, as shown in table 8.1. For all twelve items listed a significantly higher percentage of women than men believe that the illegal or dishonest behavior is never justifiable. The gap ranges from more than 9 percentage points for driving under the influence to about 4 points for claiming government benefits for which one is ineligible. In all cases the gender differences are significant at the .0001 level.

The case of greatest interest to us is "someone accepting a bribe in

TABLE 8.1. Gender and Socially Cooperative Attitudes, World Values Survey (in percentages)

The following behavior "can never be justified"	Male	Female
1. Claiming government benefits which you are not entitled to	63.7	67.9
2. Avoiding a fare on public transport	60.3	64.9
3. Cheating on taxes if you have the chance	54.4	61.5
4. Buying something you knew was stolen	72.9	79.5
5. Taking and driving away a car belonging to someone else	83.1	87.2
6. Keeping money that you found	43.9	51.6
7. Lying in your own interest	45.1	50.9
8. Someone accepting a bribe in the course of their duties	72.4	77.3
9. Fighting with the police	52.0	57.1
10. Failing to report damage you've done accidentally to a parked vehicle	61.8	67.6
11. Throwing away litter in a public place	69.1	74.4
12. Driving under the influence of alcohol	74.2	83.4

Note: Sample sizes vary between 52,107 and 83,532.
$p < .0001$

the course of their duties": 77.3 percent of women but only 72.4 percent of men agree that this behavior is "never justified." This difference implies that about one-fifth more men than women (27.6 percent compared to 22.7 percent) believe that bribery can sometimes or always be justified. Table 8.2 provides a breakdown of percentages across the 1–10 scale. As mentioned, females are more concentrated at category 1. The pattern is then slightly reversed for all the categories 2 through 10, which is not surprising, since each set of percentages must total 100.

This comparison of proportions could be misleading if men and women differed systematically in some other characteristic that also affects the attitude to bribery. In tables 8.3, 8.4, and 8.5, we show that this result is robust to tests that control for other respondent characteristics. In the first column of table 8.3 our dependent variable takes the value 1 if the respondent says that bribery is "never justified" and zero otherwise. Our main interest is in the coefficient on the gender dummy (1 if male). There is some evidence that rule-breaking is higher among young people, so we include age as a regressor. Marriage is often believed to alter public behavior; this is reflected, for instance, in lower rates of incarceration among married men, as compared to single men (Akerlof 1998). To account for this, we include a dummy that takes the value 1 if the respondent is married. Commitment to a religion is often believed to affect behavior;[6] therefore, we include a dummy that takes the value 1 if the individual responded yes to the question "are you a religious person?" We also include another dummy that takes the value 1 if the respondent frequently attends religious services. Finally, the education dummy takes the value 1 if the respondent was schooled beyond age 16.[7]

TABLE 8.2. Gender Differentials in the Attitude toward Bribery (in percentages)

	Female	Male
1 = Bribery is never justified	77.33	72.39
2	8.44	9.17
3	5.05	6.07
4	2.44	3.03
5	2.81	4.03
6	1.36	1.83
7	0.76	1.06
8	0.56	0.82
9	0.35	0.45
10 = Bribery can always be justified	0.90	1.15

In the first column of table 8.3 we pool the data across countries and estimate a probit model. In order to control for unobservable country characteristics that might otherwise bias our results, we include a dummy for each survey.[8] The coefficient on the gender dummy (1 if male) is negative and is statistically significant at any reasonable level. The marginal effect corresponding to this coefficient is −4.3 percent, that is, all else being equal, a man's likelihood of responding that accepting a bribe is "never justified" is 4.3 percentage points less than the likelihood for a woman.[9] Though this differential is not very large, it occurs with remarkable consistency, as can be seen below.

In column 2 we estimate an ordered probit model, using categories 1 through 10. The scale was reversed to allow comparability with the probit model previously reported. The male dummy coefficient is again negative and statistically significant. The marginal effect corresponding

TABLE 8.3.   Gender Differentials in the Attitude toward Bribery: Probit and Ordered Probit Estimates

	Probit	Ordered Probit
	Dependent variable = 1 if the response was 1 meaning bribery is "never justified"; =0 otherwise	Dependent variable is an integer between 1 and 10, where 1 corresponds to bribery is "always justified," 10 is "never justified"[a]
Male	−0.140	−0.142
	(0.010)**	(0.010)**
Marginal effect (%)	−4.3	−4.0
Schooled past age 16	0.039	0.062
	(0.013)**	(0.012)**
Married	0.067	0.072
	(0.012)**	(0.011)**
Attend religious services often	0.096	0.095
	(0.014)**	(0.014)**
Religious	0.135	0.122
	(0.012)**	(0.011)**
Age	0.025	0.023
	(0.002)**	(0.002)**
Age^2	−0.00013	−0.00012
	(0.00002)**	(0.00002)**
Constant	−0.507	
	(0.056)**	
N	79,645	79,645

Note: Standard error in parentheses.
[a] The scale for this dependent variable was reversed to produce estimates comparable to the others.
*p < .05   **p < .01 (two-tailed tests)

TABLE 8.4. Countrywise Probit Regression, World Values Survey Data, 1990–91

Country	N	Male Dummy Coeff.	S.e.	Marginal Effect (%)
Sweden	963	−0.360	(0.090)**	−11.6
Estonia	999	−0.327	(0.087)**	−11.5
Slovenia	1,003	−0.427	(0.096)**	−11.4
Latvia	890	−0.367	(0.099)**	−11.4
Netherlands	1,002	−0.304	(0.087)**	−10.7
Bulgaria	1,007	−0.336	(0.093)**	−9.2
Austria	1,445	−0.251	(0.073)**	−8.5
Mexico	1,497	−0.200	(0.067)**	−7.9
Japan	969	−0.227	(0.088)**	−7.8
Switzerland	1,356	−0.291	(0.082)**	−7.4
France	983	−0.197	(0.085)*	−7.3
S. Africa	2,675	−0.253	(0.057)**	−7.1
W. Germany	2,049	−0.180	(0.059)**	−6.8
Canada	1,695	−0.215	(0.069)**	−6.5
Russia	1,909	−0.279	(0.075)**	−6.3
Iceland	679	−0.246	(0.122)**	−5.7
Denmark	995	−0.367	(0.119)**	−5.6
E. Germany	1,329	−0.140	(0.073)*	−5.2
Belgium	2,671	−0.131	(0.050)**	−5.1
Ireland	996	−0.220	(0.103)*	−4.8
Britain	1,478	−0.132	(0.074)*	−4.0
N. Ireland	303	−0.182	(0.189)	−3.9
Norway	1,226	−0.134	(0.085)	−3.6
Finland	580	−0.104	(0.115)	−3.3
Brazil	1,761	−0.169	(0.080)*	−3.3
Hungary	979	−0.085	(0.085)	−3.2
Moscow	980	−0.094	(0.090)	−3.1
China	988	−0.151	(0.106)	−3.0
Argentina	986	−0.285	(0.139)*	−2.9
Spain	4,048	−0.093	(0.046)*	−2.6
Turkey	1,013	−0.153	(0.141)	−2.2
Portugal	1,148	−0.061	(0.083)	−2.0
Czech-Slovak	1,392	−0.049	(0.069)	−1.9
Chile	1,477	−0.079	(0.082)	−1.9
United States	1,754	−0.032	(0.071)	−0.9
Poland	924	−0.031	(0.101)	−0.8
Italy	2,014	0.008	(0.063)	0.2
Nigeria	979	0.024	(0.090)	0.9
India	2,476	0.052	(0.064)	1.2
S. Korea	1,245	0.082	(0.088)	1.9
Lithuania	978	0.055	(0.086)	2.1
Belarus	997	0.192	(0.089)*	6.4
Romania	1,088	0.220	(0.083)**	7.9

Note: Dependent variable = 1 if bribery is "never justified," = 0 otherwise. Standard error in parentheses.

$*p < .05$ $**p < .01$ (two-tailed tests)

to this coefficient is −4 percent, that is, all else being equal, a man's likelihood of responding that accepting a bribe is "never justified" is 4 percentage points less than the likelihood for a woman.

It is possible that a large gender differential in a subset of countries is driving the results in table 8.3. Therefore we estimated the probit model separately for each country and found, in tables 8.4 and 8.5, that the gender differential is observed in most countries, although the estimated effects vary. We estimated probit models for 43 countries for 1991 and 18 countries for 1981, using the same specification used in column 1 of table 8.3. In 1991 we see that in 36 of 43 countries the gender differential favors women; in 24 of these countries the differential is statistically significant at 5 percent. There are only 7 countries in which the gender differential favors men, and only 2 of these differentials are statistically significant at 5 percent. In the data from 1981 (table 8.5) the gender differential favors women in all 18 countries; the differential is statistically significant at 5 percent in 9 of these. Thus the gender differential in the attitude to corruption seems to be more or less a worldwide phenomenon.

Some readers have pointed out that the male dummy is negative and significant in only slightly more than half the cases. This is a fair

TABLE 8.5.   Country-wise Probit Regression, World Values Survey Data, 1981

Country	N	Male Dummy Coeff.	S.e.	Marginal Effect (%)
Netherlands	1,153	−0.355	(0.079)**	−13.1
Belgium	1,023	−0.279	(0.082)**	−10.6
Japan	1,077	−0.272	(0.081)**	−9.7
France	1,161	−0.213	(0.078)**	−8.4
Iceland	904	−0.336	(0.106)**	−8.1
Sweden	938	−0.252	(0.091)**	−7.9
Argentina	879	−0.197	(0.102)*	−5.1
Denmark	1,175	−0.370	(0.117)**	−4.6
Spain	2,205	−0.125	(0.063)*	−3.7
Norway	1,228	−0.141	(0.088)	−3.5
N. Ireland	310	−0.207	(0.204)	−3.2
Britain	1,182	−0.103	(0.085)	−3.0
Italy	1,305	−0.077	(0.076)	−2.8
W. Germany	1,301	−0.061	(0.073)	−2.3
United States	2,270	−0.071	(0.062)	−1.9
Australia	1,176	−0.047	(0.086)	−1.4
Canada	1,240	−0.042	(0.082)	−1.3
Ireland	1,145	−0.014	(0.088)	−0.4

Note: Dependent variable = 1 if bribery is "never justified," = 0 otherwise. Standard error in parentheses.
   $*p < .05$ $**p < .01$ (two-tailed tests)

point. On the other hand it should noted that if there were no gender differentials in any country, the probability of getting 54 or more negative signs out of 61 is virtually zero.

A possible response to these findings is that women may disapprove of corruption more only because they are less likely than men to be employed.[10] Persons not employed may be less able to benefit from corruption, or norms regarding bribery may be different among employed and nonemployed persons (e.g., the latter may be more naive or idealistic). Accordingly, we reestimated the model in column 1 of table 8.3, including a dummy variable for the employment status of the individual (1 if employed). The coefficient on the male dummy became larger (more negative), indicating that the gender differential in attitudes is not an artifact of male-female differences in employment rates.

The preceding analysis is based on attitudes toward the acceptability of taking bribes. In the following section we present evidence of actual behavioral differences in bribe-paying, with respect to gender, drawing on an enterprise survey in Georgia.

3. Microevidence: An Enterprise Survey in Georgia

In this section we use data from a World Bank study of corruption in Georgia, which included a survey of 350 firms.[11] The firms were in four broad sectors: trade, manufacturing, services, and agriculture. We categorize them in three groups: large (more than 50 employees), medium (between 10 and 50 employees), and small (less than 10 employees). The incidence of corruption is high, as firms reported paying an average of 233 lari per month (1.5 lari = U.S.\$1) or 9 percent of turnover on average (Anderson et al. 1999).

Managers were asked about contact with and illegal payments to 18 different agencies.[12] There are potentially 6,300 (350 firms times 18 agencies) points of contact, but only 2,954 of these actually occurred. To maximize the reliability we used only data on firms where the senior manager/owner was interviewed, which left 2,219 observations.[13] Summary statistics, by gender, are provided in table 8.6.

Our analysis starts with the response to the following question: "How frequently do the officials providing the service require unofficial payments? Please answer on a scale of 1 to 7, where 1 = Never, 2 = 1–20 percent of the time, 3 = 21–40 percent of the time, 4 = 41–60 percent of the time, 5 = 61–80 percent of the time, 6 = 81–99 percent of the time, and 7 = Always." Firms owned or managed by women gave bribes on average on 4.6 percent of the occasions that they came in contact with a government agency; the average percentage was more than twice as large for firms owned/managed by men, 12.5 percent.[14] Thus the descriptive evidence is strongly suggestive of a gender differential in involvement in bribery.[15]

How should this evidence be interpreted? The way the question is phrased, it appears that the impetus for the bribe is coming from the official, not from the owner/manager. However, questions on bribery are usually put in this way to avoid placing the onus of the bribe on the respondent, in the hope of eliciting an honest response. Therefore, an obvious interpretation of these results is that female owners/managers are less likely to offer bribes than male owners/managers. However, other interpretations are possible. It could be that women are less likely to belong to bribe-sharing old-boy networks, and hence may be less prone to be asked for bribes. It could also be that, due to less individual or collective experience in the labor force, women have not yet "learned" how to engage in corruption. Here we document the presence of a statistically robust gender differential, but do not attempt to distinguish among these alternative interpretations.

Table 8.7 examines whether this gender differential remains after

TABLE 8.6.   Means, Georgia Survey

	Unit	Whole Sample[a] (n = 2,219)	Male Owner/Senior Manager (n = 1,717)	Female Owner/Senior Manager (n = 502)
Frequency of bribes	Percent	10.7% (sd = 26.9)	12.5% (sd = 28.9)	4.6% (sd = 17.5)
Size of firms				
Small	Dummy	0.48	0.42	0.67
Medium	Dummy	0.33	0.35	0.27
Majority state ownership	Dummy	0.1	0.12	0.03
Foreign participation	Dummy	0.38	0.44	0.19
Sector				
Trade	Dummy	0.55	0.51	0.68
Manufacturing	Dummy	0.25	0.30	0.08
Services	Dummy	0.44	0.44	0.43
Education of senior manager				
University	Dummy	0.82	0.83	0.80
Postuniversity	Dummy	0.07	0.08	0.01
Scope of operation				
Local	Dummy	0.64	0.59	0.82
Regional	Dummy	0.06	0.06	0.07
National	Dummy	0.15	0.17	0.09
Percentage of sales domestic	Percent	95.41	94.18	99.6

[a] The sample of firms in which the owner/senior manager was interviewed. The proportions in various sectors add up to more than 100% because some firms are in more than one sector (e.g., Trade and Manufacturing).

TABLE 8.7. Georgian Enterprises, Patterns of Bribe Paying

Type of Procedure	Probit	Probit Marginal Effect (%)
Male owner/senior manager	0.674**	12.9
	(0.190)	
Size of firms (reference group = Large)		
Small	1.621**	39.0
	(0.326)	
Medium	1.031**	28.1
	(0.293)	
Majority state ownership	−0.791*	−12.9
	(0.326)	
Foreign participation	−0.006	−0.2
	(0.190)	
Sector (reference group = Agriculture)		
Trade	0.009	0.2
	(0.174)	
Manufacturing	0.194	4.8
	(0.203)	
Services	0.253	6.0
	(0.172)	
Education of senior manager (reference group = below University)		
University	−0.264	−6.7
	(0.238)	
Postuniversity	0.061	1.5
	(0.396)	
Scope of operation (reference group = international)		
Local	−1.175*	−31.6
	(0.488)	
Regional	−1.592**	−16.9
	(0.515)	
National	−1.148*	−17.3
	(0.500)	
% domestic sales	0.012	0.28
	(0.009)	
Constant	−2.561**	
	(0.724)	
N	2,219	
Pseudo R^2	0.165	

Note: Dummies were included for the agency with which firm was in contact. Standard errors have been corrected for within-firm autocorrelation of errors terms. Marginal effects were computed at the sample means.

$*p < .05$ $**p < .01$

we control for other firm characteristics. Given there are seven categorical outcomes that can be meaningfully ranked, one possibility is to estimate an ordered probit model. The dependent variable here takes values 1 through 7, with 1 being the category "never." However, if we are only interested in the distinction between firms that never give bribes and those that sometimes do, a probit model is appropriate. Here the dependent variable takes the value 0 if the firm never gives a bribe, and 1 if it sometimes does.

We have relied on the literature on Georgia, and on corruption more broadly, to guide our choice of control variables. Since a firm's size can affect its ability to pay, as well as its bargaining power or "connections," we include size dummies (small and medium, with large being the excluded category). For similar reasons we include dummies to reflect the firm's scale of operations (local, regional, and national, with international being the excluded category) and the percentage of the firm's output sold domestically.

Depending on the sector in which the firm operates, its dependence on governmental services and hence its temptation to bribe may vary; therefore, we have included sector dummies (manufacturing, services, and trade, with agriculture being the excluded category). We also include dummies for the level of education of the owner/manager; these could partially reflect influence or connections as, for example, in old-boy networks. The dummies are for university and postuniversity, with the excluded category being those who do not have a university education. Since some governmental agencies are likely to be more corrupt than others, we include dummies for the agency with which the firm is having contact. Because these dummies are so numerous (18 agencies, hence 17 dummies), these coefficients are not reported.[16] Participation by the state and foreign participation could also affect bribe-giving, and dummies are included for these.[17]

Column 1 of table 8.7 presents probit estimates; as mentioned, the dependent variable takes the value 0 if the firm is in the "never" category and 1 otherwise. The male dummy has a positive (and statistically significant) coefficient which suggests that, all else being equal, a firm owned/managed by a man is less likely to be in the "never" category than a firm owned/managed by a woman. Column 2 presents marginal effects, that is, the effect of a unit increase in the explanatory variable on the probability that the firm is not in the "never" category. We see that the marginal effect of a male owner/manager is 12.9 percentage points.[18] We also see that firm size, state ownership, and the scope of operations of the firm have large (and statistically significant) impacts on the probability that the firm is in the "never" category. When we estimate an ordered probit model the marginal effect of a male owner/manager (defined in the same fashion as above) is 13.7 percent.

4. Macroevidence: Cross-Country Tests

Having seen evidence from microdata-based surveys, in the next section we turn our attention to analysis of country-level data. These cross-country analyses complement the microlevel evidence in two important ways. First, as earlier mentioned, national-level corruption ratings are not self-reported, so that any gender differentials cannot be produced by male-female differences in the willingness to acknowledge corruption. Second, microlevel evidence carries no necessary implications for the macrolevel relationship between women's participation and the severity of corruption in public life. For example, male-female differences in attitudes and behavior may be too small for an increase in women's participation in commerce and government to move society from a highly corrupt to a less corrupt equilibrium. Or, women may have little influence on the way public life is conducted, even when their participation rates rise, as long as they remain in the minority.

Measurement and Data

No objective measure of corruption with broad cross-country coverage is available, so we rely on subjective indicators. The most widely known measure of corruption is Transparency International's "Corruption Perceptions Index." This index combines the information available from numerous sources, some using investor surveys and others based on assessments of country experts. The TI index can vary between 0 and 10, with higher values signifying less corruption.[19] Kaufmann, Kraay, and Ziodo-Lobaton (1999) construct a similar index, using data largely from the same sources. Their "Graft index" differs from TI's index in two major ways. First, rather than weighting all available sources equally, their statistical procedure assigns lower weights to sources that tend to agree less closely with other sources. This difference in the way the Graft index and the TI index are constructed has little impact, as the two indexes are correlated at .98. A second and more important difference between them is that the Graft index covers more countries. It is therefore used as the primary corruption measure in this section, but the main tests using a 93-country sample for the Graft index are replicated using a 68-country sample for the TI index. The Graft index is constructed to have a mean value of 0 and a standard deviation of 1 in the full Kaufmann et al. (1999) sample.

The Graft index and the TI index take into account both grand or high-level corruption as well as petty corruption, as indicated by the criteria used in the corruption ratings provided by the International Country Risk Guide (ICRG), one of the various sources used in constructing both indexes. Lower scores by ICRG indicate that "high government officials are likely to demand special payments," and that "illegal payments are generally expected throughout lower levels of government" in the form of "bribes connected with import and export licenses, exchange controls, tax assessment, police protection, or loans." The fact that the Graft index and TI index measure a combination of grand and petty corruption has implications for the ways in which women's participation should be measured in cross-country tests.

The firm-level analysis in the preceding section focused on the gender of the owner/manager. For country-level analyses, several relevant measures of women's involvement in politics and commerce are available: the proportion of legislators in the national parliament who are female,[20] the proportion of ministers and high-level government bureaucrats who are women, and women's share of the labor force. Table 8.8 provides summary statistics for the variables used in the cross-country tests.

TABLE 8.8.   Summary Statistics for 93-Country Sample

Variable	Mean	Standard Deviation	Minimum	Maximum
Graft index	.17	.95	−1.57	+2.13
TI index ($N = 68$)	5.03	2.43	1.5	10
Women in parliament (%)	9.7	8.2	0	39
Women government ministers (%)	7.8	8.3	0	44
Women in labor force (%)	38.5	7.8	10.7	53.9
Women's influence index	−.01	.79	−1.91	3.02
Log GNP per capita, 1995	8.24	1.10	5.95	9.96
Average years schooling, 1990	5.63	2.69	0.65	11.74
Catholic proportion	34.3	37.2	0	100
Muslim proportion	20.2	34.4	0	99.8
Former British colony	0.38	0.49	0	1
Never colonized	0.26	0.44	0	1
Largest ethnic group (%)	70.6	24.2	17	100
Political freedoms	4.87	1.97	1	7

Our three measures of women's participation and a composite measure we construct (described later) can at one level be considered proxies for the overall participation of women in politics and commerce. However, they can also be given more specific interpretations. The share of women in parliament can affect corruption levels in at least two ways. First, legislative corruption is itself an important dimension of governmental corruption, and if women tend to accept fewer bribes, the incidence of legislative corruption will be lower where women hold more seats. Second, members of parliament may influence the incidence of bureaucratic and judicial corruption through the passage of laws designed to deter bribery, through their influence on judicial or executive branch appointments (in some countries), or through placing corruption on the public agenda and encouraging the media and other elements of civil society to focus on the problem.

The share of ministers and top-ranking bureaucrats is a supplementary measure of women's participation in politics.[21] The incidence of bribe-taking in high-level positions in the bureaucracy may be reduced where more of those positions are held by women. Petty corruption at lower levels of the bureaucracy can also be affected, to the extent that ministers and subministers select lower-level government officials and influence the formulation and enforcement of rules against bribe-taking.

Although women's share of elite positions can influence petty corruption, it is useful to have a supplementary measure of women's representation in lower levels of the government bureaucracy as well as in the private sector. Data on the share of lower-level government positions held by women are unavailable. Women's share of the labor force overall is the closest available proxy. Women's share of the labor force is likely also to capture, to some extent, any tendency for women in the private sector to offer bribes less frequently than men.

Not surprisingly, where women are better represented in parliament, they also tend to be better represented in top ministerial/bureaucratic positions, and even in the labor force more generally. Women's share in parliament is correlated with women's share of top ministerial/bureaucratic positions at .74 (p = .0001) and with labor-force share at .33 (p = .0015). The latter two variables are correlated with each other at .26 (p = .011). Therefore, when only one of these three variables at a time—for example, women in parliament—is included in a corruption regression, its coefficient captures at least part of the effects of other dimensions of women's influence. Accordingly, we also report tests using an index of women's influence that incorporates all three variables.

Our tests of the relationship between the level of corruption and women's participation control for many other potential determinants of corruption. We control for (the log of) per capita income for two reasons. First, the development of institutions to restrain corruption may be a costly activity undertaken more easily by richer countries. Second, in some cases where survey respondents have little concrete information on which to base their assessments, they may simply infer that corruption is a problem where they observe incomes to be low. To the extent that formulation, implementation, and public knowledge of written codes and laws reduce corruption, a more educated population may be less tolerant of corruption. Therefore, we control for the average years of education completed by adults, using data from Barro and Lee 1993. Percentage of the population who are Catholic and percentage Muslim are included as proxies for cultural factors that may affect women's participation and/or corruption. For example, casual observation suggests that within Europe, Catholic countries such as Italy and Spain have lower rates of women's participation and more severe corruption than the Protestant Scandinavian nations.[22]

Corruption may also be linked to the history of colonialism. Therefore, we include a dummy that takes the value 1 if the country has never been a colony. It has also been argued that the character of British colonialism was different from others, so we include a dummy (1 if former British colony) to allow for this possibility.[23] Corruption may be higher in more ethnically divided societies. Therefore, we include the percentage of population belonging to the largest ethnic group as a regressor, using data from Sullivan 1991.

Democratic political institutions can restrain corruption in several ways. Multiparty competition may reduce corruption because each party has the incentive to expose any wrongdoing by another party.[24] By increasing the threat of exposure, an independent media can increase the costs of corrupt behavior. Independent judiciaries may reduce the incidence of corruption, at least within the executive branch. As a summary measure of democratic institutions that can restrain corruption, we use the well-known Freedom House political freedoms indicator, using ratings for 1995.[25] Values range from 1 to 7; following common practice we reverse the original scale so that higher values indicate more political freedoms.

Results

Estimates from cross-country tests using the Graft index are presented in table 8.9. In equation 1, women's share of parliamentary
seats is highly significant; the coefficient implies that a one standard
deviation increase (about 8 percentage points) is associated with an
increase in the Graft index of slightly more than one-fifth of a standard deviation. By comparison, a standard deviation increase in (the
log of) per capita income is associated with an increase in the Graft
index of slightly more than one-half of a standard deviation. Other
significant variables include the former-British-colony dummy and

**TABLE 8.9. Determinants of Corruption, Cross-Country Regressions
(Dependent Variable: Graft Index)**

Equation	1	2	3	4	5
Parliament,	2.456**			1.273	
proportion women	(0.751)			(0.853)	
Ministers, proportion		2.432**		1.444	
women		(0.567)		(0.813)	
Labor force,			2.419**	2.048*	
proportion women			(0.767)	(0.804)	
Women's influence					0.364**
index					(0.062)
Log (GNP per capita,	0.478**	0.459**	0.567**	0.551**	0.532**
1995)	(0.090)	(0.090)	(0.098)	(0.098)	(0.087)
Average years of	0.003	0.009	0.012	0.003	0.003
schooling, 1990	(0.035)	(0.037)	(0.040)	(0.035)	(0.035)
Catholic proportion	−0.281	−0.354*	−0.221	−0.139	−0.167
	(0.159)	(0.172)	(0.179)	(0.163)	(0.164)
Muslim proportion	−0.152	−0.192	−0.066	0.017	−0.014
	(0.192)	(0.197)	(0.196)	(0.198)	(0.190)
Former British	0.481**	0.467**	0.418**	0.469**	0.476**
colony	(0.131)	(0.133)	(0.134)	(0.127)	(0.126)
Never colonized	0.312	0.353*	0.229	0.183	0.209
	(0.160)	(0.165)	(0.190)	(0.174)	(0.161)
Proportion in largest	0.141	0.125	0.135	0.167	0.164
ethnic group	(0.200)	(0.191)	(0.199)	(0.192)	(0.190)
Political freedoms	0.092**	0.081*	0.078*	0.056	0.061
	(0.033)	(0.035)	(0.032)	(0.033)	(0.033)
Constant	−4.702	−4.436	−6.097	−5.976	−4.805
	(0.575)	(0.565)	(0.865)	(0.883)	(0.564)
Adj. R^2	.75	.75	.73	.76	.77
SEE	0.48	0.48	.49	.46	.46

Note: Sample size is 93. Mean of dependent variable is 0.18. White-corrected standard errors are shown in parentheses.
*$p < .05$ **$p < .01$ (two-tailed tests)

the political freedoms index. Other things equal, ex-British colonies score nearly half a standard deviation higher on the Graft index. Each 1-point improvement on the political freedoms index is associated with an increase of nearly one-tenth of a standard deviation on the Graft index.

In equation 2 the women's influence variable is the share of top ministerial/bureaucratic positions held by women. This variable is also highly significant, and its coefficient is nearly identical to that for women in parliament in equation 1. Equation 3 substitutes women's share of the labor force, which is also highly significant, with a coefficient very similar to those for the women's influence variables in equations 1 and 2. A standard-deviation increase in women's share of top ministerial/bureaucratic positions, or in women's share of the labor force, is associated with increases of about one-fifth of a standard deviation in the Graft index.

Equation 4 includes all three women's influence variables: labor force is significant, and parliament and ministers are jointly significant. A possible way of interpreting these results, where women's labor-force share and women's participation at elite levels of the government are each significant, is that the former captures women's influence in reducing petty corruption, while the latter captures primarily women's impact on reducing grand corruption. Of course, confirmation of this conjecture requires more detailed information.

Because the three women's-influence variables are correlated, and each can be interpreted as being a partial measure of the larger concept of women's participation in public life, there is a certain logic for constructing an overall index of women's participation from the separate indicators. We created such an index by standardizing the three variables (mean 0, standard deviation equal to 1) and taking the mean. The index is correlated with its parliament, ministers/bureaucrats, and labor-force components at .87, .84, and .66 respectively.[26] The index ranges from a low of −1.91 (UAE) to a high of 3.02 (Finland). In equation 5, the women's participation index has a t-statistic of nearly 6, and the adjusted R^2 indicates a slightly better fit than in equations 1 through 4. A standard deviation increase in the index is associated with an increase in the Graft index of three-tenths of a standard deviation. Figure 8.1 depicts the partial relationship, corresponding to equation 5.[27]

In section 2 we saw that the percentage of women who say corruption is "never justified" is higher than the percentage of men who give the same response. It can be argued that greater participation by

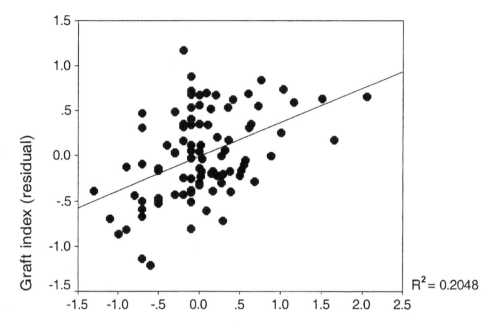

Fig. 8.1. Graft index and women's influence index (partial plot)

women in public life should have a larger impact on corruption in countries in which the gender gap (the percentage of women who say corruption is never justified minus the same percentage for men) is larger. To test this we need to estimate a model in which the women's-participation variable and the gender gap in attitudes are entered individually and also interacted; the coefficient on the interaction term should be positive. We use data on 32 nations (from the 93 nations in our cross-country sample) for which the World Values Survey could be used to compute the gender gap in attitudes toward bribery.

The regression reported in column 1 of table 8.10 is identical to equation 5 of table 8.9, with the exception that it adds as regressors the WVS gender gap[28] and its interaction with the women's participation index. The interaction between the gender gap in attitudes and the women's participation index is positive and significant at the .07 level (two-tailed test). The women's participation index has a coefficient of .24 conditional on a gender gap of 0, but increases by .034 for each percentage-point increase in the gender gap. These results are broadly consistent with the idea that the impact of women's participation on levels of corruption increases as the gender gap in attitudes becomes larger. However, this issue can be better explored when data on gender gaps in the attitude toward bribery become available for more countries.

Robustness of Results

The Graft index is constructed from numerous underlying sources. Kaufmann, Kraay, and Ziodo-Lobaton (1999) report standard errors for each country estimate. These standard errors increase with the level of disagreement among sources regarding the severity of corruption in the country, and decrease with the number of sources

TABLE 8.10. Determinants of Corruption, Cross-Country Regressions

Equation	1	2	3
Dependent Variable	Graft	Graft (WLS)	TI
Women's participation	0.240	0.380**	1.187**
index	(0.128)	(0.070)	(0.158)
Log (GNP per capita, 1995)	0.733**	0.606**	1.660**
	(0.227)	(0.069)	(0.249)
Average years of schooling,	−0.066	−0.009	−0.076
1990	(0.051)	(0.030)	(0.088)
Catholic proportion	0.025	−0.131	−0.645
	(0.261)	(0.163)	(0.493)
Muslim proportion	−0.325	0.021	0.426
	(0.295)	(0.185)	(0.524)
Former British colony	0.565*	0.480**	0.840*
	(0.240)	(0.123)	(0.391)
Never colonized	0.203	0.144	−0.372
	(0.246)	(0.149)	(0.428)
Proportion in largest ethnic	−0.085	0.178	0.806
group	(0.824)	(0.235)	(0.591)
Political freedoms	0.092**	0.076*	0.203
	(0.033)	(0.032)	(0.110)
WVS gender gap	−0.016		
	(0.025)		
WVS gap*participation index	0.034		
	(0.018)		
Constant	−6.161	−5.473	−10.368
	(1.288)	(0.469)	(1.571)
Adj. R^2	.81	.80	.81
N	32	93	68

Note: White-corrected standard errors are shown in parentheses. R^2 does not have its usual interpretation in WLS.
*$p < .05$ **$p < .01$ (two-tailed tests)

available for the country. Higher standard errors reflect greater uncertainty about the "true" level of corruption. In equation 2 of table
8.10, the (inverse of the) standard errors are used to weight observations, to reduce the sensitivity of estimates to the inclusion of countries for which there is less reliable information on the severity of
corruption. Results from this weighted least-squares regression are
very similar to those from OLS in equation 5 of table 8.9, for the
women's participation index and for the other regressors.

The TI index is based on a different approach to data-quality issues, requiring, for a value to be published, that a minimum of three
sources be available for a nation. The TI index therefore covers fewer
countries. Equation 3 of table 8.10 replicates equation 5 of table 8.9,
but substituting the TI index for the Graft index. Despite the change
in sample size from 93 to 68, results are very similar: the same variables that were significant using the Graft index are also significant
using the TI index. A standard deviation increase in the women's participation index is associated with an increase in the TI index of two-
fifths of a standard deviation, or about 1 point on the 0–10 TI scale.

Results are also not sensitive to the inclusion of outlying observations. To conserve space, table 8.11 reports only the coefficients and
standard errors for the women's participation variables, from regressions analogous to equations 5 and 1 through 3 respectively in table
8.9, using the Graft index. Each row of table 8.11 thus summarizes the
results from four regressions. The first row duplicates the coefficients
and standard errors for the women's participation variables from
equations 5 and 1 through 3, respectively. The next two rows of table
8.11 show that when we run median or robust regressions, which
downweight the influence of outliers, results for the women's participation variables are unaffected.

The fourth set of coefficients in table 8.11 is estimated deleting
Denmark, Finland, Norway, and Sweden, which all rate at or very
near the top on all of the women's participation variables as well as
on the Graft index. The women's variables all remain significant, with
magnitudes little affected.

Results are also insensitive to the addition of several regressors
not included in table 8.9. Treisman (2000) found that federal states
were more corrupt than nations with centralized governments. We
use a dummy variable from the Polity IV (2000) data set, which classifies 16 of the 93 nations in our sample as federal states. The fifth row
of coefficients in table 8.11 indicates that the inclusion of this feder-
alism dummy has no impact on the women's participation results.

Similarly, adding a trade-openness dummy (for 1994, using data from Sachs and Warner 1996) or the black market currency exchange premium—as measures of opportunities for bribe seeking—does not substantially alter the estimated impact of women's participation on corruption.[29] It is often claimed that public officials are more likely to seek bribes when they are poorly paid (e.g., Haque and Sahay 1996). Therefore, we include the average government wage as a multiple of per capita GDP.[30] Civil service pay turns out to be unrelated to corruption in our regressions, and its inclusion does not materially affect the women's participation coefficients, despite a reduction in sample size from 93 to 64.

TABLE 8.11.   Gender and the Graft Index: Alternative Samples, Specifications, and Methods

Change in Method, Sample, or Specification	Index of Women's Participation	Women's Share in Parliament	Women's Ministerial Positions	Women's Share in the Labor Force
From table 8.9: equations 5, 1–3	0.364**	2.456**	2.432**	2.419**
	(0.062)	(0.751)	(0.567)	(0.767)
Median regression	0.335**	3.185**	3.413**	2.965
	(0.101)	(1.107)	(1.046)	(1.612)
Robust regression	0.370**	2.702**	2.444**	2.656**
	(0.086)	(0.745)	(0.747)	(1.022)
Scandinavia dropped ($N = 89$)	0.405**	2.197*	2.559**	2.264**
	(0.092)	(1.063)	(0.913)	(0.773)
Federalism dummy added	0.363**	2.424**	2.438**	2.437**
	(0.061)	(0.752)	(0.561)	(0.768)
Trade openness dummy added	0.375**	2.539**	2.508**	2.434**
	(0.064)	(0.791)	(0.585)	(0.759)
Black market exchange premium added ($N = 83$)	0.334**	2.452**	1.861**	2.813**
	(0.061)	(0.620)	(0.579)	(0.660)
Civil service pay added GDP ($N = 63$)	0.330**	2.516**	2.455**	1.898*
	(0.061)	(0.680)	(0.591)	(0.927)
Continent dummies added	0.248**	1.731**	1.610**	1.590
	(0.069)	(0.646)	(0.579)	(0.812)
Life expectancy gap added	0.344**	2.349**	2.504**	1.906*
	(0.063)	(0.763)	(0.567)	(0.793)
Education attainment gap added ($N = 88$)	0.317**	2.293**	1.914**	2.359**
	(0.061)	(0.680)	(0.527)	(0.803)
Herfindahl index of party representation added ($N = 86$)	0.358**	2.425**	2.534**	2.222*
	(0.063)	(0.725)	(0.573)	(0.866)

Note: Cell entries indicate coefficients and standard errors for women's participation variables. Dependent variable is the Graft index from Kaufmann, Kraay, and Ziodo-Lobaton (1999). Except where indicated, independent variables are the same as in table 8.9. Standard errors are White-corrected, except in median and robust regression.
*$p < .05$ **$p < .01$ (two-tailed tests)

Ethnic homogeneity was not significant in table 8.9; an alternative indicator of social cohesion that might be related to corruption is the distribution of income. Including the Gini measure of income inequality has little impact on the women's participation coefficients (not reported in table 8.11), and they all remain significant.

We added a set of continent dummies (sub-Saharan Africa, Middle East and North Africa, Latin America and the Caribbean, and Asia, with the OECD as the omitted category), to account for any omitted variables related to corruption or women's participation rates that vary primarily across continents or country groupings. For example, it is conceivable that the low corruption, high women's participation countries are all developed countries, and that corruption and women's participation are unrelated within the group of developed countries, or within the group of developing countries. As shown in table 8.11, the inclusion of the continent dummies reduces the women's participation coefficients, but all remain significant (labor force only at the .06 level).

It could be that more corrupt countries also discriminate more against women, which leads to lower levels of participation by them. In this scenario the observed correlation between women's participation and corruption is spurious, and driven by the omitted variable "level of discrimination against women." We evaluated (and ruled out) this possibility by controlling for the level of gender discrimination using the gap between men's and women's educational attainment, and the gap between men's and women's life expectancy. Inclusion of these controls changes the women's participation estimates only slightly, as shown in table 8.11. In results not shown in table 8.11, results for the women's participation variables also proved insensitive to the inclusion of Humana's (1992) indexes of "political and legal equality" and "social and economic equality" between men and women.

Studies of the determinants of the presence of women in parliament find that proportional representation (PR) matters (Reynolds 1999; Matland and Studlar 1996). In a PR system as opposed to a plurality system a certain number of women can be elected even if a large majority of voters in every district is disinclined to vote for women candidates. Electoral rules can potentially affect the incidence of corruption also. Myerson (1999) argues that it is easier under PR than under plurality voting to launch a new party that adopts policy positions similar to those of an existing party, but that promises to reduce corruption. On the other hand, as Myerson notes, reforms in Italy to reduce the number of seats allocated through PR are motivated by the goal of reducing corruption—apparently because PR is blamed for the Christian Democrats' long-standing dominance of the governing coalition. Thus, because proportional representation can affect the incidence of corruption as well as the presence of women in parliament, its omission could bias our estimates. Using data from Beck et al. 2000 we identify 38 nations in our 93-country sample that elect the majority of their (lower house) legislators via PR. A PR dummy when added to our regressions is associated with a one-fifth of a standard deviation decline in the Graft index (significant at .10 for a two-tailed test), but this does not reduce the magnitude or significance of the women-in-parliament coefficient (2.878, s.e. of 0.680).

Reynolds (1999) also finds that more fragmented multiparty systems are associated with lower women's representation in parliament, attributing this result to the likelihood that smaller parties have a smaller pool of "safe seats" for which they can nominate women candidates. If the extent of fragmentation affects the level of corruption as well as women's representation, its omission is a potential source of bias. A Herfindahl index of party representation in the legislature (from Beck et al. 2000) is not significant when added to our corruption regressions, and its inclusion does not affect the relationship between corruption and women's share of parliamentary seats, as can be seen in the last row of table 8.11.

Four countries in our sample have minimum quotas or reserved seats for women in parliament, and 22 more had some political parties with quotas. Dummy variables for these national and party quotas are not significant in our corruption regressions, and their inclusion has no impact on the women in parliament estimates.[31]

Despite our efforts, the possibility of omitted variable bias in a cross-sectional regression can never be entirely ruled out. For example, it might be argued that societies in which "traditional" political values and clientelistic attitudes are prevalent may tend to choose "strong" male leaders and may also be more tolerant of corruption, with no causal connection between these two phenomena. A powerful way of addressing this problem of potential omitted variable bias is by looking at the correlation between the changes in women's participation and the extent of corruption *within* countries over time; we can then be confident that our estimates are not affected by the omission of any time-invariant country-specific variable that affects the level of corruption. Time-series data on corruption are very sparse:

the TI index is updated annually but was first released only in 1995. The Graft index is even newer and has been produced for only one year thus far. The only available source covering a substantial period of time and a large sample of countries is the "corruption in government" index from the International Country Risk Guide (ICRG). The ICRG corruption index, one of the sources used in constructing the TI index and the Graft index, varies from 0 to 6, with higher values representing less corruption.[32] Correlations of the ICRG corruption index for 1997 with the TI and Graft indexes respectively are .80 and .77. Because the TI and Graft indexes aggregate information from numerous sources, the ICRG index—based on a single source— is likely to be a noisier measure.

Time-series data are available on two of the women's participation variables: women in the labor force is available annually, and women in parliament is available for 1994, 1990, 1985, and 1975. Time-series data on our control variables are available for two of the three control variables that are statistically significant in table 8.9: per capita income and the political freedoms index. The other one—the ex-British colony dummy—does not vary over time. Most of the other control variables in table 8.9 (e.g., percent Catholic) are unlikely to vary much over a fifteen-year period.

The dependent variable in our time-series tests in table 8.12 is the change in the ICRG corruption index from 1982 (or the first avail-

TABLE 8.12. Determinants of Corruption Changes, Cross-Country Regressions (Dependent Variable: Change in ICRG Corruption Index from 1982 to 1997)

Equation	1	2
Parliament, percentage women (1994 minus 1975)	3.948**	
	(1.531)	
Labor force, percentage women (change in)		7.603*
		(3.458)
% change in GNP per capita, 1982–96	0.124	0.086
	(0.295)	(0.275)
Change in political freedoms	0.084	0.086*
	(0.056)	(0.042)
Initial value of corruption index	−0.607**	−0.577**
	(0.057)	(0.057)
Constant	1.956	1.742
	(0.208)	(0.199)
Adj. R^2	.51	.51
N	85	98

*$p < .05$ **$p < .01$ (two-tailed tests)

able year) to 1997. Changes vary from −4 (Niger) to +3 (Bahamas, Haiti, Iran, Philippines, and Syria). Control variables include the initial corruption index value, to control for regression-to-the-mean effects, the percentage change in per capita income over the period, and the change in the political freedoms measure. Women's participation variables are the change in women's share of parliamentary seats (equation 1) and the change in women's share of the labor force (equation 2). The former varies from −27 percentage points (Albania) to +25 points (Guyana), while the latter varies from −2.3 percentage points (Botswana) to +12.1 points (Kuwait).

The ICRG index shows a strong regression-to-the-mean effect, as the initial value of the index has a coefficient of −0.6 and a t-statistic of about −10 in both regressions. Increases in income are not associated with significant improvements in corruption ratings. Change in political freedoms has a positive coefficient as expected, but it is significant only in equation 2. Coefficients for both women's participation variables are positive and significant. In equation 1, an increase of 25 percentage points in women's share in parliament is associated with a 1-point improvement in the ICRG corruption rating. In equation 2, an increase of about 13 percentage points in women's share of the labor force is associated with a 1-point improvement in the ICRG corruption rating. These results suggest that our central finding is not driven by a time-invariant, country-specific omitted variable. Of course we still cannot entirely rule out bias due to a time-varying omitted variable (say, social "modernization").

5. Interpretation of Findings and
Concluding Remarks

Though questions can be raised regarding each of the three sets of evidence we have assembled, they reinforce each other, and taken together they make a strong case. For instance, the World Values Survey results can be criticized on the grounds that they represent hypothetical choices, and the data on corruption from Georgia can be questioned because they are self-reported. But neither of these charges holds true for the cross-country data. The results from Georgia can be questioned on grounds of selection bias; if employers discriminate against women, only those women who are exceptionally capable or honest may become owners/managers, and the gender differential we are observing may be the difference between average men and exceptional women. Arguing along similar lines, greater representation of women in government and in market work could improve average outcomes because participation rates for women are still low, and women participants are from the "better" part of the women's distribution, rather than because the distribution of attitudes toward corruption differs between men and women. However, in the World Values Survey we have random samples of the whole population (no room for selection bias), and there is still a gender differential. Moreover, controlling for discrimination against women does not change our cross-country results. We are making a simple point: to question the central finding of this essay one needs to argue that the results of careful analyses of several distinct data sets have, by sheer fluke, all been biased in the same direction. Our conclusion, that there is indeed a gender differential in tolerance for corruption, is more plausible.

We are reassured to learn that our evidence is entirely consistent with the findings of leading criminologists. For instance, Gottfredson and Hirschi (1990, 194) show, using U.S. Department of Justice figures, that arrests for embezzlement per 100,000 white-collar workers are higher for men for every age group. They also cite a variety of sources to make the case that across age groups, countries, and types of crime, the evidence regarding higher participation of men is remarkably uniform. The following summary statement from a study conducted by the National Academy of Sciences of the United States reflects the confidence with which the gender differential has been identified in the criminology literature:[33] "The most consistent pattern with respect to gender is the extent to which male criminal participation in serious crimes at any age greatly exceeds that of females, regardless of the source of data, crime type, level of involvement, or measure of participation."

This essay has primarily focused on identifying an empirical regularity, a "stylized fact." Ideally, we would like to conclude with an explanation of this stylized fact. Criminologists have developed many theories that are potentially relevant. Women may be brought up to be more honest or more risk averse than men, or even to feel there is a greater probability of being caught (Paternoster and Simpson 1996). Women, who are typically more involved in raising children, may find they have to practice honesty in order to teach their children the appropriate values. Women may feel more than men—the physically stronger sex—that laws exist to protect them and therefore be more willing to follow rules. More generally, girls may be brought up to have higher levels of self-control than boys, which affects their propensity to indulge in criminal behavior (Gottfredson and Hirschi 1990, 149).

Though these theories are generally consistent with our findings, our data are not sufficiently detailed to specifically support any one of them. Indeed, even in heavily researched areas such as male-female differences in sexual behavior and propensity for violence, researchers are very far from having reached a consensus on the underlying causes. Since at least the mid-1970s sociobiologists have argued that behavioral differences between human males and females have parallels among other species, and that common explanations can be provided for these differences, based primarily on the roles of males and females in reproduction and child rearing.[34] However many sociologists, especially those of feminist persuasion, have seen in these arguments the potential for biological justification of gender inequity; some have accused sociobiologists of "biological essentialism," that is, an emphasis on biology to the point where culture is treated as peripheral to behavior, and the social construction of gender roles is severely underestimated (Bem 1993; Epstein 1988). But there is disagreement even among feminists; some radical feminists have implicitly appealed to biology to theorize a greater propensity for nurturing and cooperative behavior in women, following from their role in reproduction and child rearing.[35] Despite decades of debate, these issues are far from resolved; it is clear that empirical identification of the sources of gender differentials in behavior is a very difficult (not to mention politically charged) task even for researchers who have much richer sources of data than we do. Therefore, though there is a plethora of theories regarding the sources of gender differentials in crime, with potential applications to corruption, we are reluctant to take a position on this issue.

We do need to comment, however, on one policy-related matter. If gender differentials in tolerance for corruption are culturally based, it is worth asking whether they will persist as the position of women in society changes and their participation in the labor force increases. We suspect the differentials will persist, at least in the medium term, for three reasons. First, in our evidence from the World Values Survey, the gender differential is robust to controlling for employment status. Second, in the same survey, the gender differential can also be seen in the OECD countries, where women have been in the labor force in large numbers for some decades. Finally, it used to be routinely assumed by criminologists that with greater equality of status between men and women, crime rates would equalize. However, in the United States, large differentials have persisted despite the increase in women's participation in the labor force (Gottfredson and

Hirschi 1990, 146–47). Given this evidence, we suspect the gender differential in corruption will be stable in the medium term, and policy initiatives like those discussed at the beginning of this essay will indeed reduce corruption.

Notes

This chapter was originally published under the same title in the *Journal of Development Economics* 64 (1) (February 2001): 25–55. It is reprinted with permission from Elsevier Science.

1. For example, Fukuyama (1998, 24) reports that the percentages of American women who supported U.S. involvement in World War II, the Korean War, the Vietnam War, and the Gulf War were 7 to 10 points less than the corresponding percentages for men. A study by the Center for American Women in Politics (Dodson and Carroll 1991) documents substantial differences between men and women in their attitudes toward prohibition of abortion (79 percent women oppose versus 61 percent men), toward the death penalty (49 percent women oppose versus 33 percent men), and toward more nuclear plants (84 percent women oppose, compared to 71 percent men). Htun and Jones (1999) find that there are significant differences by gender in committee membership and bills introduced to the Argentinean legislature, with women overrepresented on health and education committees and underrepresented on finance, defense, and foreign policy.

2. Kaufmann (1998) presents a scatterplot showing a cross-country correlation between corruption and an index of women's rights and emphasizes the need for more detailed investigation of this association.

3. We chose Georgia (rather than any other country) purely because of access to microdata on corruption: the World Bank was kind enough to allow us to use this survey.

4. The adverse consequences of corruption have been discussed by Klitgaard (1988), Mauro (1995, 1998), and Olson, Sarna, and Swamy (2000).

5. Inglehart et al. (1998) provide details on the procedures followed in the various surveys in the 1990s. The surveys in the Western countries were carried out by experienced survey organizations, many linked with the Gallup chain. In other countries they were carried out by academies of science, or by university-based institutes. Inglehart et al. write: "In most countries stratified multistage random sampling was used, with samples selected in two stages. First a random selection of sample locations was made ensuring that all types of location were represented in proportion to their population. Next, a random selection of individuals was drawn up" (471).

6. This could be because, as argued by Strate et al. (1989, 452), "Church attendance involves a sense of personal affiliation with an institution in which communal values and social obligations are regularly emphasized."

7. Inclusion of additional education dummies did not alter our central result regarding the gender differential. The data do not allow us to construct a variable equal to years of education completed.

8. So, for instance, there are separate dummies for Canada in 1981 and 1991.

9. We reestimated the probit model perturbing the dependent variable in two ways: (a) dependent variable = 1 if the respondent chose categories 1 or 2 and (b) dependent variable = 1 if respondent chose categories 1, 2, or 3. We saw in the summary table 8.2 that while a larger percentage of women are in category 1, the gender differential is slightly reversed for categories 2 through 10. Consistent with this we found that while the male dummy is negative and significant, the marginal effects are slightly smaller (less negative), at −3.5 percent and −2.7 percent for cases (a) and (b) respectively.

10. We thank Margaret Madajewicz for this point.

11. We are grateful to the World Bank for making these data available to us.

12. The full list of contact agencies is as follows: phone installation, enterprise registration, water, electricity, inspection of weights and measurements, fire inspection, sanitary inspection, tax and finance inspection, tax clearance (for example in government privatization), other clearance to participate in government procurement, export license or permit, import license or permit, customs at border crossing, registration of property ownership, lease of state-owned commercial real estate, state banking services, building permits, and road police.

13. Results are very similar if we use the full sample; see below.

14. A value in the range 21 to 40 percent was converted to 30 percent, and so on. We then took the average of these converted values by gender.

15. If we use the full sample the average percentages for firms run by men and women are 10 percent and 4.1 percent, respectively.

16. The most corrupt agencies in terms of frequency of receiving bribes are traffic police, customs, import/export licensing, and tax inspection. The amounts of the bribes are relatively large for customs, import/export licensing, building permits, tax inspection, and enterprise registration.

17. State ownership should reduce bribe-giving if this gives the firm better contacts within the government. Miller et al. (1999) report that in formerly communist countries officials treat other officials better than they do private citizens. Foreign ownership may increase bribe-giving, since foreign-owned firms may be perceived to be richer, and more able to pay.

18. Estimating a probit model using the full sample yields a slightly smaller gender differential, 9.7 percent.

19. Details of the method of construction are provided by Lambsdorff (2000).

20. This measure is based on legislators in both houses of parliament, for countries that have upper and lower chambers. All results using this measure

are robust to using alternatively the proportion of lower-house members who are women.

21. Included are cabinet ministers, deputy and vice ministers, permanent secretaries, deputy permanent secretaries, and heads of Central Banks. The data are published in the UN's 1999 Human Development Report and are collected from the *Worldwide Government Directory,* published by Worldwide Government Directories, Bethesda, MD.

22. Disputes at the 1995 UN women's conference in Beijing and in a special UN session on gender and development in June 2000 usually pitted Western delegates against delegates from predominantly Catholic and Islamic nations (see, for example, *Washington Post,* June 10, 2000, A20).

23. Using the TI index, Treisman (2000) finds that ex-British colonies are rated as less corrupt on average.

24. For a discussion of this and related issues see Shleifer and Vishny 1998 and Myerson 1999.

25. The Freedom House civil liberties index is equally relevant as the political freedoms index, but the former is not used because it is correlated by construction with corruption, as it includes "freedom from gross government indifference and corruption" among its evaluative criteria. The political freedoms and civil liberties indexes for 1995 are correlated at .89 in our sample. In tests not reported in tables, we alternatively controlled for corruption-restraining institutions using several indexes from Humana 1992 that evaluate the independence of the courts, the degree of multiparty competition, press censorship, independence of newspapers, and independence of television and radio. The major difference with results using the political freedoms index is a reduction in the sample size; coefficients on the women's participation variables are unaffected.

26. Alpha, a measure of index reliability, equals .70 for this index. Alpha varies from 0 to 1, and increases with the degree of intercorrelation among the index items and with the number of items in the index.

27. The slope of the least-squares line in figure 8.1 is .364, the coefficient for the women's participation index in equation 5.

28. For countries represented in both WVS survey waves, the gap is the mean of the gaps for 1981 and 1990.

29. Government consumption as a share of GDP also proved to be unrelated to corruption, and its inclusion did not affect the estimates on the women's participation variables.

30. These data were assembled for the early 1990s by Schiavo-Campo et al. (1997).

31. Countries with quotas are identified from Inter-Parliamentary Union (1997), which conducted a survey of national parliaments in 1996. However, some parliaments did not respond to the survey. In most cases the dates of quota adoption are not available, and some of these quotas may not have been in effect when parliaments of 1994, which is the most re-

cent year for which we have data, were elected. Htun and Jones (1999) discuss why quotas have had limited effectiveness in increasing women's representation. Other determinants of women's representation in parliament have been identified in the political science literature (see Reynolds 1999 and Darcy, Welch, and Clark 1994). However, these determinants—such as the date women were first granted the vote or the right to run for office—can be viewed as alternative and less precise measures of women's participation in the context of the current study, rather than as omitted variables that could influence the relationship between women's participation and corruption.

32. We follow others who have used this measure in using the annual values calculated by Knack and Keefer (chapter 3, this volume) from the monthly ICRG issues dating back to 1982.

33. Blumstein et al. 1986, cited in Gottfredson and Hirschi 1990, 145.

34. Early influential works in sociobiology include Wilson 1975, 1978. Pinker 1997 provides an accessible summary.

35. Jaggar 1983 provides a critical overview of various feminist perspectives.

References

Akerlof, G. 1998. "Men without Children." *Economic Journal* 108:287–309.

Anderson, J., O. Azfar, D. Kaufmann, Y. Lee, A. Mukherjee, and R. Ryterman. 1999. "Corruption in Georgia: Survey Evidence." Mimeo, World Bank.

Barro, Robert J., and Jong-Wha Lee. 1993. "International Comparisons of Educational Attainment." *Journal of Monetary Economics* 32 (3): 363–94.

Beck, T., G. Clarke, A. Groff, P. Keefer, and P. Walsh. 2000. "New Tools and New Tests in Comparative Political Economy: The Database of Political Institutions." World Bank Policy Research Working Paper 2283.

Bem, Sandra Lipsitz. 1993. *The Lenses of Gender: Transforming the Debate on Sexual Inequality.* New Haven and London: Yale University Press.

Blumstein, A., J. Cohen, J. Roth, and C. Visher. 1986. *Criminal Careers and "Career Criminals."* Washington, DC: National Academy Press.

Bureau of Justice Statistics. 1996. *Sourcebook of Criminal Statistics.* Washington, DC.

Darcy, R., Susan Welch, and Janet Clark. 1994. *Women, Elections, and Representation.* 2d ed. Lincoln: University of Nebraska Press.

Dodson, D. L., and S. J. Carroll. 1991. *Reshaping the Agenda: Women in State Legislatures.* Center for American Women and Politics. New Brunswick: Rutgers University Press.

The Economist. 2000. "Liberty, Equality, Sorority." May 13: 51.

Epstein, C. 1988. *Deceptive Distinctions.* New Haven and London: Yale University Press.

Fukuyama, Francis. 1998. "Women and the Evolution of World Politics." *Foreign Affairs* 77 (5): 24–40.

Gottfredson, M. R., and T. Hirschi. 1990. *A General Theory of Crime.* Stanford: Stanford University Press.

Haque, Nadeem U., and Ratna Sahay. 1996. "Do Government Wage Cuts Close Budget Deficits? Costs of Corruption." *IMF Staff Papers* 43 (4): 754–78.

Htun, M. N., and M. P. Jones. 1999. "Engendering the Right to Participate in Decision-Making: Electoral Quotas and Women's Leadership in Latin America." Manuscript.

Humana, Charles 1992. *World Human Rights Guide.* 2d ed. New York: Oxford University Press.

———. 1996. *World Human Rights Guide.* 3d ed. New York: Oxford University Press.

Inglehart, R., M. Basanez, and A. Moreno. 1998. *Human Values and Beliefs: A Cross-cultural Sourcebook. Political, Religious, Sexual, and Economic Norms in 43 Societies: Findings from the 1990–1993 World Values Survey.* Ann Arbor: University of Michigan Press.

Inter-Parliamentary Union. 1997. *Men and Women in Politics: Democracy Still in the Making.* Geneva: Inter-Parliamentary Union.

Jaggar, A. 1983. *Feminist Politics and Human Nature.* Totowa, NJ: Rowman and Allenheld.

Kaufmann, D. 1998. "Challenges in the Next Stage of Corruption." In *New Perspectives in Combating Corruption.* Washington, DC: Transparency International and the World Bank.

Kaufmann, D., A. Kraay, and P. Ziodo-Lobaton. 1999. "Aggregating Governance Indicators." World Bank Policy Research Working Paper 2196.

Klitgaard, Robert. 1988. *Controlling Corruption.* Berkeley: University of California Press.

Lambsdorff, J. G. 2000. Corruption Perceptions Index: Framework Document, <http://www.gwdg.de/~uwvw/1999_CPI_FD.pdf> (accessed April 2002).

Matland, R., and D. Studlar. 1996. "The Contagion of Women Candidates in Single-Member Districts and Proportional Representation Electoral Systems: Canada and Norway." *Journal of Politics* 58 (3): 707–33.

Mauro, Paolo. 1995. "Corruption and Growth." *Quarterly Journal of Economics* 110:681–712.

———. 1998. "Corruption and the Composition of Public Expenditure." *Journal of Public Economics* 69:263–79.

McDermott, Jeremy. 1999. "International: Women Police Ride in on a Ticket of Honesty." *Daily Telegraph,* London, July 31.

Miller, W., A. Grodeland, and T. Koshechkina. 1999. "Caught between State and Citizen: The View from behind the Official's Desk." Paper prepared for the NISP Acee seventh annual conference, Sofia, March 25–27.

Moore, Molly. 1999. "Mexico City's Stop Sign to Bribery: To Halt Corruption, Women Traffic Cops Replace Men." *Washington Post,* July 31.

Myerson, Roger M. 1999. "Theoretical Comparisons of Electoral Systems." *European Economic Review* 43:7671–97.

Olson, M., N. Sarna, and A. Swamy. 2000. "Governance and Growth: A Simple Hypothesis Explaining Cross-Country Differences in Productivity Growth." *Public Choice* 102:341–64.

Paternoster, R., and S. Simpson. 1996. "Sanction Threats and Appeals to Morality: Testing a Rational Choice Model of Corporate Crime." *Law and Society Review* 30 (3): 549–83.

Pinker, Steven. 1997. *How the Mind Works.* New York: Norton.

Polity IV Project. 2000. *Polity IV Dataset* [computer file]. College Park, MD: Center for International Development and Conflict Management, University of Maryland. Accessed at <http://www.bsos.umd.edu/cidcm/inscr/polity/index.htm data>.

Reynolds, Andrew. 1999. "Women in the Legislatures and Executives of the World: Knocking at the Highest Glass Ceiling." *World Politics* 51:547–72.

Sachs, Jeffrey, and Andrew Warner. 1996. "Economic Reform and the Process of Global Integration." *Brookings Papers on Economic Activity* 1:1–118.

Schiavo-Campo, S., G. Tommaso, and A. Mukherjee. 1997. "An International Statistical Survey of Government Employment and Wages." World Bank Policy Research Working Paper 1806.

Shleifer, Andrei, and Robert Vishny. 1998. *The Grabbing Hand: Government Pathologies and Their Cures.* Cambridge: Harvard University Press.

Strate, J. M., C. J. Parrish, C. D. Elder, and C. Ford III. 1989. "Life Span Civic Development and Voting Participation." *American Political Science Review* 83 (2): 443–64.

Sullivan, Michael J. 1991. *Measuring Global Values.* New York: Greenwood Press.

Treisman, Daniel. 2000. "The Causes of Corruption: A Cross-National Study." *Journal of Public Economics* 76 (3): 399–457.

United Nations Development Program. 2000. World Income Inequality Database, <http://www.undp.org/poverty/initiatives/wider/wiid.htm> (accessed April 2002).

United Nations Publications. 1994. *Women's Indicators and Statistics Database (WISTAT).* Version 3, CD-ROM. New York: United Nations.

Washington Post. 2000. "Women's Rights Dispute Rages." June 10: A20.

Wilson, E. O. 1975. *Sociobiology: The New Synthesis.* Cambridge: Belknap Press of Harvard University Press.

———. 1978. *On Human Nature.* Cambridge: Harvard University Press.

Social Capital and Development

Conjoint action is possible just in proportion as human beings can rely on each other. There are countries in Europe, of first-rate industrial capabilities, where the most serious impediment to conducting business concerns on a large scale, is the rarity of persons who are supposed fit to be trusted with the receipt and expenditure of large sums of money.

—*John Stuart Mill (Principles of Political Economy, 1848)*

The two chapters comprising part 3 analyze the relationships between institutions and development—the topic of part 1 of this volume—as well as the determinants of institutions—the focus of part 2. Chapters 9 and 10 differ from earlier chapters in addressing softer institutions such as norms and interpersonal trust, in contrast to harder institutions such as legal mechanisms for enforcing contracts. The two chapters have several other notable points in common. Both stress interrelationships between formal and informal mechanisms for enforcing agreements and ensuring cooperation, and both emphasize that informal mechanisms or social capital can be used for socially inefficient as well as efficient purposes.

"Rule Obedience, Organizational Loyalty, and Economic Development" (chapter 9) was first published in the *Journal for Institutional and Theoretical Economics* in 1993. Christopher Clague defines *rule obedience* as the tendency of people to follow society's rules, including laws and customs, affecting their interactions with each other and with the government. He argues that a minimum level of rule obedience is lacking in many societies, adversely affecting incentives for physical and human capital formation, the quantity and quality of public goods, and the rate of technological progress. In a model of tax compliance, Clague analyzes the determinants of rule obedience, arguing that incentives and their mutually reinforcing relationship with attitudes lead societies toward one of two equilibria, one with a high level and one with a low level of rule obedience. Clague's final paragraph notes that "societal differences in rule obedience ... are quantifiable to some degree" and urges empirical testing of his hypotheses. Chapter 10 by Stephen Knack and Philip Keefer provides some evidence consistent with Clague's ideas, although they do not use the term *rule obedience*.

"Does Social Capital Have an Economic Payoff?" was first published in the *Quarterly Journal of Economics* in November 1997. In this chapter, Stephen Knack and Philip Keefer show that economic performance is positively associated across countries with interpersonal trust and with an index of civic norms that is conceptually very closely related to Clague's rule obedience. Putnam's favorite social capital indicator—associational activity—fares less well: countries with more group memberships, as determined from surveys, do not grow faster, and actually have slightly lower investment rates, than other countries. One explanation for this finding is that any positive impacts of associational activity on economic performance are canceled out by the rent-seeking functions of groups emphasized by Olson (1982). However, when Knack and Keefer attempt to distinguish "Putnam groups" (with mostly social functions) from "Olson groups" (with mostly political and redistributive functions), they find no evidence that the latter are more damaging than the former; in fact, the only statistically significant result is an *inverse* link between membership in Putnam groups and investment rates. Knack and Keefer present some cross-country evidence consistent with Putnam's (1993) finding of a positive relationship between social capital and government efficiency and responsiveness across Italian regions. However, they argue that causality between informal and formal institutions goes in both directions; for example, trust may be conducive to citizens' efforts to make government accountable, but efficient government mechanisms to enforce private agreements in turn can be an important underpinning of interpersonal trust.

CHAPTER 9

Rule Obedience, Organizational Loyalty, and Economic Development

Christopher Clague

1. Introduction

Societies differ greatly in their economic and social institutions. Some societies have well-functioning institutions that channel individuals' energies into socially productive activities leading to economic and social progress, while in other societies the poor quality of the institutional infrastructure frustrates attempts at reforms and perpetuates stagnation. The quality of a society's institutional infrastructure depends not only on the content of the norms and rules but also on the degree to which people actually follow these norms and rules, or in other words, on the degree of rule obedience. A minimum level of rule obedience, it will be argued, is required for a well-functioning societal institutional infrastructure, and this level of rule obedience is lacking in many societies.

In societies that display more than this minimal level of rule obedience, institutional efficiency is supported by constructive kinds of internalization of goals, which lead to socially beneficial behavior that goes well beyond merely following the rules. Goal internalization may apply to the society as a whole and to subunits within the society, such as the town, the social class, or the extended family. The focus in this essay will be goal internalization within organizations. Some organizations are characterized by intensive interaction among individuals, which leads in some cases to a high degree of goal internalization. In turn this leads individuals to act on behalf of the group interest in ways that go far beyond mere rule obedience. These individuals exert extra effort, take the initiative to start new projects, and take on responsibility for matters that fall between the cracks of other people's jurisdictions. This type of behavior involving effort, initiative, and responsibility will be called EIR behavior; it seems to be the key to effective organizations.[1]

Both rule obedience and EIR behavior may be motivated by self-interest or by internalization of group goals. What internalization means in this context is that individuals incorporate group goals into their own utility functions. Individuals with such utility functions are not necessarily disadvantaged relative to those with purely self-oriented motivations;[2] moreover, recognition of such arguments in utility functions is eminently realistic, as attested by many studies in social psychology (see, for example, Turner 1987).

The present essay attempts to advance our understanding of institutional differences across societies by exploring some of the determinants of rule obedience and EIR behavior. A basic idea in the essay is that there are forces that lead societies to evolve to very different levels of rule obedience; in other words, there can be multiple equilibria, in one of which there is a high level of rule obedience and in another a very low level. The forces sustaining these different levels include both narrow considerations of self-interest and the evolution of attitudes that reinforce past patterns of behavior. A similar idea is claimed in the essay to apply to EIR behavior within organizations; such behavior tends to be more highly rewarded and more highly valued as it becomes more common. Some organizations develop a high level of group loyalty, or *esprit de corps,* which tends to enhance rule obedience and EIR behavior. In a competitive environment, business organizations with low levels of rule obedience and EIR behavior will tend to be driven out of business. Rule obedience in the society and organizational effectiveness tend to support one another in a variety of ways (with obvious qualifications with regard to the purposes of the organizations at issue).

This essay draws heavily on ideas in the New Institutional Economics, which has refocused economists' attention on the important role of institutions and institutional change in the emergence of capitalism and in the explanation of economic growth and development (North 1990; Nabli and Nugent 1989; Bardhan 1989; Adelman and Thorbecke 1989). In this literature, institutions are understood to include not only the public policy environment that has long been the focus of much economic analysis, but also such rules of the game as property rights and the security of such rights, the types of contracts in use and the degree of contract enforcement, and the norms and patterns of behavior in the business community. The logic of these institutions has been illuminated by transaction cost economics (Williamson 1985; Miller 1992), which emphasizes the importance of trust within organizations as well as across markets. The essay also draws on theories of cooperation (Axelrod 1984) and theories of the evolution of conventions and norms (Schotter 1981; Sugden 1986), which explain how expectations of the behavior of others interact with self-interest to generate different social outcomes, especially with respect to following conventions and obeying norms. Finally, the essay makes use of some concepts in social psychology such as cognitive dissonance and self-categorization (Festinger 1957; Turner 1987) to help to explain how attitude formation may reinforce societal differences in rule obedience and organizational effectiveness.

The next section discusses different types of rule obedience and the evolution of one type with the aid of a simple model. Section 3 then explains how the evolution of attitudes reinforces the conclusions of the model. Organizational effectiveness is taken up in section 4, and a model of organizational behavior is presented in section 5. Concluding observations are contained in section 6.

2. The Evolution of Rule Obedience

Rule obedience is defined as the tendency of people in a society to follow society's rules. A rule is a constraint on behavior originating in social relations that is generally recognized to be obligatory and that is commonly (though not necessarily uniformly, nor even nearly uniformly) obeyed. Two types of rule obedience may be distinguished: bureaucratic rule obedience refers to the tendency of individuals within an organization to follow the rules of that organization.[3] Citizen rule obedience is the tendency of citizens and businesses to obey the laws and customs affecting their interactions with each other (for example, with respect to contracts) and with the government (for example, in the payment of taxes). In modern societies, enforcement of the laws affecting citizen and business behavior depends on the behavior of bureaucracies (the police, the courts, the tax collection authorities), and therefore citizen rule obedience in such personally painful areas as the payment of taxes is not likely to be very high if bureaucratic rule obedience is very low. Moreover, in such areas as credit scams and customer fraud, while most business people might be obeying the rules because of reputational considerations or internalization of norms (Macaulay 1963), there would seem always to be a plentiful supply of people who would engage in these potentially profitable activities if there were not bureaucracies that made them generally unprofitable. In traditional societies and the rural sectors of many contemporary societies, on the other hand, where much interpersonal contact is not anonymous, social pressure and authority relationships may well induce a fairly high degree of citizen rule-obedience even in the absence of functioning bureaucracies.

There is a fairly close connection between the notion of a rule-obedient society and James Coleman's concept of a society with a high level of social capital (1988). Social capital consists of aspects of the social structure that individual actors can use as resources to achieve their objectives. One of the forms of social capital is the network of obligations in a community, which consist of the credits that one has accumulated and the obligations that one has incurred, along with the trustworthiness of the environment, which affects the degree to which the obligations will be repaid. Another form of social capital is the set of norms in the community, which can be enforced by both internal and external sanctions. An important difference between the concept of a rule-obedient society and one with a high level of social capital is that rule obedience does not imply anything about the content of the rules. With an inefficient set of rules, a highly rule-obedient society may have very inefficient patterns of behavior. For example, the rules may permit special-interest lobbying and campaign contributions that lead to institutional sclerosis (Olson 1982). Yet one may say that in general a society with a good set of rules and a high degree of rule obedience will have a high level of social capital. Moreover, the social characteristics described by Coleman that support the formation of social capital (such as closure of social networks and multiplex relations) are very relevant to the forces supporting rule obedience.

It is clear that societies differ very sharply in their degree of rule obedience. This point seems rather obvious from descriptive literature on the way people think and behave in different countries. In particular the degree of bureaucratic rule-obedience appears to be much higher in the developed democracies of today than in these countries before 1800 or in the majority of less-developed countries today (see Wraith and Simpkins 1963; Scott 1972; Myrdal 1968).

The difficulties of large-scale organization in poor and backward societies have been emphasized in an interesting article by Olson (1987). He describes the problems created by poor transportation and communication systems and the cultural traits that are functional in such societies but are inimical to efficient large-scale organization. These difficulties are especially great in government agencies, which suffer from the lack of clear measure of output (such as profits) and from the lack of bottom-line termination mechanism.[4] But the difficulties stemming from underdevelopment also apply to organizations in the private sector.[5]

While there is undoubtedly a connection between overall economic development and the level of bureaucratic rule-obedience (and the causation runs both ways), there also seem to be large differences in rule obedience among societies at similar levels of economic development. Theoretical considerations support the proposition that these differences exist and are persistent. A model is presented below in which individuals decide whether to obey the rules by considering the expected costs and benefits of doing so. The model involves the interaction of the citizenry with a bureaucratic agency of the government; it thus concerns only one mechanism of enforcement of rule obedience. Much of the enforcement of rule obedience involves social sanctions (Coleman 1988), which should be modeled in a different way. Nevertheless, the point that the model illustrates seems to be a general one: when the overall level of rule obedience is high, most people find it in their interest to obey the rules; when the overall level of rule obedience is low, many people will choose not to obey the rules. The considerations addressed in the model help to explain why different societies exhibit persistently different degrees of rule obedience.

Model of Rule Obedience

For concreteness, let us think of a taxpayer who is deciding whether to pay or to evade the taxes owed. The logic of the model also applies to businesses deciding whether to obey regulations or to employees in a bureaucracy deciding whether or not to accept bribes, or whether or not to shirk on the job.

The payoffs for the taxpayer are expressed in money or monetary equivalents; for simplicity, risk neutrality is assumed. The taxpayer has a (0,1) decision; either pay in full or do not pay.[6] If he does not pay, he either escapes entirely or is caught and punished. The expected value (EV_i) of breaking the law (evading taxes) for taxpayer i is

$$EV_i = G - p(L + b) - a_i$$

where G is the (monetary) gain from evasion, p is the probability of getting caught and punished, L is the (monetary value of the) punishment in the form of a fine or imprisonment, and a_i and b are parameters reflecting the "psychological" cost of breaking the law. The psychological cost is in two parts: a_i is the guilt from breaking the law, which is incurred even if the individual is not caught, and b is the shame of getting caught. For simplicity, b is assumed to be the same for all taxpayers, but a_i varies across individuals.[7]

The individual's decision is illustrated in figure 9.1. The downward-sloping line $G - pL$ measures the monetary gain from breaking the law as a function of the probability of apprehension and punishment. The upward-sloping line $a_i + bp$ measures the psychological cost. The intersection of the two curves determines the critical probability p^*. This particular taxpayer will evade taxes if the probability of punishment is less than p^* and will pay if it exceeds p^*.

Next, it is assumed that there is a distribution of personality types in the population. Specifically, the guilt parameter a_i is distributed according to a rectangular distribution between the values a^0 (lower end) and a^1 (upper end). Individuals near the lower end of the distribution are less squeamish about breaking the law than the others. Let p as before be the probability of apprehension, and let $f(p)$ be the fraction of the population that will obey the law (pay their taxes) given this probability. Simple algebra shows that the law-abiding fraction will be

$$f(P) = \frac{a^1 - G}{a^1 - a^0} + \frac{L + b}{a^1 - a^0} p. \tag{1}$$

The first term shows the fraction of the population that will obey the law even when there is no chance of getting caught, while the second term shows the fraction that are law-abiding at least in part because of the probability of punishment.

Next the probability of punishment is modeled. The internal revenue service (IRS) initially examines a sample of the population and divides the sample into those who have paid and those who need to be further investigated. It is assumed the costs of this determination are negligible. However, the costs of apprehension and conviction of delinquents are substantial; it costs an amount c per conviction. The IRS has R resources at its disposal. It proceeds against all the delinquents in its first sample, and if it has resources left over, it goes on to a second sample and follows the same procedure. All the necessary samples are drawn within a given period. The result is that the probability of apprehension and punishment depends on the number of

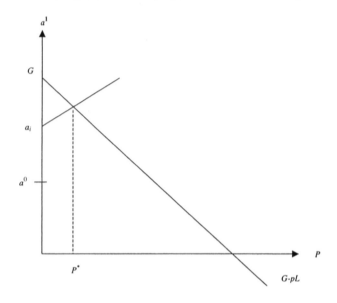

Fig. 9.1. The individual's decision

cases the IRS can pursue (which is R/c) and on the number of delinquents (which is $(1 - f)$ times the population, where f is the law-abiding fraction of the population). Thus we have

$$p(f) = \frac{R/c}{(1 - f)Population} = \frac{r/c}{1 - f}, \qquad (2)$$

where $r = R/Population$, or IRS resources per capita.

The equilibrium is illustrated in figure 9.2. The obedience curve plots equation (1), or the fraction (f) of the population that obeys the rule as a function of the probability of punishment (p).

The punishment curve plots equation (2), or the probability of punishment as a function of the fraction of the population that is rule obedient. To illustrate the diagram, let us start with a given level of rule obedience (f_1) and move horizontally to the point A on the punishment curve. This gives the value of the probability of punishment (p). But when the probability of punishment is p, the level of rule obedience in the next period drops down to point B on the obedience curve; this gives the new level of rule obedience f_2. It is easy to see that the intersection E_1 is a stable equilibrium, while E_2 is unstable. The

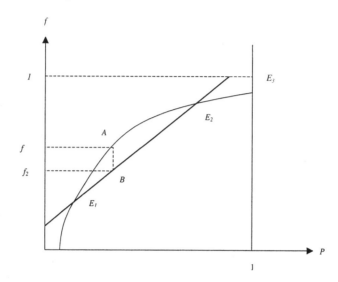

Fig. 9.2. The equilibrium

point E_3 is another stable equilibrium. Thus the diagram shows how countries may be stuck in a low-level equilibrium (E_1) or may evolve toward the high-level equilibrium (E_3), if the country starts from a point above E_2.

A rightward shift in the distribution of the guilt parameters (the a_i) shifts the obedience curve upward; some reasons why this shift may occur are explained in the next section. An increase in the government allocation of funds toward enforcement or a decrease in the cost of apprehending and punishing violators of the rule shifts the punishment curve to the right: this increase moves the low-level equilibrium upward and will eventually move the society into the region where it evolves toward the point E_3. But for this evolution to occur the society must develop rule-obedient bureaucracies. The development of such bureaucracies is also discussed in the next section, following our discussion of changes in people's attitudes and goals.

The larger social context (as described in Coleman 1988) will affect the parameters of the model. The probability p is affected by the willingness of people to report violators; the shame parameter is affected by society's attitude toward rule violations, as is the punishment L. In addition, as mentioned earlier there may be other social sanctions against rule violations, such as the loss of business opportunities.

3. Attitudes and Behavior

Evolution may take place not only with respect to behavior but also with respect to attitudes. A plausible hypothesis is that people's attitudes toward rules are affected by their behavior. That is, if people behave according to certain patterns, they tend to develop the attitude that these patterns are appropriate. In terms of the model presented above, the a_i would tend to drift upward over time in a society where rule obedience is normal. It seems likely that the degree of rule obedience may differ from one context to another within the same society, and certainly from one organization to another, but there is probably also some spillover from one context to another, as people observe the successful functioning of bureaucracies and the culture of the organization man spreads.

Social psychology supports the proposition that behavior affects attitudes. The behavior of others affects one's attitudes in that people take their values from the values of others, especially from individuals they admire and with whom they identify (see the discussion of conformity in Aronson 1979, chap. 2). If people believe that others are cheating on their taxes, they are more likely to feel like chumps for not doing so as well, but if they believe that most others (including those they admire) are honest, they will tend to value tax honesty in their own behavior. In addition, the theory of cognitive dissonance suggests that one's own behavior affects one's attitudes. As originally stated by Festinger (1957), the theory says that if an individual holds two cognitions (ideas, attitudes, beliefs, opinions) that are psychologically inconsistent or dissonant, he will modify them so as to reduce the dissonance (see Aronson 1979, chap. 4, for a clear exposition with many examples; Akerlof and Dickens 1982 gives additional examples and explores some economic consequences of the theory). The cognition "I cheat on my taxes" is dissonant with the belief "I am a decent person." The dissonance can be reduced by searching out information that cheating is widespread, that the government wastes the money it collects, and so forth. On the other hand, people who obey the rules are likely to strengthen their attitudes against breaking them.

Psychologists have conducted many experiments that support and refine the theory of cognitive dissonance. For example, after a person has purchased a particular brand of a product, he is less interested in seeking information that might reveal that he made a poor choice. Workers in benzene factories deny that they are working with dangerous chemicals. People who went through a painful initiation procedure to join a study group report that the group is more interesting than those whose initiation procedure was not very painful. Students who were induced to write an essay contrary to their prior attitudes (in this case an essay supporting the behavior of police in recent riots) displayed a greater change in attitude toward the police if their reward for writing the essay was small rather than large. These examples suggest that people who decide to pay their taxes when the probability of detection is very low are likely to form stronger attitudes in favor of obeying the tax laws than those who decide to pay their taxes under conditions where the probability of detection is very high. If so, then a population may become very rule-obedient even without much expenditure on enforcement.

A particularly interesting experiment showing the effects of decisions on attitudes was conducted on a sample of sixth graders by Judson Mills. As described by Aronson:

> Mills first measured their attitudes toward cheating. He then had them participate in a competitive exam with prizes being offered to the winners. The situation was arranged so that it was almost impossible to win without cheating and so that it was easy for the children to cheat, thinking that they would not be detected. As one might expect, some of the students cheated and others did not. The next day, the sixth graders were again asked to indicate how they felt about cheating. In general, those children who had cheated became more lenient toward cheating, and those who had resisted the temptation to cheat adopted a harsher attitude toward cheating. (1979, 118)

4. Organizational Loyalty and Effectiveness

Thus attitude formation interacts with self-interest in the evolution of citizen rule-obedience. Similar mechanisms operate in the evolution of bureaucratic rule-obedience. Let us consider first such readily observable behavior as arriving at work on time and not taking excessive coffee breaks. If punctuality is normal, then failure to be punctual is conspicuous. Moreover, firing workers for rule violations is less costly to the organization when these violations are rare.

With respect to employee behavior that is costly for supervisors to observe, there is a mechanism that is quite analogous to the taxpayer model. When an organization's rule obedience is fairly high, monitoring activity can be directed toward new employees and toward the minority of employees who show signs of violating the rules. Where rule obedience is low, employees can fairly safely violate the rules.

As mentioned in the introduction, organizational effectiveness is not just a matter of rule obedience; well-functioning organizations also take advantage of employee internalization of the goals of the organization. Herbert Simon, whose Nobel Prize in economics derives in considerable part from his study of organizations, explains why organizational loyalty must be incorporated into our understanding of organizational behavior (1991). First, to do their jobs properly employees need to take responsibility for evaluating alternatives and choosing among them, bringing items to the attention of their superiors, and acting in other ways that are not simply following rules mechanically; in our terminology, they need to display EIR behavior. Second, for evolutionary reasons people are susceptible to acquiring organizational pride and loyalty under the right conditions. Simon uses these insights to criticize theories of organizational behavior that rely exclusively on self-interested motivation, and he remarks that there appear to be substantial intercultural differences in the degree to which societies foster organizational identification.

A recent book by Miller (1992) forcefully makes the point that efficiency within an organization cannot be achieved by relying on incentive mechanisms alone. Hierarchies can be more efficient than markets in certain circumstances, but the task of making the organization operate efficiently is not simply that of designing an efficient set of individual incentives. The leaders of the organization need to foster the development of a corporate culture, to build a reputation for honoring commitments even when high-level executives have a temptation to renege on them, and to communicate directly and symbolically with employees in such a way as to elicit organizational loyalty. The task of building an effective organization involves creating and then respecting property rights, which is conceptually similar to the phenomenon of the emergence of the institutions supportive of a market economy, as described by North and others.

Granted that organizational loyalties are important to the functioning of an organization, a critical issue is whether the members' loyalty is directed toward the whole organization or toward subunits such as the immediate workgroup. As Miller (1992) explains in his analysis of managerial dilemmas, loyalty to subunits can be very detrimental to the efficiency of the whole organization, as when workgroups impose social sanctions on "rate-busting" workers or functional divisions of a corporation engage in tribal warfare. Again, the possibility of multiple equilibria seems very prominent, as different patterns of loyalty and trust could easily become established and perpetuated. Turner's theory of psychological group formation based on self-categorization helps to explain why very different patterns of loyalty could emerge. Turner's theory states, in consonance with economists' formulation of the logic of collective action (e.g., Olson 1982), that cooperation does not automatically emerge out of the existence of common interests, as was suggested by the interdependence theory of social psychology (see Turner 1987, chap. 2). Instead cooperation depends on the prior perception of the existence of a psychological group. The perception of a group depends on the perceived identity of oneself and other group members, which leads to a perceived identity of needs, goals, and motives. Individuals categorize themselves into groups at different levels (for example, as Europeans, as Italians, as Fiat employees, as members of a small workgroup) and the salience of these self-categorizations into psychological groups can be altered by the flow of information (for example, the behavior of respected others) and by the attitude formation consequent to one's own behavior. The theory seems to be consistent with a substantial role for organizational leaders in molding corporate culture.[8]

In a given society, different organizations will of course develop different degrees of organizational loyalty, or esprit de crops (Clague 1977). The term *esprit de corps* will be used here to denote the loyalty to a firm rather than to a subunit of the firm. A high level of esprit de corps can enhance the efficiency and profitability of a firm in a variety of ways. Some of these are captured in a model of organizational efficiency that is presented in the next section. The model highlights the role of information sharing on the employee's effort decision and is somewhat analogous to the model of tax compliance presented earlier. Some other ways in which esprit de corps affects organizational efficiency are discussed after the presentation of the formal model.

5. A Model of Organizational Effectiveness

Let us imagine a firm operating in a competitive environment, hiring employees who produce output. Each employee's contribution to output depends on both his talent and his effort; the owner-manager of the firm observes neither talent nor effort but does observe the employee's contribution to output, although with an error of measurement.

The owner sets the salary of each employee and the minimum standard of performance; if the employee's measured performance falls below the minimum standard, the employee is fired, and the firm must incur a cost to replace him. The owner also spends her time and money on supervising and evaluating employee performance and makes a profit-maximizing decision with respect to these costs.

We could think of the firm hiring a cohort of executives and evaluating them after five years. Some are promoted and kept by the firm, and the others are let go. We do not explicitly model the time dimension of the problem.

The employee maximizes expected utility by selecting the level of effort, in light of his distaste for effort, the minimum standard of performance, the measurement error, and the utility of his present job compared to the next best alternative.

The owner-manager sets the minimum standard of performance and the level of supervision costs. These costs should be thought of as primarily consisting of the time of the owner-manager rather than as monetary outlays. The idea is that the owner-manager spends part of her time supervising her junior managers, ensuring that their jobs are done well and at the same time evaluating them, and part of her time thinking about the future direction for her firm, that is, being entrepreneurial. The more time she spends in supervision, the less entrepreneurial she can be.

The key to the model is the existence of esprit de corps within the firm. This variable reflects the attitudes of the employees toward the firm, including the degree to which the employees internalize the goals of the owner-manager. If esprit de corps is high, then employees, who in the course of their work observe the performance of their fellow employees, share this information with the owner-manager. Thus esprit de corps reduces supervision costs of the owner and also increases the accuracy of assessment of employee performance.

The owner would like to establish a high level of esprit de corps within her firm, and it is assumed that she does whatever she can along these lines by her leadership, which involves communicating with her employees, setting an example, and building up their trust in her competence and fairness (see the discussion of leadership in Miller 1992, chap. 11). An increase in the owner's effort in supervising employees increases esprit de corps, because employees appreciate being judged fairly, but on the other hand, an excess of supervision may reduce esprit de corps, because employees appreciate being trusted with the responsibility to carry out their tasks without supervision. It is assumed, perhaps not entirely realistically, that the supervision is kept within the range where increases in it have a positive effect on esprit de corps.

The model is presented next, with a verbal summary for the reader not interested in the algebra. Then the implications of the model and some extensions are described.

The Employee's Effort Decision

The employee's expected utility is equal to the probability of keeping his current job times the utility of that job plus the probability of getting fired times the utility of that outcome. The employee's utility function reflects an assumption of risk neutrality.

$$u = \phi(x)[w(1 - bx)](1 + e) + [1 - \phi(x)]u^*$$

Here $\phi(x)$ is the probability of keeping his job, which is a function of his effort x; w is his salary, b is a parameter reflecting his distaste for effort, e represents his esprit de corps, and u^* is his utility in the case where he gets fired. Note that esprit de corps raises the utility of the current job but does not otherwise affect the relative utilities of income (w) and on-the-job leisure. The only decision the employee has to make is how much effort (x) to exert. The first-order condition for utility maximization is

$$b\phi(x) = \phi'(x)\left[\frac{(1-bx)-u^*}{w(1+e)}\right]. \tag{3}$$

The intuition behind this result is very simple. The left-hand side represents the disutility of another unit of effort, multiplied by the probability of still being in the present job. The right-hand side (RHS) represents the effect of another unit of effort on the probability of keeping his job multiplied by the difference in utility between the current job and the state of the world in which he gets fired. The term in brackets [ ] might be called the rent the employee receives from his current job.

The employee's measured performance, q, is equal to his effective labor supply (tx) plus an error of measurement (t is the employee's level of talent, which is here assumed to be the same for all employees).

$$q = tx + \varepsilon$$

To keep matters simple e is assumed to have a uniform density function over the interval $(tx - c, tx + c)$. The mean of e is zero. Figure 9.3 illustrates the density function. The minimum standard of performance is q^*. The probability of not getting fired is illustrated in figure 9.3 and is given by

$$\phi(x) = (tx + c - q^*)/2c.$$

The derivative of $\phi(x)$ is simply

$$\phi'(x) = t/2c.$$

Putting these into the first-order condition (3) gives

$$b(tx + c - q^*)\, t[(1 - bx) - u^*/w(1 + e)],$$

which becomes

$$x = \left(\frac{1}{2b}\right)\left(1 - \frac{u^*}{w(1+e)}\right) + \left(\frac{1}{2t}\right)(q^* - c). \tag{4}$$

The level of effort x is reduced by an increase in the distaste for effort (b). It is increased by an increase in the wage w or a decrease in the utility of the alternative job u^*. An exogenous increase in esprit de corps e will affect effort (x) indirectly. A higher e means that the current job has a greater attractiveness over the next best alternative, and thus the employee has a greater incentive to try to avoid getting fired.[9]

Next let us consider how the employee responds to changes in working conditions (c and q^*). We assume that a rise in the minimum standard adversely affects esprit de corps, as it represents an increased risk of getting fired. We also assume that employees feel more positively toward the firm if they feel that their output is measured more accurately, or in other words if c is reduced. Thus esprit de corps is a negative function of the measurement error c. Hence we have

$$e(c,q^*); \qquad e_c < 0; \qquad e_q < 0.$$

To see how the employee responds to changes in working conditions (c and q^*), take the total differential of the first-order condition.

density

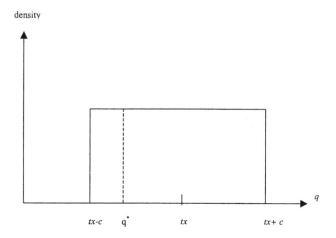

Fig. 9.3.   **The probability of not getting fired**

$$dx = \left(\frac{1}{2t}\right)(dq^* - dc) + \frac{u^*}{2bw(1+e)^2}\,(e_c dc + e_q dq^*). \qquad (5)$$

The effects of changes in working conditions (q^* and c) may be divided into the direct effect and the indirect ones that operate through changes in esprit de corps. The direct effects may be seen in the first term on the right-hand side of (5). A rise in the minimum standard q^* increases effort because each unit of effort has a larger effect on the probability of keeping one's job. Conversely, an increase in the measurement error c reduces effort by reducing the effect of effort on the probability of keeping one's job. However, increasing the minimum standard and the measurement error have an adverse effect on esprit de corps and hence on the rent from the current job. These effects reduce the employee's optimal effort, as can be seen in the second term on the RHS of (5), where both e_c and e_q are negative.

In summary, the worker increases effort in response to a rise in the wage and an exogenous increase in his own esprit de corps, and he decreases effort in response to a rise in the utility of the alternative job. An increase in the accuracy of measurement of performance (a decrease in c) increases effort unambiguously, while a rise in the minimum standard has an ambiguous effect, depending on the strength of the direct influence (which is positive) and the indirect effect (through esprit de corps, which is negative).

The Firm's Decisions

The firm's decision variables are the minimum standard $q*$ and the supervision costs. Although these costs consist primarily of the time of the owner, for ease of exposition they are measured here in monetary terms. The firm's profits per employee can be written

$$Q = F(gtx) - w - [1 - \phi(x;c,q*)]R - M, \tag{6}$$

where $F(g\,t\,x)$ is the average level of output (sales) per employee (ignore the term g for the moment), w is the salary, R is the cost of replacing one employee who is fired, and M is the supervision cost per employee (for simplicity we take the number of employees as given and we let the firm's maximand be profits per employee).

The term g may vary over firms and across industries, but it is given for a particular firm. This term reflects the fact that different firms may have different degrees of sensitivity to talent, perhaps because of the talent of the owner-entrepreneur, and industries differ in their skill intensities.

Now we write the measurement error, c, as a function of supervision costs M and esprit de corps, on the idea that a high esprit de corps induces the employees to share information with the owner-manager. But esprit de corps is a function of c and $q*$, or $e(c, q*)$, so we have $c[M, e(c, q*)]$ and

$$dc \,/\, dM = c_M + c_e e_c c_M = c_M(1 + c_e e_c) = \gamma'. \tag{7}$$

We write $c = \gamma(M)$ and $dc = \gamma' dM$ where γ' is negative. As the firm increases its supervision cost M it gets a better measure of employee performance directly, and it induces the employees to share information so it gets an indirect benefit.

The logic of the firm's decision problem can be spelled out as follows. The firm's profit function is $Q(x, M, q^*)$, and employee effort is the function $x = X(M, q^*)$. The firm maximizes profits by selecting M and q^* to maximize Q subject to the employee response. Writing out the total differentials, we have

$$dQ = Q_x dx + Q_M dM + Q_q dq* = 0 \tag{8}$$

$$dx = X_M dM + X_q dq* \tag{9}$$

$$dQ = dM(Q_M + Q_x X_M) + dq* (Q_q + Q_x X_q). \tag{10}$$

Rewriting (5), making use of $dc = \gamma' dM$, yields

$$dx = dM\left(-\frac{\gamma'}{2t} + \frac{u^*e_c\gamma'}{2bw(1+e)^2}\right) + dq^*\left(\frac{1}{2t} + \frac{u^*e_q}{2bw(1+e)^2}\right).$$

Hence

$$X_M = \frac{-\gamma'}{2t} + \frac{u^*e_c\gamma'}{2bw(1+e)^2} \tag{11}$$

$$X_q = \frac{1}{2t} + \frac{u^*e_q}{2bw(1+e)^2} \tag{12}$$

Recall that

$$\phi(x,c,q^*) = (tx + c - q^*)/2c.$$

Hence

$$\phi_x = t/2c; \qquad \phi_q = -1/2c; \qquad \phi_c = (q^* - tx)2c^2 \tag{13}$$

From (6) we have

$$\partial Q/\partial x = Q_x + F'gt + R\phi_x = F'gt + Rt/2c \tag{14}$$

$$\partial Q/\partial M = Q_M = R\phi_c\frac{dc}{dM} - 1 = \frac{R(q^* - tx)}{2c^2}y' - 1 \tag{15}$$

$$\partial Q/\partial q = Q_q = R(\phi_c c_e e_q + \phi_q) = -\frac{R}{2c} + \frac{R(q^* - tx)}{2c^2}c_e e_q. \tag{16}$$

Now we substitute (9)–(16) into (10). The optimal value of supervision costs M is found by setting the expression in (10) multiplying dM equal to zero ($Q_M + Q_x X_M = 0$). This yields

$$\frac{R(q^* - tx)}{2c^2}y' - 1 - \frac{Q_x\gamma'}{2t} + \frac{Q_x u^*e_c y'}{2bw(1+e)^2} = 0 \tag{17}$$

$$-\frac{dM}{dc} = -\frac{1}{y'} = \frac{Q_x}{2t} + \frac{R(tx - q^*)}{2c^2} - \frac{Q_x u^*e_c}{2bw(1+e)^2}.$$

The term $-1/\gamma'$ is the monetary cost of reducing c by one unit. On the right we have various benefits of the reduction in c. The first term represents the effect on sales of the greater effort induced by the more accurate measurement of effort (the reduction in c). The second term is the reduction in replacement costs from making fewer errors of measurement (note that this term would be negative if the minimum standard $q*$ were higher than tx, but normally this would not be the case). The last term on the right reflects the greater effort induced by the increase in rent on the current job brought about by the rise in esprit de corps caused by the reduction in c.[10]

To find the optimal value of the minimum standard, we gather the $dq*$ terms in (10) and set the resulting expression $(Q_q + Q_x X_q)$ equal to zero. This yields

$$\frac{-R}{2_c} + \frac{R(q* - tx)}{2c^2}c_e e_q + \frac{Q_x}{2t} + \frac{Q_x u* e_q}{2bw(1+e)^2} = 0 \tag{18}$$

$$\frac{Q_x}{2t} = \frac{R}{2_c} + \frac{R(tx - q*)}{2c^2}e_c e_q - \frac{Q_x u* e_q}{2bw(1+e)^2}. \tag{19}$$

The left side reflects the additional revenue from raising $q*$, achieved through a higher level of x. The right side shows the various costs of raising $q*$. $R/2c$ are replacement costs of the additional firings. The next term reflects the fact that a higher $q*$ reduces esprit de corps, which raises c, which causes additional firings. The last term reflects the fact that higher $q*$ reduces esprit de corps and reduces effort because it reduces the rent attached to the current job.

In summary, the firm increases the minimum standard to the point where the value of the increased employee effort is equal to the additional cost of replacing workers who are fired as a result of the higher standard, with due allowance in both cases for the effects of changing the minimum standard on esprit de corps. With regard to supervision costs, the firm increases these to the point where the marginal cost of increasing the accuracy of performance measurement is equal to the reduction in the cost of replacing fired workers plus the value of the increased effort resulting from more accurate measurement, again with due allowance for the effects of accurate measurement of esprit de corps.

Implications of the Model and of Other Considerations

The model has described an owner-manager with a set of employees. The model need not refer to a firm in a market; it could apply to any organization with a measured net output that the "owner" of the organization tries to maximize. The model could apply to a subunit within a firm or to an office in a government bureaucracy, provided that the office's net output is measured and that the office head attempts to maximize that net output.

Suppose that organizations differ in esprit de corps, partly because owner-managers differ in their ability to cultivate it and partly because of chance variations in personal interactions. Considering now firms in a competitive market, these firms will differ in their profitability. The high profits of successful firms will not necessarily be competed away, because esprit de corps is not something that can be manufactured automatically. Esprit de corps for a firm is to some extent a non-importable factor of production, just as for a poor country a good institutional structure is a non-importable requirement for development (Olson 1987). To be sure, there is a market in owner-managers, and competitive pressure will drive out of business those owner-managers who impede the development of esprit de corps within their firms, but the winnowing process is less than perfect because esprit de corps depends in part on factors over which the owner-manager has no control.

Esprit de corps plays two roles in the model. It adds to the utility of the current job, increasing thereby the rent on this job and adding to the employee's desire not to get fired. It also induces the employee to share information with the owner-manager about the performance of fellow employees, thereby increasing the accuracy of measurement of employee performance. It would be reasonable to associate still another effect with esprit de corps. The concept captures the degree to which the employee internalizes the goals of the owner (which become also the goals of fellow employees). An employee who internalizes these goals may exert effort even in a situation in which there is no possibility of being observed and rewarded. Or to put it another way, the employee may exert effort without thinking very much about whether he will be rewarded for doing so. This effect could be incorporated into the model simply by letting the distaste-for-work parameter b be a negative function of esprit de crops. Moreover, esprit de corps affects the degree to which employees withhold or reveal private information about projects that the firm might undertake. An employee may be positively or adversely affected by the decision to undertake a particular new project (it might represent either a welcome or an unwelcome addition to his responsibilities), and a self-interested employee would have reason to transmit information selectively to the owner. Employees with esprit de corps will be less opportunistic. This effect could be captured in the model by letting production itself be a positive function of esprit de corps.

It is important to emphasize that a new employee entering an organization where there is a high level of esprit de corps has a purely selfish motive for exerting effort, even if he does not internalize the goals of the organization. The reason is that there is accurate measurement of performance, and slackers will be fired.

It seems clear that allowing firms to differ in wage rates and in the talent of their recruits will reinforce the conclusion that firms will differ in esprit de corps, EIR behavior, and organizational effectiveness. Profitable firms will pay higher wages, recruit more talented workers, and set higher minimum standards of performance. Successful organizations acquire prestige and can even more effectively attract the most talented and energetic workers. A firm with very high standards of performance will tend to recruit not only talented workers but also those willing to work hard. A socialization process may take place in which workaholism becomes the norm (in a model, the b parameters of the employees start out rather small and become smaller over time). This virtuous circle of developing esprit de corps and EIR behavior is reinforced if the organizational effectiveness generates higher revenues, from which still higher salaries can be paid. This process clearly operates for private companies in a competitive environment, but it can also exist for public agencies that can capture a larger budget through successful performance.

Organizational effectiveness is likely to spread from one organization to another within a society, in part via competition within the business sphere and in part by example. Individuals also move from one organization to another, and their receptiveness to rule obedience and to organizational loyalty is influenced by their past experiences.

6. Concluding Observations

This essay has argued that in explaining many economic phenomena economists need to recognize that there are large differences in rule obedience and organizational effectiveness across societies. A model of tax compliance suggests that countries are likely to evolve toward very different levels of rule obedience and that these differences are likely to be persistent. A society with very low levels of rule obedience cannot, it is argued, have a set of institutions that is conducive to economic progress. Rule obedience is by no means sufficient for economic progress, but a certain level of it seems to be necessary. Where the level of rule obedience is satisfactory and the content of the rules is favorable, a society will tend to develop business and governmental organizations that instill organizational loyalty and esprit de corps.

The essay argues that efficient bureaucracies provide incentives for rule obedience and that rule-obedient behavior molds attitudes favorable to rule obedience. An interesting but essentially unresearchable question concerns the degree to which societal differences in rule obedience are due to differences in incentives as opposed to differences in attitudes. The model suggests that incentives and attitudes reinforce one another in a cumulative fashion such that untangling the separate effects of each is virtually impossible. However, certain questions are researchable. I submit that the level of rule obedience and the degree of organizational effectiveness in a society will affect many aspects of its economic development, including the incentives for physical and human capital accumulation, the quantity and quality of public goods, the nature of the economy's comparative advantage, the rate of technological progress, and so forth. Societal differences in rule obedience and organizational effectiveness are quantifiable to some degree, and research based on such quantification could confirm or reject hypotheses about the effects of rule obedience and organizational effectiveness on economic patterns. Perhaps more important, a focus on rule obedience and organizational effectiveness may lead to greater insight into the strategies that government might follow to promote a more favorable evolution of institutions. While economists can claim no monopoly on the study of social norms and organizational behavior, economic reasoning is likely to continue to prove valuable in deepening our understanding of these economically relevant phenomena.

Notes

This chapter was originally published under the same title in the *Journal of Institutional and Theoretical Economics* 149 (2) (June 1993): 393–414. It is reprinted with the permission of the author.

1. Williamson (1975) makes a distinction between consummate and perfunctory cooperation on the part of employees in a firm. Consummate coop-

eration implies EIR behavior. In fact, in his discussion of consummate cooperation, Williamson quotes from a study by Blau and Scott that observes that the legal employment contract does not embody the essence of the employer-employee relationship because the contract "does not encourage employees to exert effort, to accept responsibilities, or to exercise initiative" (69).

2. One reason for this statement is that having a conscience makes a person more trustworthy, as explained by Frank (1987, 1990). That is, a conscience reduces the ability of a person to act on behalf of immediate self-interest, and this characteristic leads others to be willing to trust this individual. Since trust permits cooperation that would not otherwise occur, the individual with a conscience may turn out to be better off than one without. A second point is that incorporating group goals into one's utility function is not the same thing as adding a constraint (e.g., obey the rules) to the task of maximizing an individualistic utility function. Many have thought that higher satisfactions in life are attained by concerning oneself with the welfare of other people.

3. The classic description of bureaucracy is by Max Weber (1992). A convenient source for Weber's original statement of the "ideal type" of bureaucracy, together with sociological discussion, is Merton 1952. For our purposes the essential characteristics of bureaucracy are (1) a hierarchical set of offices, with (2) impersonal rules of procedure for carrying out the organization's tasks and (3) impersonal rules of procedure for selection and promotion of employees, and (4) the ability of the organization to continue functioning as individuals change offices or are replaced by others.

4. A partial exception to this generalization arises in the military, where there is a clear measure of output (winning battles) and a termination mechanism (conquest). The important role of bureaucratic organization in military improvements in Europe prior to the Industrial Revolution is described in McNeil 1982, chaps. 4, 5.

5. The emergence of modern management in the Industrial Revolution in Britain is described in Pollard 1965. The importance of transportation and communication systems for the efficient operation of bureaucracy is also emphasized in Weber (see Merton 1952, 26, 68).

6. This assumption simplifies the analysis but of course is unrealistic. Incorporating partial payment of taxes would lead to a less clear-cut set of outcomes and would probably increase the chances for unraveling of the equilibrium with a high degree of rule obedience (see below).

7. On the relative importance of shame and guilt in traditional and modern societies, see Posner 1983, 277–78.

8. Some very interesting experiments on the effect of group identity on the degree of cooperation within a group are described in Dawes, van de Kragt, and Orbell 1990. The experiments were devised to distinguish among the motivations of self-interest, altruism, and group identity. Group identity was fostered in the experiments by allowing the members of the group (who

were strangers to each other) to discuss their mutual problem before making their anonymous decisions.

9. The worker's motivation to keep his job is similar to that in Shapiro and Stiglitz 1984, where the cost of losing one's job depends on the rate of unemployment.

10. As c is reduced beyond some point the marginal cost of reducing it further will increase at an increasing rate and thus there will be an interior solution.

References

Adelman, I., and E. Thorbecke, eds. 1989. "Institutions and Economic Development: A Symposium." *World Development* 17 (9): 1317–1483.

Akerlof, G., and W. T. Dickens. 1982. "The Economic Consequences of Cognitive Dissonance." *American Economic Review* 72:307–19.

Aronson, E. 1979. *The Social Animal.* San Francisco: W. H. Freeman.

Axelrod, R. 1984. *The Evolution of Cooperation.* New York: Basic Books.

Bardhan, J., ed. 1989. *The Economic Theory of Agrarian Institutions.* Oxford: Clarendon.

Clague, C. 1977. "Information Costs, Corporate Hierarchies, and Earnings Inequality." *American Economic Review Papers and Proceedings* 67:81–85.

Coleman, J. 1988. "Social Capital in the Creation of Human Capital." *American Journal of Sociology* 94 (supplement): S95–S120.

Dawes, R. M., A. J. C. van der Kragt, and J. M. Orbell. 1990. "Cooperation for the Benefit of Us—Not Me, or My Conscience." In Jane J. Mansbridge, ed., *Beyond Self-Interest.* Chicago: University of Chicago Press.

Festinger, L. 1957. *A Theory of Cognitive Dissonance.* Stanford: Stanford University Press.

Frank, R. H. 1987. "If Homo Economicus Could Choose His Own Utility Function, Would He Want One with a Conscience?" *American Economic Review* 77:593–604.

———. 1990. *Passions within Reason: The Strategic Role of the Emotions.* New York: Norton.

Macaulay, S. 1963. "Non-Contractual Relations in Business." *American Sociological Review* 28:55–70.

McNeil, W. 1982. *The Pursuit of Power.* Chicago: University of Chicago Press.

Merton, R. 1952. *Reader in Bureaucracy.* New York: Free Press.

Miller, G. 1992. *Managerial Dilemmas: The Political Economy of Hierarchy.* Cambridge: Cambridge University Press.

Myrdal, G. 1968. *Asian Drama,* vol. 2. New York: Twentieth Century Fund.

Nabli, M., and J. B. Nugent, eds. 1989. *The New Institutional Economics and Development: Theory and Applications to Tunisia.* Amsterdam: North-Holland.

North, D. C. 1990. *Institutions, Institutional Change and Economic Performance.* New York: Cambridge University Press.

Olson, M. 1982. *The Rise and Decline of Nations.* New Haven: Yale University Press.

———. 1987. "Diseconomies of Scale and Development." *Cato Journal* 7: 77–97.

Pollard, S. 1965. *The Genesis of Modern Management.* Cambridge: Harvard University Press.

Posner, R. 1983. *The Economic Theory of Justice.* Cambridge: Harvard University Press.

Schotter, A. 1981. *The Economic Theory of Social Institutions.* New York: Cambridge University Press.

Scott, J. C. 1972. *Comparative Political Corruption.* Englewood Cliffs, NJ: Prentice-Hall.

Shapiro, C., and J. E. Stiglitz. 1984. "Equilibrium Unemployment as a Worker Disciplining Device." *American Economic Review* 74:433–44.

Simon, H. 1991. "Organizations and Markets." *Journal of Economic Perspectives* 5:25–44.

Sugden, Robert. 1986. *The Economics of Rights, Co-operation, and Welfare.* New York: Basil Blackwell.

Turner, J. C. 1987. *Rediscovering the Social Group: A Self-Categorization Theory.* Oxford: Basil Blackwell.

Weber, M. 1992. *Wirtschaft und Gesellschaft.* Tubingen: J. C. B. Mohr.

Williamson, O. 1975. *Markets and Hierarchies.* New York: Free Press.

———. 1985. *The Economic Institutions of Capitalism.* New York: Free Press.

Wraith, R., and E. Simpkins. 1963. *Corruption in Developing Countries.* New York: Norton.

CHAPTER 10

Does Social Capital Have an Economic Payoff? A Cross-Country Investigation

Stephen Knack and Philip Keefer

1. Introduction

The notion of social capital has attracted great academic and journalistic attention, particularly with the publication of Putnam's *Making Democracy Work* (1993), in which the concept is used to explain differences in the economic and government performance of northern and southern Italy. We explore in this essay the following issues related to social capital and economic performance:

1. the relationship between interpersonal trust, norms of civic cooperation, and economic performance, and some of the policy and other links through which these dimensions of social capital may have economic effects;
2. the conflicting hypotheses of Putnam (1993) and Olson (1982), on the relationship between associational activity and growth; and
3. the determinants of trust and norms of civic cooperation, including levels of associational activity and formal institutions.

Trust, cooperative norms, and associations within groups all fall within the elastic definitions that most scholars have given to the term *social capital.* Coleman (1990, 300–301) writes that "authority relations, relations of trust, and consensual allocations of rights which establish norms" can be viewed as resources for individuals, noting that Loury (1977) introduced the term *social capital* to describe these resources. Following Granovetter (1973), Putnam points to the potential importance of weak ties across kinship groups. Both Coleman and Putnam refer to trust and norms of civic-minded behavior as other manifestations of social capital.

Our analysis arrives at three major conclusions. First, trust and civic cooperation are associated with stronger economic performance. Second, associational activity is not correlated with economic performance—contrary to Putnam's (1993) findings across Italian regions. Third, we find that trust and norms of civic cooperation are stronger in countries with formal institutions that effectively protect property and contract rights, and in countries that are less polarized along lines of class or ethnicity.

2. How Can Trust Affect Economic Performance?

Economic activities that require some agents to rely on the future actions of others are accomplished at lower cost in higher-trust environments. According to Arrow, "Virtually every commercial transaction has within itself an element of trust, certainly any transaction conducted over a period of time. It can be plausibly argued that much of the economic backwardness in the world can be explained by the lack of mutual confidence" (1972, 357). Trust-sensitive transactions include those in which goods and services are provided in exchange for future payment, employment contracts in which managers rely on employees to accomplish tasks that are difficult to monitor, and investment and savings decisions that rely on assurances by governments or banks that they will not expropriate these assets. Individuals in higher-trust societies spend less to protect themselves from being exploited in economic transactions. Written contracts are less likely to be needed, and they do not have to specify every possible contingency. Litigation may be less frequent. Individuals in high-trust societies are also likely to divert fewer resources to protecting themselves—through tax payments, bribes, or private security services and equipment—from unlawful (criminal) violations of their property rights. Low trust can also discourage innovation. If entrepreneurs must devote more time to monitoring possible malfeasance by partners, employees, and suppliers, they have less time to devote to innovation in new products or processes.[1]

Societies characterized by high levels of trust also are less dependent on formal institutions to enforce agreements. Informal credit markets dependent on strong interpersonal trust can facilitate investment where there is no well-developed formal system of financial intermediation, or where lack of assets limits access to bank credit.

Interpersonal trust can also provide an imperfect substitute for government-backed property rights or contract enforcement where governments are unable or unwilling to provide them.

Government officials in societies with higher trust may be perceived as more trustworthy, and their policy pronouncements as thus being more credible. To the extent that this is true, trust also triggers greater investment and other economic activity. Promises by central bankers that they will not raise interest rates, assurances by ministers of finance that a nominal exchange rate anchor is fixed in stone, and guarantees that tax legislation will not be rapidly amended are all likely to be more credible in societies where people trust each other more. As a consequence, in such societies people adopt more appropriate horizons in making investment decisions and choose production technologies that are optimal over the long, rather than short, run.

Trusting societies not only have stronger incentives to innovate and to accumulate physical capital, but are also likely to have higher returns to accumulation of human capital. Where trust improves access to credit for the poor, enrollment in secondary education—which, unlike primary education, has a high cost in forgone income—may be higher (Galor and Zeira 1993). As shown in section 4, trust and civic involvement are linked to better performance of government institutions, including publicly provided education (Putnam 1993; La Porta et al. 1997; Coleman 1988). Higher-quality schools increase the return to education. Where trust facilitates the enforcement of contracts, the return to specialized education will increase. Finally, in low-trust societies, hiring decisions will be influenced more by trustworthy personal attributes of applicants, such as blood ties or personal knowledge, and less by educational credentials, than in high-trust societies—reducing the returns to acquisition of educational credentials in low-trust societies.

Norms of civic cooperation can be linked with economic outcomes in some of the same ways as trust. Cooperative norms act as constraints on narrow self-interest, leading individuals to contribute to the provision of public goods of various kinds. Internal (e.g., guilt) and external (e.g., shame and ostracism) sanctions associated with norms alter the costs and benefits of cooperating and defecting in Prisoner's Dilemmas (Coleman 1990).

For many collective action problems, norms leading to cooperative solutions impose serious negative externalities on nonplayers. For example, in the classic Prisoner's Dilemma game, the payoffs to two cooperating criminals are higher than if they both defect. "Civic norms"—such as the norm against littering—are defined here as those that resolve Prisoner's Dilemmas without imposing substantial external costs on other parties (unlike cartel arrangements, for example). They improve allocative efficiency from a societal standpoint: the total benefits to society from attaining cooperative outcomes far exceed the total costs. To the extent that civic norms effectively constrain opportunism, the costs of monitoring and enforcing contracts are likely to be lower, raising the payoffs to many investments and other economic transactions.

In addition to the more direct effects on economic activity outlined previously, trust and civic norms may improve economic outcomes indirectly, through political channels. They may improve governmental performance and the quality of economic policies, by affecting the level and character of political participation. Knowledge of politics and public affairs by large numbers of citizens, and their participation, are important potential checks on the ability of politicians and bureaucrats to enrich themselves or narrow interests that they are allied with. But self-interested citizens will rationally decline to vote or to acquire information about the performance of officials. Civic norms help voters (principals) overcome the collective action problem in monitoring officials (agents). Putnam (1993) has shown that regional governments in the more-trusting, more civic-minded northern and central parts of Italy provide public services more effectively than do those in the less-trusting, less civic south. Moreover, citizen-initiated contacts with government officials in the south tend to involve issues of narrowly personal concerns, while contacts in the more trusting regions tend to involve larger issues with implications for the welfare of the region as a whole.[2] Survey evidence from the United States is consistent with these findings. Among respondents in the 1992 American National Elections Study (NES), interpersonal trust is a significant predictor of various participatory attitudes and behaviors. Controlling for income and education, trust is associated with an 8.6 percentage-point increase in the probability of voting, and with similar increases in interest in political campaigns and in public affairs generally, and with agreement that voting is a civic duty.[3]

3. Measuring Trust and Civic Norms

In a critique of Fukuyama 1995, Solow argues that if social capital is to be more than a "buzzword" its stock "should somehow be measurable, even inexactly," but "measurement seems very far away" (1995, 36). In this study, we use survey indicators that are no doubt inexact—due to translation difficulties, sampling error, and response bias—but which produce values that are consistent with data from independent sources (as described below).

The World Values Survey contains survey data on thousands of respondents from 29 market economies: 21 in the 1981 surveys, and 28 in the 1990–91 surveys, with 29 represented in at least one of these two survey waves.[4] Some groups—for example city-dwellers and the better-educated—are oversampled in some countries (Inglehart 1994). As a correction, we use the weight variable provided in the data in computing country-level means. Higher-status groups still tend to be overrepresented, particularly in the less developed countries, even with use of the weight variable (Inglehart 1994). This problem should have the effect of attenuating the variation in our measures of trust and civic cooperation—which tend to be positively correlated with income and education levels—making it more difficult to reject null hypotheses involving these variables.

The question used to assess the level of trust in a society is: "Generally speaking, would you say that most people can be trusted, or that you can't be too careful in dealing with people?" Our trust indicator (TRUST) is the percentage of respondents in each nation replying "most people can be trusted" (after deleting the "don't know" responses). The mean value is 35.8 percent, with a standard deviation of 14 percent (see appendix for country values).

This trust item is somewhat ambiguous with respect to which "people" respondents have in mind. The term *people* is general enough that responses should not merely reflect expectations about the behavior of friends and family.[5] Responses, however, could easily reflect a varying mix of two concepts across individuals: how much trust one places in people who are not close friends or relatives, and the frequency of encounters with such persons. People in low-trust environments will transact more with close friends and relatives than with strangers, compared to people in high-trust environments. If by "most people" respondents consider most people that they transact with, the variation in our trust measure will be reduced, making it more difficult to reject null hypotheses regarding the effects of trust.

The strength of norms of civic cooperation is assessed from responses to questions about whether each of the following behaviors "can always be justified, never be justified or something in between."

1. claiming government benefits which you are not entitled to
2. avoiding a fare on public transport
3. cheating on taxes if you have the chance
4. keeping money that you have found
5. failing to report damage you've done accidentally to a parked vehicle

Respondents chose a number from 1 (always justifiable) to 10 (never justifiable). We reversed these scales, so that larger values indicate greater cooperation, and summed values over the five items to create a scale (CIVIC) with a 50-point maximum. Each of these five items reflects the strength of civic norms as that concept is defined above; cooperative solutions to these Prisoner's Dilemmas impose little or no costs on nonplayers. The mean value for CIVIC is 39.4, with a standard deviation of only 2.

As it is based on multiple survey items, each with numerous response categories, CIVIC may be more discriminating than TRUST, which is based on an item with only two response categories. On the other hand, respondents are likely to be far more reluctant to admit to cheating the government, taxpayers, or other people than to agree that others cheat. This problem may introduce substantial measurement error into CIVIC, likely accounting in part for its low variation across countries. We use TRUST as our primary social capital indicator in our empirical tests, because it is more directly relevant to economic activity—as indicated by the greater attention the concept has received in the literature—and because CIVIC exhibits so little variation across countries. However, results for CIVIC are in most cases very similar, and we often report results using both measures.

Data from experiments conducted by the *Reader's Digest* provide reassuring behavioral evidence for the validity of these survey measures (*Economist,* June 22, 1996). Twenty wallets containing $50 worth of cash and the addresses and phone numbers of their putative owners were "accidentally" dropped in each of 20 cities, selected from 14 different western European countries. Ten wallets were similarly "lost" in each of 12 U.S. cities. The number of wallets returned with their contents intact was recorded for each city. The percentage of wallets returned in each country closely tracks the WVS measures: it is correlated with TRUST at .67, and with the fourth item of the CIVIC index, on the acceptability of "keeping money that you have found" at .52 (partial correlations controlling for per capita income are even higher). Correlations with the other four CIVIC items are all somewhat lower.

This evidence indicates that nonrandom samples, translation problems, and discrepancies between professed attitudes and actual behaviors do not introduce severe noise into our survey-based measures of social capital.

The high correlation of TRUST with the percentage of wallets returned (by strangers) and its relatively low correlation with trust in family members indicate that TRUST is primarily capturing "generalized" trust as opposed to "specific" trust placed in people one has repeated interactions with. Similarly, CIVIC is defined by attitudes toward cooperating with anonymous others in Prisoner's Dilemma settings. These characteristics of our social capital measures reduce the chances that they are measuring trust and cooperation largely at the level of limited groups based on kinship, ethnic, or special interest ties, which have potentially large negative effects on economic performance. Cooperation and trust among these limited groups may facilitate their organization for rent-seeking purposes or even for violent conflict.

The variables TRUST and CIVIC are in some sense mirror images of each other. The survey item on trust measures expectations of whether others will act opportunistically at one's expense; TRUST therefore reflects the percentage of people in a society who expect that most others will act cooperatively in Prisoner's Dilemma contexts. Our measure of civic cooperation reflects respondents' own stated willingness to cooperate when faced with a collective action problem; it thus can be thought of as trustworthiness.

One would naturally expect trust and trustworthiness to be positively correlated across societies: where fewer people prove to be trustworthy, fewer people will be trusting (Hardin 1992, 161). Causation likely runs the other way, also, as many people are "conditional cooperators" who act cooperatively only when they have high expectations that others will reciprocate (Hardin 1982), in contrast to "Kantians" who follow moral rules prescribing cooperation regardless of what others do. Thus, "not only do expectations affect honest behavior, but over time honest behavior affects expectations" (Platteau 1994, 760). Figure 10.1 depicts the positive relationship between TRUST and CIVIC in our sample.[6]

4. Trust, Civic Cooperation, and Economic Performance

Little evidence directly connects trust and civic cooperation to economic performance. Narayan and Pritchett (1999) find for a sample

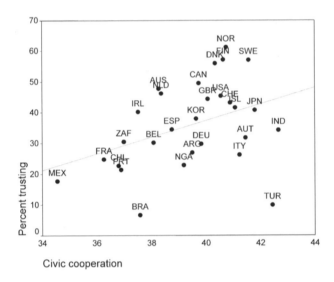

Fig. 10.1.

of Tanzanian villages that higher levels of associational memberships are related to higher incomes. Economic historians have documented cases where trust resulting from repeated interaction between parties, with the expectation that the present value of rewards from future interactions outweighs the benefits from reneging on current deals, was associated with expanded trade and economic activity. For example, Greif (1989) shows that the development of formal institutions that promote trust (self-enforcing agreements) had a dramatic impact on the spread of long-distance trade in the Middle Ages.

Helliwell and Putnam (1995) show that, holding initial income constant, regions of Italy with a more developed "civic community" had higher growth rates over the 1950–90 period. They measure "civic community" by a composite index of newspaper readership, the density of sports and cultural associations, turnout in referenda, and the incidence of preference voting. Using WVS data, Helliwell (1996) finds trust (and group memberships) to be significantly and negatively related to productivity growth in a sample of seventeen OECD members.[7]

We test the impact of trust and civic norms on both growth and investment rates using the WVS indicators described above. To minimize endogeneity problems, we measure performance subsequent to the measurement of trust and civic cooperation wherever possible.

As other explanatory variables we include, following much of the literature since Barro 1991, the proportion of eligible students enrolled in secondary and primary schools in 1960, per capita income at the beginning of the period, and the price level of investment goods, relative to the United States.[8]

The dependent variable in equations 1–3 of table 10.1 is average annual growth in per capita income over the 1980–92 period. Our 29-nation sample over this period behaves similarly to the larger sample and longer time periods used by Barro (1991). Incomes converge, conditional on the other variables. School enrollment is positively related to growth, and investment goods prices are negatively related to growth.

The social capital variables exhibit a strong and significant relationship to growth. The coefficient for TRUST in equation 1 indicates that

TABLE 10.1. Trust, Civic Cooperation, and Economic Performance, 1980–92

Equation	1	2	3	4	5	6	7
Method	OLS	OLS	OLS	OLS	2SLS	OLS	OLS
Dependent variable		Growth				Investment/GDP	
Constant	−0.935	−10.476	−9.593	−2.829	−1.037	9.617	−23.893
	(1.280)	(4.730)	(4.520)	(1.895)	(1.898)	(3.820)	(11.998)
GDP80	−0.361	−0.273	−0.375	0.152	−0.366	0.162	0.273
	(0.131)	(0.126)	(0.127)	(0.274)	(0.127)	(0.403)	(0.364)
PRIM60	6.192	5.930	7.061	4.818	6.270	11.655	13.030
	(1.051)	(1.164)	(1.224)	(1.709)	(1.759)	(3.558)	(3.274)
SEC60	2.194	3.457	1.648	1.256	2.085	−0.431	0.495
	(1.632)	(1.543)	(1.485)	(1.930)	(2.133)	(8.286)	(7.067)
PI80	−3.693	−3.117	−3.535	−3.930	−3.713	−4.435	−3.170
	(0.867)	(1.100)	(0.935)	(0.755)	(0.809)	(1.993)	(2.154)
TRUST	0.082		0.076	0.192	0.086	0.146	
	(0.030)		(0.030)	(0.060)	(0.039)	(0.078)	
CIVIC		0.272	0.207				0.872
		(0.098)	(0.092)				(0.301)
TRUST* GDP80				−0.013			
				(0.006)			
Adj. R^2	.55	.44	.56	.60	.52	.37	.38
SEE	1.37	1.52	1.35	1.29	1.37	4.43	4.38
Mean, D.V.	1.45	1.45	1.45	1.45	1.45	22.4	22.4

Note: White [1980]-corrected standard errors in parentheses. Instruments for TRUST in equation 4 include law students/total postsecondary students, Sullivan's homogeneity indicator, GDP80, SEC60, PRIM60, and PI80. Note R^2 and SEE do not have their usual interpretations in 2SLS. R^2s without social capital variables are .41 (growth) and .33 (investment/GDP). All equations have 29 observations.

a 10-percentage-point rise in that variable is associated with an increase in growth of four-fifths of a percentage point. A one-standard-deviation change in trust (14 percentage points) is associated with a change in growth of more than one-half (.56) of a standard deviation, nearly as large as the standardized coefficient for PRIM60 (.64). Each 4-point rise in the 50-point CIVIC scale in equation 2 is associated with an increase in growth of more than 1 percentage point. When both social capital variables are entered together in equation 3, their coefficients drop slightly but remain significant.

Equation 4 introduces an interaction term, equal to TRUST × GDP80. The impact of TRUST on growth should be higher in poorer countries, if trust is more essential where contracts are not reliably enforced by the legal system, and where access to formal sources of credit is more limited due to an underdeveloped financial sector.[9] On the other hand, if greater specialization increases the number of transactions between strangers, and over time and across space (Platteau 1994, 541), trust should reduce transaction costs more in richer than in poorer countries (Putnam 1993, 178). The negative and significant coefficient on TRUST*GDP80 in equation 4 provides support for the former argument. For a country with a per capita GDP in 1980 of $1,000, TRUST's coefficient is .179, more than double the average effect over the whole sample.

The social capital variables are measured near the beginning of our sample period for 21 of our 29 countries. For the other 8, measuring trust in 1990 could introduce reverse causation problems. Deleting these 8 reduces the significance of all of the regressors, particularly GDP80, SEC60, and PI80. Coefficients for the social capital variables rise in most cases when these 8 countries are deleted, suggesting that reverse causality is not driving our results. This result is not surprising in light of the fact that for the twenty countries with TRUST values for both 1981 and 1990, the correlation between the two is .91.

In equation 5 of table 10.1, we instrument for TRUST to correct for endogeneity problems, or possible measurement error. Sullivan (1991) measures the percentage of a country's population belonging to the largest "ethnolinguistic" group, where groups are identified by race, language, or religion depending on which of these appears to be the most important source of cleavages in a society. As a second instrument, we use the number of law students in 1963 as a percentage of all postsecondary students.[10] Instrumenting for TRUST with these two variables and all of the other right-hand-side variables, TRUST remains a significant predictor of growth (equation 5).[11]

We would expect TRUST and CIVIC to affect growth through innovations that increase total factor productivity, and through factor accumulation. When investment's share of GDP is included as a regressor in growth equations, coefficients for TRUST and CIVIC remain positive but are no longer statistically significant, suggesting that accumulation is the more important channel.[12]

Similar effects are observed with measures of human capital accumulation. When secondary enrollment is omitted from the regressions, TRUST and CIVIC coefficients rise, as expected, given the arguments from section 2 that social capital influences human capital accumulation. Substituting attainment measures for the enrollment variables reduces the TRUST and CIVIC coefficients somewhat. The growth effects of TRUST and CIVIC remain significant using literacy rates, or Kyriacou's (1991) estimates of average years of completed education for 1980. The social capital coefficients diminish much more using average years of completed education for 1980 as estimated by Barro and Lee (1993),[13] but even then the log of TRUST remains a significant predictor of growth.[14]

Equations 6 and 7 of table 10.1 examine the impact of social capital on investment/GDP, averaged over the 1980–92 period, controlling for other determinants of investment. Trust is positively correlated with investment in equation 6, but is significant at the .05 level only for a 1-tailed test. Each 7-percentage-point rise in trust is associated with a 1-point rise in investment's share of GDP. Civic norms are highly significant in equation 7, with each 1-point rise in the index associated with an increase in investment of nearly 1 percentage point.

The results in table 10.1 are fairly insensitive to changes in specification, the exclusion of influential observations, and the inclusion of additional regressors. These findings are especially remarkable given the small sample size.

As about half of our sample consists of Western European countries, autocorrelated errors due to spatial correlation or to common membership in the EC are potentially serious problems. Residuals among the subset of EC members (or Western European countries) were not found to differ significantly from those for nonmembers, however.[15]

The most influential individual case in table 10.1 regressions is Korea. The first row of table 10.2 (labeled "None") repeats the regression coefficients and standard errors for TRUST and CIVIC from table 10.1. Succeeding rows report the effects of TRUST and

CIVIC on growth and investment when the indicated change is made to the relevant equation from table 10.1. The second row shows results when the observation in each equation with the largest positive influence on the slope of the social capital coefficient is deleted. For TRUST's effect on growth and investment, and the effect of CIVIC on growth, that observation is Korea. In two of these three cases, the social capital variable remains statistically significant when Korea is deleted. Switzerland is the most influential observation increasing CIVIC's relationship to investment; this relationship remains significant when this case is deleted.

The third row of table 10.2 deletes the two cases most favorable

TABLE 10.2. Robustness to Alternative Specifications

Dependent Variable:	Growth		Investment/GDP	
Equation[a]	1	2	6	7
Specification change	TRUST	CIVIC	TRUST	CIVIC
None (from table 10.1)	0.082	0.272	0.146	0.872
	(0.030)	(0.098)	(0.078)	(0.301)
Influential observation deleted	0.054	0.223	0.081	0.657
	(0.020)	(0.081)	(0.061)	(0.270)
2 influential observations deleted	0.038	0.202	0.051	0.575
	(0.016)	(0.082)	(0.060)	(0.233)
Labor force growth	0.082	0.312	0.146	0.928
	(0.027)	(0.105)	(0.075)	(0.311)
(Exports + Imports)/GDP	0.071	0.334	0.141	0.930
	(0.025)	(0.116)	(0.072)	(0.310)
M_2/GDP	0.076	0.185	0.130	0.652
	(0.029)	(0.106)	(0.079)	(0.289)
Black market premium	0.070	0.225	0.128	0.806
	(0.029)	(0.094)	(0.080)	(0.300)
Property rights (ICRG)	0.083	0.300	0.155	0.917
	(0.039)	(0.084)	(0.096)	(0.311)
Currency depreciation	0.047	0.221	0.108	0.808
	(0.023)	(0.103)	(0.078)	(0.303)
Institutional investor credit rating	0.065	0.229	0.115	0.799
	(0.024)	(0.086)	(0.079)	(0.290)
Gini (income)	0.059	0.099	0.143	0.814
	(0.028)	(0.101)	(0.073)	(0.418)
1970–92 growth, investment	0.039	0.126	0.160	0.773
	(0.022)	(0.088)	(0.059)	(0.328)
1960–92 growth, investment	0.029	0.121	0.160	0.807
	(0.017)	(0.096)	(0.058)	(0.321)

Note: Standard errors (in parentheses) are White-corrected. Iceland is missing data for Gini. For all other equations where influential observations are not deleted, $N = 29$. Independent variables include PRIM60, SEC60, initial income, and initial investment goods prices.

[a] Equation number is from table 10.1.

for social capital's impact on economic performance. This procedure deletes Korea and Brazil (TRUST and growth; see figure 10.2), Korea and Switzerland (CIVIC and growth), Korea and the United States (TRUST and investment), and Switzerland and Japan (CIVIC and investment). All three coefficients that were still significant when the single most influential observation was omitted remain significant after deleting these second observations from our 29-nation sample. Neither Nigeria nor Mexico—each an oil-exporting low-trust nation with low or negative growth in the 1980s following rapid petroleum-led growth in the 1970s—is among these influential observations.

The effects of TRUST and CIVIC prove to be robust to the inclusion of other variables often used in growth regressions, indicating that they are not merely capturing the effects of important omitted variables. Table 10.2 (beginning with the fourth row) indicates how coefficients and standard errors for TRUST and CIVIC change when the indicated additional regressor is included in the relevant growth or investment equation. Most of the added regressors are significant predictors of growth, but not of investment, in our sample.

Estimates for TRUST and CIVIC are changed little by adding labor force growth, trade openness (as measured by exports plus imports divided by GDP), M_2/GDP (the primary measure of financial development measure used in King and Levine 1993), the black market premium, or the property rights indicator from ICRG (International Country Risk Guide) introduced by Knack and Keefer (see chapter 3, this volume). In results not shown in table 10.2, TRUST and CIVIC also prove insensitive to the inclusion of the mineral sector's share of GDP, or the government size and political instability indicators used in Barro 1991.

Other policy variables affect the social capital estimates to a somewhat greater extent, but in ways that are consistent with our theory. These are policies that are particularly sensitive to social polarization, which we expect to be associated with (and measured in part by) low trust and weaker civic norms. For example, difficulty in implementing stabilization programs has been attributed to polarization associated with inequalities in income and wealth, and with ethnic tensions (Berg and Sachs 1988; Keefer and Knack 2002). In more polarized societies, groups are more willing to impose costs on society, for example, by failing to compromise on a reform program in a timely way. High inflation and government debt could therefore be a product in part of low social cohesiveness. Table 10.2 shows that coefficients for TRUST and CIVIC fall—although usually remaining

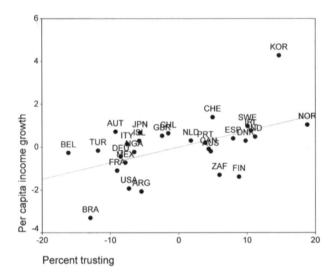

Fig. 10.2.

significant—when currency depreciation,[16] or international bankers' evaluations of the creditworthiness of governments, are added to the regressions.[17]

A more direct approach to social polarization is to examine inequality, a source of polarization that has been linked to unstable macropolicy and to uncertain property rights.[18] There are theoretical reasons to expect inequality to lower trust and weaken civic norms (this issue is addressed in more detail in section 7). The Gini coefficient for income inequality is strongly correlated with TRUST ($r = -.65$) and with CIVIC ($-.43$). When this Gini is added to our regressions (see table 10.2), the TRUST coefficient declines to .059 (but remaining significant at the .05 level), while the CIVIC slope drops to .099. Inequality is not significant in investment equations, however, where it has little impact on TRUST and CIVIC.[19] While there appears to be an important relationship between inequality and social capital, the social capital variables remain significant in three out of four cases with inequality in the model, suggesting that TRUST and CIVIC in table 10.1 are not solely capturing redistributional or other effects of inequality.

If trust and civic norms are viewed as culture variables that change only slowly over time, TRUST and CIVIC as measured in the early 1980s should explain cross-country variation in long-term economic performance, as measured by investment or growth rates over twenty- or thirty-year periods, or even by per capita income levels. This assumption may be reasonable, as TRUST values for 1980 and 1990 are correlated at .91. Moreover, changes in TRUST over the decade are uncorrelated with growth rates. However, there are both theoretical and empirical reasons for caution regarding the assumption that trust and the strength of civic norms are stable over long periods of time. Cooperative equilibria can unravel very quickly, as Yugoslavia demonstrates. The United States, the one country with a long time-series on the trust survey measure, shows a steady decline in trust from 55 to 60 percent in surveys from the late 1950 and early 1960s, to the mid- and upper 30s in the 1990s. With these caveats, we report tests of long-term performance below, investigating longer-period growth and investment rates as well as levels of output per worker.

The last two rows of table 10.2 show the association of TRUST and CIVIC on investment levels and income growth for the 1970–92 and 1960–92 periods.[20] Investment results are very similar to those for the shorter period; the TRUST coefficient rises somewhat while the standard error falls. Figure 10.3 depicts the simple correlation of TRUST and investment/GDP for the 1960–92 period. Coefficients in growth regressions fall by more than one-half, relative to the shorter period. The effect of TRUST, but not CIVIC, remains significant at the .05 level for a one-tailed test.[21]

The weaker relationship between social capital and growth in the longer periods is driven mainly by three low-trust countries that grew slowly, if at all, in the 1980–92 period, but rapidly in the 1960s and 1970s—in part through dramatic increases in oil prices in the case of Nigeria, large inflows of debt in the case of Brazil, and a combination of the two in the case of Mexico. An (admittedly ex post facto) explanation of the experiences of these countries may be consistent with our theory. If trust is weak, leaders are more likely to direct revenue windfalls toward consumption than toward productive investments. Because of low trust, leaders cannot credibly promise supporters future benefits from worthwhile investments. To maintain support, leaders must divert resources to supporters who, again because of low trust, do not find it advantageous to invest these resources in productive investments inside the country—making the country more vulnerable to crisis. Moreover, once crisis hits, the lack of social cohesiveness reflected in low values of TRUST and CIVIC makes it less likely that a consensus on needed policy reforms can be built.

We also analyze the relationship between TRUST and levels of

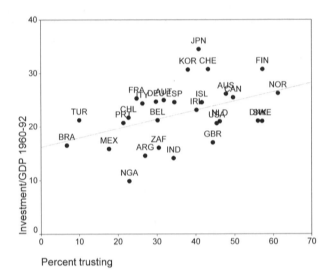

Fig. 10.3.

output per worker, physical and human capital per worker, and total factor productivity (TFP), following the levels accounting approach of Hall and Jones (1996) and using data provided by them. Table 10.3 reports the relationship of TRUST with (1) the log of output per worker, net of mineral production, for 1988 (from Summers and Heston 1991), (2) the Hall and Jones estimate of (the log of) capital per worker for 1988 (using investment data from Summers and Heston 1991), (3) human capital per worker (the attainment measure for 1985 from Barro and Lee 1993), and (the log of) TFP for 1988, estimated by Hall and Jones (1996) as a residual. Column 1 of table 10.3 reports coefficients and standard errors for TRUST from four bivariate regressions: TRUST is positively and significantly correlated with output, capital, and schooling, while the correlation with TFP is positive but insignificant.[22]

Hall and Jones report regressions of each of these four variables on a set of variables (listed in the note to table 10.3) that they contend are exogenous and that measure "basic characteristics" of an economy. When TRUST is added to their full model, its coefficient is significant only for schooling (column 2 of table 10.3). Theory and evidence provided elsewhere in this essay strongly suggest that policy is endogenous to trust: accordingly, in column 3 of table 10.3 we delete from the regressions the two policy variables used by Hall and

Jones—the ICRG property rights index, from Knack and Keefer (chapter 3, this volume), and the openness measure from Sachs and Warner 1995. As in the simple bivariate regressions, output, capital, and schooling are all significantly related to TRUST when these policy variables are dropped. The most powerful "determinant" of output, factor accumulation, and TFP in Hall and Jones 1996 is latitude (distance in degrees from the equator), a variable with an ambiguous theoretical interpretation, and which is highly correlated with TRUST. When latitude and the two policy variables are dropped from the models in column 4 of table 10.3, coefficients for TRUST are all larger than in the bivariate regressions, although still not significant in the case of TFP.

Causality could go in both directions for income and trust, and for education and trust. For example, trust could be a product of optimism (Uslaner 2002) generated by high or growing incomes. But if trust were largely a product rather than a cause of high incomes, it should follow rather than lead per capita income levels. In fact, TRUST is more strongly correlated with per capita incomes in later years, such as 1990, than with income in earlier years, such as 1970.

Similarly, education may strengthen trust and civic norms, for example, if ignorance breeds distrust, or if learning reduces uncertainty about the behavior of others, or if students are taught to behave cooperatively (Mueller 1989, 364–65).[23] However, TRUST is more

TABLE 10.3.   Trust and Levels of Output, Factor Accumulation, and TFP

Equation	1	2	3	4
Independent variables	Trust only	Full Hall-Jones model	No ICRG, years open	No ICRG, years open, or latitude
Dependent variable				
Log output/ worker	.0258	.0035	.0197	.0397
	(.0061)	(.0081)	(.0085)	(.0177)
Log capital/ worker	.0336	.0015	.0223	.0454
	(.0062)	(.0107)	(.0102)	(.0198)
School/worker	.1533	.0977	.1312	.1667
	(.0156)	(.0298)	(.0268)	(.0427)
Log TFP	.0023	−.0056	.0025	.0127
	(.0038)	(.0048)	(.0046)	(.0094)

Note: Cells of table report TRUST coefficients; White-corrected standard errors are in parentheses. Full Hall-Jones model includes latitude (distance from the equator), percent English-speaking, percent speaking another "international language," a dummy for "capitalist-statist" systems (as contrasted to "capitalist"), fraction of years, 1950–94, with open economy (from Sachs and Warner 1995), and the ICRG property rights index. Sample size is 29.

highly correlated with recent than with past measures of attainment or enrollment, suggesting that causality does not run solely from education to social capital.

5. Associational Activity and Economic Performance

The importance of trust in expanding economic activity is perhaps not surprising, although not previously empirically substantiated at the cross-country level. The role of associational activity is a subject of greater contention. Putnam attributes the economic success and governmental efficiency of northern Italy, relative to the south, in large part to its richer associational life, claiming that associations "instill in their members habits of cooperation, solidarity, and public-spiritedness" (Putnam 1993, 89–90). This cooperation and solidarity may be invoked most commonly to resolve collective action problems at the level of smaller groups, however. If the economic goals of a group conflict with those of other groups or of unorganized interests, the overall effect of group memberships and activities on economic performance could be negative. Adam Smith noted that when "people of the same trade" meet "even for merriment and diversion" the result is often "a conspiracy against the public" or "some contrivance to raise prices" (quoted in Granovetter 1985, 484). In a more extreme example, Marx blamed the inability of the nineteenth-century French peasantry to overthrow capitalism on the absence of dense networks of social interaction: the peasants did not enter into "manifold relations with one another" (quoted in Hardin 1982, 189). Similarly, Olson (1982) observes that horizontal associations can hurt growth because many of them act as special interest groups lobbying for preferential policies that impose disproportionate costs on society.

Keefer and Knack (1993) provide some evidence for the conflicting influences of associational activity on growth, using a variable from Banks and Textor (1963) called "interest articulation" which assesses (on a subjective scale ranging from 1 to 4) how effectively groups articulate their policy preferences to government. Although the ability of groups to express their interests is likely to be an important restraint on government, it also provides groups a way to capture private benefits at the expense of society. Consistent with the view that these two effects tend to counteract each other, "interest articulation" proves to be an insignificant predictor of growth when introduced into Barro-type cross-country tests.

We obtain a similar result here on the influence of horizontal associations. Respondents in the World Values Survey were asked whether they belonged to any of the following types of organizations:

1. social welfare services for elderly, handicapped or deprived people;
2. religious or church organizations;
3. education, arts, music or cultural activities;
4. trade unions;
5. political parties or groups;
6. local community action on issues like poverty, employment, housing, racial equality;
7. third world development or human rights;
8. conservation, the environment, ecology;
9. professional associations;
10. youth work (e.g., scouts, guides, youth clubs, etc.).[24]

Our measure of the density of associational activity (GROUPS) is the average number of groups cited per respondent in each country (see appendix for values). This indicator unfortunately does not measure the intensity of participation in groups. Assuming that group memberships are correlated with levels of activity, GROUPS constitutes a reasonable approximation of Putnam's notion of the density of horizontal networks in a society.[25] Independent data on union memberships as a proportion of the labor force are available from Wallerstein 1989 for 18 of the countries in our sample (for the late 1970s), permitting a check on the reliability of the survey data. The correlation of this variable with item (d) on trade union memberships is a reassuring .68.

In table 10.4, we test the relationship between GROUPS and economic performance, using models similar to those in table 10.1. Group membership is not significant in either growth or investment equations.[26] An obvious possible explanation for this result is that the harmful effects of groups as rent-seeking organizations theorized by Olson (1982) are offsetting any positive effects posited by Putnam (1993).

We explored this possibility further by attempting to differentiate "Olsonian" from "Putnam-esque" groups. Groups 2, 3, and 10 from the above list were identified as those groups least likely to act as "distributional coalitions" but which involve social interactions that can build trust and cooperative habits. The total memberships per respondent in these three Putnam categories (P-GROUPS) range from

.83 (for the United States) to .06 (Finland). Groups 4, 5, and 9 were deemed most representative of groups with redistributive goals; total memberships in these Olson groups per respondent (O-GROUPS) range from .76 (Iceland) to .12 (Korea).

Membership in Olson groups is not significant in either the growth or investment equations (equations 2 and 4). Perversely, Putnam groups appear to harm investment (equation 4). These results are little changed by tinkering with the definitions of Putnam and Olson groups, for example, by leaving out religious and church organizations from P-GROUPS, on the grounds that hierarchical religions weaken trust (Putnam 1993), or by deleting political parties and groups from O-GROUPS, on the grounds that parties may be relatively "encompassing," aggregating the preferences of many different groups (Olson 1982).

This attempt at distinguishing types of groups thus provides no empirical support for our conjecture that groups have neutral effects on performance because positive Putnam forces are counterbalanced by negative Olson influences.[27] These tests can be regarded as only preliminary, however: the categories of groups are overly broad, it is

TABLE 10.4.   Group Membership and Economic Performance, 1980–92

Equation	1	2	3	4
Dependent variable	Growth, 1980–92		Investment/GDP, 1980–92	
Constant	1.156	1.558	21.676	22.698
	(3.323)	(3.618)	(8.210)	(8.528)
GDP80	−0.219	−0.274	0.648	0.448
	(0.153)	(0.164)	(0.414)	(0.455)
PRIM60	4.421	4.800	1.933	2.968
	(1.641)	(1.482)	(5.302)	(5.383)
SEC60	4.196	4.065	4.237	5.098
	(1.995)	(2.061)	(7.076)	(7.328)
PI80	−3.102	−3.601	−2.954	−4.235
	(1.657)	(1.767)	(3.118)	(3.316)
GROUPS	−0.232		−6.199	
	(0.872)		(3.306)	
O-GROUPS		2.186		−1.200
		(1.551)		(5.980)
P-GROUPS		−1.303		−10.589
		(1.412)		(3.890)
Adj. R^2	.19	.18	.19	.16
SEE	1.71	1.72	4.50	4.59
Mean, D.V.	1.54	1.54	23.2	23.2

Note: White-corrected standard errors are in parentheses. Sample size is 26.

not clear what some of these groups do, and the depth of involvement is not measured. While TRUST and CIVIC appear to capture *generalized* trust and norms of *civic* cooperation, our data on groups do not permit us to convincingly distinguish between socially efficient and inefficient memberships and activities.

6. Additional Links from Trust to Growth

This section further explores the channels through which trust might affect economic outcomes. Some of these channels must remain largely unexplored due to data limitations, for example, on the extent and damage of rent-seeking coalitions. Following arguments in section 2, we consider two possible channels here: the impact of trust on the strength of property and contractual rights, and the impact of trust on the performance of government.

We constructed an index of perceived government performance from items in the WVS. Respondents were asked "how much confidence" they had in various governmental and societal institutions, with responses ranging from "a great deal," "quite a lot," and "not very much," to "none at all." The index was built from responses to items concerning the education system (largely government-run in most countries), the legal system, the police, and the civil service. For each of these, we calculated the percentage of respondents in each country with either "a great deal" or "quite a lot" of confidence. The mean of the four percentages is used as a measure of perceived overall government performance (see appendix for values).[28]

Equation 1 of table 10.5 regresses this index on TRUST, controlling for per capita income and education enrollments.[29] The only significant determinant of government performance in this equation is TRUST: each 2-percentage-point rise is associated with a rise in confidence of about 1 percentage point.

For alternative subjective measures of governmental performance, we use data from two firms that evaluate risks to foreign investors. For one index of bureaucratic efficiency, we create an additive index from two variables from *International Country Risk Guide* (ICRG): "corruption in government" and "quality of the bureaucracy." The maximum possible value for this index is 12; higher scores indicate less corruption and higher-quality bureaucracies. For a second index of bureaucratic efficiency, we add two variables from Business Environmental Risk Intelligence (BERI): "bureaucratic delays" and "transportation and communications quality." The maximum possible score is 8, with higher scores indicating shorter delays and better infrastructure.[30]

These ICRG and BERI variables are shown in chapter 3 (this volume) to be strong predictors of investment and growth. Equations 2 and 3 of table 10.5 show that these bureaucratic efficiency indices are positively and significantly related to TRUST. This evidence suggests that the relationship between "social capital" and governmental performance Putnam discovered for Italy may generalize across countries.

Table 10.5 also demonstrates strong relationships between TRUST and two subjective measures of property rights security. In equations 4 and 5, the dependent variable is an index of two ICRG variables, "risk of repudiation of government contracts" and "risk of expropriation" of assets. The maximum possible value is 20, with higher scores indicating lower risks. In equations 6 and 7, the dependent variable is "contract enforceability," a BERI measure with a maximum value of 4. Consistent with our tests of the determinants of government performance, we control for income and education.[31] In equations 4 and 6, TRUST is significantly related to the ICRG and BERI property rights indicators. Equations 5 and 7 control for formal sources of secure property rights, with "executive constraints," a subjective variable coded by Gurr (1990) in his *Polity II* data set. Countries are scored on a 1 to 7 scale on the extent to which the executive of a

TABLE 10.5. Links from Trust to Growth

Equation	1	2	3	4	5	6	7
Dependent variable	Confidence in Government (WVS)	Bureaucratic Efficiency		Property Rights (ICRG)		Contract Enforceability (BERI)	
		ICRG	BERI				
Constant	0.626	2.662	2.065	4.812	2.647	1.395	1.266
	(0.074)	(1.244)	(0.755)	(1.102)	(1.100)	(0.281)	(0.318)
GDP80	.0085	0.235	0.134	0.293	0.170	0.065	0.057
	(.0091)	(0.102)	(0.056)	(0.149)	(0.104)	(0.029)	(0.031)
PRIM60	−0.162	2.195	0.750	5.765	6.483	0.054	0.101
	(0.093)	(1.263)	(0.578)	(1.468)	(0.954)	(0.333)	(0.360)
SEC60	−0.215	2.220	0.675	1.938	1.586	0.485	0.465
	(0.145)	(1.412)	(0.964)	(1.847)	(1.507)	(0.426)	(0.421)
TRUST	.0045	0.050	0.018	0.065	0.037	0.015	0.014
	(.0013)	(0.025)	(0.010)	(0.020)	(0.029)	(0.005)	(0.005)
Executive constraint					0.616		0.037
					(0.260)		(0.039)
Adj. R^2	.20	.73	.69	.74	.82	.73	.73
SEE	.096	1.33	.645	1.81	1.51	.324	.324
N	28	29	28	29	29	28	28
Mean, D.V.	.605	9.66	4.91	16.3	16.3	2.75	2.75

Note: White-corrected standard errors are shown in parentheses.

country is able to rule by decree (coded as 1) or must gain the consent of others before acting (coded 7). The independent effect of TRUST on the ICRG index is reduced somewhat (equation 5), but TRUST remains a significant determinant of the BERI measure.

These preliminary explorations into the links between social capital and growth have provided some suggestive evidence that trust may improve governmental efficiency and increase investors' confidence that contracts will be enforced. The evidence is not entirely unambiguous, however. We have not attempted to develop complete models of governmental performance or of the security of property rights, or enforceability of contracts. The ICRG and BERI measures that are strongly linked to economic performance in chapter 3 are not significant predictors of investment and growth in the small sample used here. The "confidence in government" index constructed from WVS items does not predict investment rates and is of only borderline significance in a growth equation (slope = .035; SE = .019). Thus, we cannot directly explain the paths by which economic performance is related to TRUST and CIVIC in table 10.1. Neither have we addressed empirically the possibility of reverse causality, as the behavior of governments can influence levels of trust and civic cooperation (Gambetta 1988, 158–63; Hardin 1992). For example, where the police violate traffic laws and norms, cooperative equilibria among drivers will tend to unravel. Finally, table 10.5 results are much weaker when CIVIC is substituted for our primary indicator, TRUST.[32]

7. Determinants of Trust and Civic Cooperation

Using the survey results and other data sources, we undertake a preliminary investigation of the determinants of trust and civic cooperation, an issue of special interest to policymakers. We test the effects of group memberships, income inequality and ethnic polarization, formal institutions for protecting property and contract rights, per capita income, and education rates. In section 5, we argue that associational activity has ambiguous effects on economic performance: it may increase trust, but also facilitate rent seeking. Here, we argue that even the relationship between associations and trust is double-edged. Involvement in formal or informal groups and associations (the density of networks of horizontal association) may build trust and civic-minded behavior (Putnam 1993). The underlying idea is that such relationships either break down information asymmetries or create a pattern of repeated interactions that allow self-enforcing agreements to be reached; people who belong to such networks "trust" others who belong to them, and they are more likely to exhibit civic behavior.

However, many societies are polarized by ethnic, political, religious, or income differences. Associations in such societies will often form along (e.g.) ethnic lines. These relatively homogeneous associations in heterogeneous societies may strengthen trust and cooperative norms within an ethnic group, but weaken trust and cooperation between those groups. This effect creates the potential for a negative relationship between horizontal associations and trust or norms of civic cooperation when measured at the national level. Additionally, participation in formal groups may constitute only a small percentage of the social interactions that can build trust and cooperative norms.

We therefore hypothesize that at best horizontal associations are only weakly related to trust or norms of civic cooperation. Even if a positive correlation were found, it could be attributable to reverse causality: high-trust individuals are more likely to join formal associations in which many transactions at least initially will involve interacting with strangers.

Social polarization is a second possible determinant of trust and civic cooperation. Polarization by definition implies greater distances between preferences of individuals in a society. Individuals and groups in such a society have a greater incentive to renege on policy agreements (Keefer and Knack 2002). When policy coalitions are unstable, trust relations among individuals often break down.[33] In polarized societies, individuals are less likely to share common backgrounds and mutual expectations about behavior, so it is more difficult to make self-enforcing agreements (see Platteau 1994 for examples of the importance of religious and linguistic homogeneity in facilitating trade in West Africa). Finally, polarization can increase rent-seeking activities—whether legal, through the political system, or illegal, through theft—that undermine trust. Through any of these various channels, polarization can erode trust and weaken cooperative norms. We proxy for polarization using income inequality and ethnic homogeneity.

A third possible determinant of trust and civic norms is the formal institutional structure of a country. Where these institutions restrain arbitrary behavior by government leaders, for example, government policies are likely to be more credible (or trustworthy). If formal institutions enforce private agreements and laws more effectively, trust and adherence to civic norms among private citizens may be strengthened:[34] "In a Hobbesian view . . . trust is underwritten by a strong government to enforce contracts and to punish theft. Without such a government, cooperation would be nearly impossible and trust would be irrational" (Hardin 1992, 161). There is little empirical or theoretical research to provide guidance as to other determinants of trust and the strength of civic norms.[35] We control here for 1980 per capita income, and school enrollment in 1960, recognizing that causality is likely not unidirectional.

Tables 10.6 and 10.7 report results on the determinants of trust and civic cooperation. The effect of income is always positive, as expected, and is significant in most of the TRUST equations. The effect of secondary education is uniformly positive and often significant. Coefficients for primary education are always negative and sometimes significant.

As Putnam (1995b) has noted, there is a strong bivariate relation-

TABLE 10.6.   Determinants of Trust and Civic Cooperation: Group Memberships and Governmental Institutions

Equation	1	2	3	4	5	6	7
Dependent variable	TRUST	CIVIC	TRUST	CIVIC	TRUST	CIVIC	TRUST
Constant	34.391	39.053	34.746	39.172	23.425	40.217	25.921
	(16.275)	(3.600)	(14.415)	(3.387)	(7.397)	(1.951)	(3.497)
GDP80	1.403	0.213	1.047	0.122	1.118	0.013	1.256
	(0.604)	(0.137)	(0.645)	(0.131)	(0.547)	(0.163)	(0.532)
PRIM60	−22.959	−2.770	−20.947	−2.352	−16.234	−3.944	−35.782
	(13.107)	(3.168)	(11.780)	(2.954)	(6.082)	(1.604)	(8.227)
SEC60	22.824	3.168	18.987	2.685	25.008	2.700	16.540
	(11.682)	(2.288)	(10.923)	(2.218)	(10.484)	(2.351)	(10.263)
GROUPS	5.052	−0.447					
	(6.378)	(0.903)					
P-GROUPS			−4.993	−3.119			
			(8.568)	(1.128)			
O-GROUPS			27.019	3.896			
			(14.035)	(1.345)			
Executive constraints					1.522	0.345	
					(0.933)	(0.203)	
Independence of courts							8.192
							(2.220)
Adj. R^2	.46	.30	.51	.42	.51	.24	.60
SEE	9.94	1.61	9.46	1.46	9.77	1.75	9.05
N	26	26	26	26	29	29	28
Mean, D.V.	37.4	39.2	37.4	39.2	35.8	39.4	35.6

Note: White-corrected standard errors are shown in parentheses. Iceland is missing data on independence of courts. India, Nigeria, and Turkey are missing data on group memberships.

ship between trust and group memberships across countries.[36] However, we find in equations 1 and 2 of table 10.6 that horizontal associations have no significant effect on TRUST or CIVIC when income and education are controlled for, consistent with the ambiguities noted above on the effects of group memberships. A possible explanation for this result is that groups with social goals are better than those with political goals at building trust and cooperative habits. In equations 3 and 4, we investigate this possibility using the distinction made in section 5 between Putnam groups and Olson groups. Memberships in the more politically oriented Olson groups are associated, surprisingly, with stronger trust and cooperative attitudes, while the Putnam groups have no effect on trust (equation 3) and appear to reduce civic cooperation (equation 4).[37]

"Executive constraints" is positively and (marginally) significantly related to both TRUST (equation 5) and CIVIC (equation 6). Each 1-point rise in the 7-point Executive Constraints scale is associated with a rise in TRUST of 1.5 percentage points. As a second proxy for formal institutions, we use a variable called "Independence of the courts" from Humana 1987. This variable is a 4-point scale, with higher numbers indicating greater independence of the judiciary

TABLE 10.7. Determinants of Trust and Civic Cooperation: Polarization

Equation	1	2	3	4
Dependent variable	TRUST	CIVIC	TRUST	CIVIC
Constant	57.938	47.704	25.717	39.883
	(12.108)	(2.112)	(4.645)	(1.710)
GDP80	1.341	0.054	1.776	0.224
	(0.516)	(0.143)	(0.473)	(0.150)
PRIM60	−24.228	−5.509	−25.660	−8.305
	(7.137)	(1.511)	(8.219)	(1.766)
SEC60	17.425	0.906	5.968	1.313
	(9.566)	(2.667)	(9.350)	(2.413)
Gini (income)	−0.453	−0.099		
	(0.173)	(0.027)		
Ethnic Homogeneity			0.349	0.064
			(0.107)	(0.023)
Lawyers (1963)			−1.254	0.012
			(0.194)	(0.068)
Adj. R^2	.55	.31	.73	.30
SEE	9.53	1.68	7.32	1.68
N	28	28	29	29
Mean, D.V.	35.6	39.4	35.8	39.4

Note: White-corrected standard errors are shown in parentheses.

from the chief executive. It is strongly related to TRUST (equation 7), with each 1-point rise associated with an 8-percentage-point increase in TRUST. There is no relationship between independence of the judiciary and CIVIC, however (results not shown). These results on formal institutions, although perhaps fraught with multiple directions of causation, constitute important evidence for the interaction of formal and informal institutions.

Table 10.7 analyzes the relationship between polarization and our measures of social capital. The Gini coefficient for income inequality is strongly associated with lower trust and civic cooperation (equations 1 and 2). Both TRUST and CIVIC increase significantly with ethnic homogeneity (equations 3 and 4). With each 3-point increase in the percentage belonging to the largest ethnic group, TRUST rises by 1 point. Each 15-point increase in homogeneity increases CIVIC by 1 point.[38] Lawyers are also associated with low trust, whether as a signal of social polarization or through some other channel. Each 1-percentage-point increase in law students (as a percentage of all postsecondary students in 1963) is associated with a decline in TRUST of more than 1 percentage point (equation 3). Lawyers are unrelated to CIVIC, however (equation 4).

This section offers evidence for the following propositions. Income equality and checks on executive power are associated with higher levels of trust and stronger norms of civic cooperation. Ethnic and linguistic divisions coincide with weakened trust and civic norms.[39] Group memberships, in contrast, are unrelated to trust and norms.

We also explored the effects of several other possible determinants of trust and civic cooperation, which are less well-developed conceptually here for reasons of space. Urbanization, population, population density, and government size all proved insignificant.[40] Putnam (1993) views "hierarchical" religions such as Catholicism in terms of horizontal ties and trust. Inglehart (1990) and Fukuyama (1995), citing Weber, link Protestantism to higher trust. La Porta et al. (1996) report that trust is lower in countries with "dominant hierarchical religions" as measured by percentage of the population that is Catholic, Orthodox Christian, or Muslim. We find that Protestantism is associated with significantly greater trust: each 5-percentage-point rise in the number of Protestants (from Taylor and Jodice 1983) is associated with a 1-point rise in TRUST. When percent Protestant, percent Catholic, and percent Muslim are all included in a TRUST regression, coefficients for the latter two regressors are significantly negative, while percent Protestant is positive but not significant.[41]

8. Conclusion and Policy Implications

The notion of social capital is emerging with greater frequency in discussions of development, whether of poor countries or of chronically poor areas of industrialized countries. The elasticity of the term *social capital* has made progress in these discussions difficult. Nevertheless, all concepts have in common the idea that trust and norms of civic cooperation are essential to well-functioning societies and to the economic progress of those societies. This essay makes three contributions to these discussions. First, it provides some idea of the importance of these dimensions of social capital, supplying the strongest evidence to date that trust and civic cooperation have significant impacts on aggregate economic activity.

Our second contribution is a negative one. Disputes about the role of social capital arise when one attempts to define how trust and norms of civic cooperation in a society can be strengthened. Putnam (1993) has suggested that dense horizontal networks reinforce trust and civic norms. However, we find that horizontal networks—as measured by membership in groups—are unrelated to trust and civic norms (controlling for education and income) and to economic performance. The stronger impact on economic performance of trust and civic norms suggests that if declining social capital in the United States has adverse implications for growth, it is the erosion of trust and civic cooperation as documented by Knack (1992) that are of greater concern than the decline in associational life emphasized by Putnam (1995a, 1995b).[42]

Our third contribution is to demonstrate the importance of two sources of trust and civic norms. Social polarization and formal institutional rules that constrain the government from acting arbitrarily are associated with the development of cooperative norms and trust. These results carry several implications for policy. Trust's relationship to growth in our study is especially large in poorer countries, which may be attributable to their less well-developed financial sectors, insecure property rights, and unreliable enforceability of contracts. Interpersonal trust seems to be more important in facilitating economic activity where formal substitutes are unavailable. This finding suggests that where interpersonal trust is low and unlikely to improve rapidly, institutional reforms providing better formal mechanisms for the reliable enforcement of contracts and access to credit are even more important than where trust is higher.

Promoting horizontal associations through encouraging the formation of and participation in groups may be counterproductive, according to our findings. Group memberships are not directly related to economic performance and are unrelated to trust. On the positive side, secondary education is shown here to be associated with trust, although determining causality is problematic. Reforms in this area, already strongly supported by international agencies and donors for other reasons, may improve economic performance through increasing interpersonal trust. Our findings also reinforce the case for reducing income disparities in developing countries. These policies—often advocated on other grounds—have not proven easy to implement, however. The building of social capital has been broached as a significant new road to development. Our results suggest that this road is no less difficult than the more heavily traveled ones.

Appendix

Country	Trust	Civic	Groups	O-Groups	P-Groups	Confidence in Government	Ethnic Homogeneity
Norway	61.2	40.75	1.09	0.24	0.63	0.72	98
Finland	57.2	40.64	0.40	0.06	0.29	0.66	90
Sweden	57.1	41.57	1.08	0.27	0.64	0.65	88
Denmark	56.0	40.34	0.97	0.24	0.61	0.76	95
Canada	49.6	39.74	1.03	0.52	0.29	0.70	70
Australia	47.8	38.27	1.01	0.45	0.35	0.64	98
Netherlands	46.2	38.36	1.11	0.53	0.25	0.63	99
U.S.	45.4	40.55	1.50	0.83	0.42	0.61	81
UK	44.4	40.07	0.92	0.38	0.36	0.54	82
Switzerland	43.2	40.89	0.73	0.22	0.29		72
Iceland	41.6	41.07	1.70	0.63	0.76	0.73	100
Japan	40.8	41.79	0.38	0.14	0.21	0.46	99
Ireland	40.2	37.51	0.85	0.48	0.24	0.73	94
Korea	38.0	39.64	0.47	0.31	0.12	0.61	100
Spain	34.5	38.75	0.45	0.23	0.14	0.55	75
India	34.3	42.65	—	—	—	0.67	72
Austria	31.8	41.45	0.76	0.26	0.37	0.60	99
South Africa	30.5	36.99	0.84	0.52	0.16	0.70	73
Belgium	30.2	38.08	0.56	0.26	0.20	0.60	57
Germany	29.8	39.83	0.74	0.22	0.35	0.54	99
Argentina	27.0	39.50	0.47	0.19	0.21	0.28	91
Italy	26.3	41.23	0.38	0.12	0.20	0.44	99
France	24.8	36.26	0.42	0.16	0.18	0.62	94
Nigeria	22.9	39.19	—	—	—	0.73	32
Chile	22.7	36.80	0.59	0.33	0.14	0.64	78
Portugal	21.4	36.89	0.43	0.21	0.14	0.45	99
Mexico	17.7	34.55	0.57	0.28	0.14	0.53	58
Turkey	10.0	42.43	—	—	—	0.61	82
Brazil	6.7	37.58	0.68	0.31	0.16	0.55	88

Notes

This chapter was originally published under the same title in the *Quarterly Journal of Economics* 112, no. 4 (November 1997): 1252–88. It is reprinted with the permission of the MIT Press, © 1997 by the President and Fellows of Harvard College and the Massachusetts Institute of Technology.

1. This assumption is contained in Clague's model of "rule obedience" and organizational performance (chapter 9, this volume).

2. Political participation can be motivated by groups based on class, ethnic, or other ties seeking to use government for their own ends at the expense of the larger society. Putnam (1993) implicitly assumes that these inefficient effects of enhanced participation are outweighed by the efficient effects. Our measures of trust and civic norms, as explained below, appear to reflect attitudes toward cooperation more broadly, not only with those one associates or identifies with.

3. See Knack 1992 for related evidence.

4. Both "Britain" and Northern Ireland are included in the surveys. We treat Britain's values as representing the United Kingdom (Northern Ireland accounts for less than 3 percent of the latter's population). Many nonmarket economies were included in the 1990–91 surveys. Following Barro (1991) and others, we have not included them in our analyses, because of the lack of available data on education and other variables, and because economic performance is driven by different processes in nonmarket economies. The Eastern European nations and ex-Soviet republics tend to have low values for our trust measure; China's 60.3 percent ranks among the highest, however.

5. In 26 countries in our sample, respondents in the 1990 surveys were asked how much they trusted "your family." Responses were on a 5-point scale ranging from "trust them completely" to "do not trust them at all." Means of this scale were correlated with TRUST across countries at only .24. Trust in the family—unlike TRUST, as shown below—is uncorrelated with economic and governmental performance, formal constraints on chief executives, income equality, and ethnic homogeneity.

6. The simple correlation is .39; the partial correlation (controlling for per capita GDP) is .33.

7. His sample omits the poor and middle-income nations for which we report below that trust has the largest effects. He also uses 1990 data on trust, rather than data from the early 1980s, and controls only for initial income.

8. Growth, investment, and investment goods prices are all from the Penn World Tables version 5.6 (Summers and Heston 1991). Education enrollment data, collected by UNESCO, are from the Barro-Wolf data set used in Barro 1991.

9. Rotating credit associations and similar informal institutions "seem in general to disappear as capital markets develop" (Besley 1995, 121).

10. The source is the 1965 UNESCO Statistical Yearbook. Data are from 1962–64. Murphy, Shleifer, and Vishny (1991) used similar measures of law

and engineering students. Less trusting, more litigious, and more crime-ridden societies will have a higher demand for lawyers, as will more polarized societies in which special interests lobby governments for rent. But lawyers may also be in higher demand where formal institutions such as courts work better. For example, Putnam (1993, 126–27) attributes the proliferation of "notaries, lawyers, and judges" in the Italian city-states to the "unusual confidence in written agreements, in negotiation, and in the law" rather than to "contentiousness." In our sample, there is a strong, negative relationship between TRUST and lawyers. A Hausman test of the overidentifying restrictions indicates that the homogeneity and law students variables do not belong in the growth regression directly.

11. Instrumenting for TRUST with distance from the equator, as measured by Hall and Jones (1996), produces a 2SLS coefficient estimate for TRUST of .158 (SE = .086). Hall and Jones use this variable as a climate indicator, arguing that temperate regions have an advantage over tropical or polar regions; they find empirically, however, that income per worker increases (roughly) linearly with latitude over the observable range. This variable is correlated with TRUST in our sample at .63. A Hausman test indicates that latitude does not influence growth independent of its effects on trust in our sample.

12. The social capital measures could nevertheless influence innovation, as productive knowledge may be embodied in machinery and other investments, or in human capital.

13. The correlation between TRUST and Barro-Lee attainment for 1980 is .83, the highest correlation with TRUST found for any variable.

14. Since the marginal impact of social capital on performance appears to be greatest at lower levels of TRUST and CIVIC, we considered log specifications. The logged values of TRUST and CIVIC generally produce stronger results than those reported in table 10.1.

15. DeLong and Summers (1991) found no significant spatial correlation in their sample, using more rigorous tests that took into account the distance of each pair of national capitals from each other. They report that the three Southern Cone countries (only two of which are in our sample) had similar residuals, but that the European countries exhibited no geographic pattern.

16. If trust is reduced by untrustworthy behavior by government officials, its impact on economic performance could be associated with policy credibility. This possibility is a second explanation of why the TRUST coefficient may decline when currency depreciation is included in the equation.

17. These variables are averages over the 1980–90 period. Institutional Investor conducts the survey of international bankers; this measure of creditworthiness is also used in chapter 6.

18. See Berg and Sachs 1988 and Keefer and Knack 2002.

19. Inequality is measured as near to 1980 as the data permit. Iceland is

missing data for inequality. Sources are the World Development Report and Milanovic 1994.

20. Initial income and investment goods prices are measured in 1970 or 1960 as appropriate.

21. For these longer periods, TRUST and CIVIC remain significantly related to investment when additional regressors listed in table 10.2 (appropriately modified for the longer period) are added. For growth, TRUST and CIVIC coefficients remain positive in every case but are rarely significant when other regressors are added.

22. Measurement error may be partly responsible for this low correlation, as implausibly high TFP estimates are concentrated among low-trust countries in our sample. For example, TFP estimates are far higher for Mexico, Italy, and Brazil than for Norway, Finland, Denmark, and Sweden (and higher than for Germany, Switzerland, and the United States).

23. The rise of Japan in the late nineteenth century coincided with a government-initiated shift from "limited-group" morality to a more generalized morality, using the system of universal compulsory education as an important tool in this campaign (Platteau 1994).

24. "Sports and recreation clubs"—of particular interest in Putnam's work—and other groups were also included in the survey, but for too few countries to be analyzed. Group memberships for most countries are from the 1981 wave of surveys, and from the 1990 wave for the others, as with TRUST and CIVIC.

25. Putnam 1995b uses similar measures of associations from the WVS and, for the United States, from the General Social Survey.

26. The sample size drops from 29 in table 10.1 to 26 in table 10.4, as there are no data on group memberships for India, Nigeria, or Turkey. The greater measured impact of TRUST and CIVIC relative to GROUPS is not due to the changing sample, however: coefficients for TRUST and CIVIC in table 10.1 actually rise when those three countries are dropped.

27. Membership in groups classified here as Putnam groups could simply be proxying stronger preferences for leisure, which might harm measurable economic performance. Trade associations—Olson groups—do more than lobby for legal barriers to entry and tax breaks. They may have positive effects on economic performance by establishing ethical codes and standards (Bergsten 1985) or by reducing transaction costs, e.g., by spreading information about the identity of cheaters. See Greif 1996 and Granovetter 1985.

28. Switzerland is the only one from our 29-country sample in which these questions were not asked. While rankings suggest a certain amount of face validity for this index, there are several anomalies. Japan scores poorly (46 percent) and Nigeria scores very highly (73.1 percent). It is unclear to what extent these confidence items reflect how responsive the government is to the narrowly self-interested demands of respondents, or how effectively it carries out its legally mandated responsibilities, or something else.

29. Where incomes are higher, governments may have access to more tax revenue to provide better services, and better-educated citizens may place more effective demands on government to provide services efficiently.

30. These indexes were created using averages over the 1980–90 period for BERI and 1982–90 for ICRG. All countries in our sample are included in ICRG data. Iceland is missing in BERI.

31. High incomes may proxy the number and size of business transactions, which will be related to the demand for enforceable contracts, and may give the government access to more revenue to establish an effective judicial system.

32. When GROUPS is substituted for TRUST in table 10.5, it is significantly and positively related to two of the four dependent variables: confidence in government, consistent with Putnam's (1993) results, and the BERI contract enforceability measure.

33. Weingast 1993 provides multiple examples, including the former Yugoslavia, arguing that institutional guarantees of policy bargains related to interethnic distributional issues disappeared with the fall of communist regimes, leading in short order to the breakdown of trust between individuals from different ethnic groups.

34. The relationship between trust and civic cooperation, on the one hand, and property rights and government performance, on the other, is likely to be complex, with each influencing the other. Formal institutions can be substitutes for—as well as causes of—trust and civic cooperation. Societies with low trust require more robust formal institutions if they are to undertake the exchanges that are crucial to growth.

35. Using individual-level data on group memberships for the United States, Germany, and Sweden from the WVS and other sources, Stolle and Rochon (1998) find memberships increase trust, controlling for age, education, and income. They find mixed evidence on whether groups that are more diverse (in terms of age, socioeconomic status, ideology, and sex) produce more trust among members. They acknowledge that their results could be influenced by self-selection. Helliwell (1998), using individual-level WVS data for the United States and Canada, finds group members are more trusting, controlling for education and region. He finds no difference in the strength of this effect across different types of groups. Note that such individual-level analyses, unlike our aggregate-level analysis, cannot capture the effects of group memberships on the trust and trustworthiness of nonmembers.

36. However, the marked decline in trust in the United States since the 1960s has not been accompanied by a decline in group memberships. Even if the two variables were correlated, causality arguably runs primarily from trust to groups rather than the other way around, as more trusting individuals may have a greater propensity to affiliate with strangers in groups.

37. These results—as with those in section 5 on group memberships and economic performance—are not sensitive to deleting religious organizations from P-GROUPS.

38. Using individual-level WVS data, Helliwell (1996b) found that U.S. and Canadian respondents classifying themselves first in terms of ethnicity (e.g., Asian-American or French-Canadian) and only secondarily in terms of nationality (e.g., American or Canadian) were less trusting, controlling for education and region.

39. As discussed above, the WVS indicators appear to measure generalized trust and civic norms. Inequality and ethnic heterogeneity may well strengthen cooperation and trust within certain limited groups.

40. Taylor (1976) claims that large governments "crowd out" norms. Buchanan (1965) among others argues that the force of ethical rules weakens with larger numbers.

41. Results available on request.

42. Moreover, survey evidence indicates that membership in groups has been fairly stable in recent years in the United States. Putnam's "decline" results from adjusting for the rise in education levels over time, which he justifies on the basis of a positive cross-sectional relationship between years of education and group memberships.

References

Arrow, Kenneth. 1972. "Gifts and Exchanges." *Philosophy and Public Affairs* 1:343–62.

Banks, Arthur S., and Robert S. Textor. 1963. *A Cross-Polity Survey.* Cambridge: MIT Press.

Barro, Robert. 1991. "Economic Growth in a Cross-Section of Countries." *Quarterly Journal of Economics* 106:407–44.

Barro, Robert, and Jong-Wha Lee. 1993. "International Comparisons of Educational Attainment." *Journal of Monetary Economics* 32:363–94.

Berg, Andrew, and Jeffrey Sachs. 1988. "The Debt Crisis: Structural Explanations of Country Performance." *Journal of Development Economics* 29:271–306.

Bergsten, Gordon S. 1985. "On the Role of Social Norms in a Market Economy." *Public Choice* 45:113–37.

Besley, Timothy. 1995. "Nonmarket Institutions for Credit and Risk Sharing in Low-Income Countries." *Journal of Economic Perspectives* 9:115–27.

Buchanan, James. 1965. "Ethical Rules, Expected Values, and Large Numbers." *Ethics* 76:1–13.

Coleman, James S. 1988. "Social Capital in the Creation of Human Capital." *American Journal of Sociology* 94 (Supplement): S95–S120.

———. 1990. *Foundations of Social Theory.* Cambridge: Harvard University Press.

DeLong, J. Bradford, and Lawrence H. Summers. 1991. "Equipment Investment and Economic Growth." *Quarterly Journal of Economics* 106: 445–502.

Fukuyama, Francis. 1995. *Trust: The Social Virtues and the Creation of Prosperity.* New York: Free Press.

Galor, Oded, and J. Zeira. 1993. "Income Distribution and Macroeconomics." *Review of Economic Studies* 60:35–52.

Gambetta, Diego. 1988. *Trust: Making and Breaking Cooperative Relations.* Oxford: Blackwell.

Granovetter, Mark. 1973. "The Strength of Weak Ties." *American Journal of Sociology* 78:1360–80.

———. 1985. "Economic Action and Social Structure: The Problem of Embeddedness." *American Journal of Sociology* 91:481–510.

Greif, Avner. 1989. "Reputation and Coalitions in Medieval Trade: Maghribi Traders." *Journal of Economic History* 59:857–82.

———. 1996. "Contracting, Enforcement, and Efficiency: Economics beyond the Law." Presented at the World Bank Conference on Development Economics, Washington, DC, April.

Gurr, Ted Robert. 1990. *Polity II: Political Structures and Regime Change, 1800–1986.* Ann Arbor, MI: Inter-University Consortium for Political and Social Research.

Hall, Robert E., and Charles I. Jones. 1996. "The Productivity of Nations." NBER Working Paper No. 5812.

Hardin, Russell. 1982. *Collective Action.* Baltimore: Resources for the Future.

———. 1992. "The Street-Level Epistemology of Trust." *Analyse & Kritik* 14 (1992):152–76.

Helliwell, John. 1996. "Economic Growth and Social Capital in Asia." NBER Working Paper No. 5470.

———. 1998. *How Much Do National Borders Matter?* Washington, DC: Brookings Institution.

Helliwell, John, and Robert Putnam. 1995. "Economic Growth and Social Capital in Italy." *Eastern Economic Journal* 21:295–307.

Humana, Charles. 1987. *World Human Rights Guide.* London: Hodder and Stoughton.

Inglehart, Ronald. 1990. *Culture Shift in Advanced Industrial Society.* Princeton: Princeton University Press.

———. 1994. *Codebook for World Values Surveys.* Ann Arbor: Institute for Social Research.

Keefer, Philip, and Stephen Knack. 1993. "Why Don't Poor Countries Catch Up? A Cross-National Test of an Institutional Explanation." IRIS Center Working Paper No. 60, University of Maryland, College Park.

———. 2002. "Polarization, Politics and Property Rights: Links between Inequality and Growth." *Public Choice* 111 (1–2): 127–54.

King, Robert G., and Ross Levine. 1993. "Finance and Growth: Schumpeter Might Be Right." *Quarterly Journal of Economics* 108:717–37.

Knack, Stephen. 1992. "Civic Norms, Social Sanctions, and Voter Turnout." *Rationality and Society* 4:133–56.

Kyriacou, George A. 1991. "Level and Growth Effects of Human Capital." C. V. Starr Working Paper No. 91-26.

La Porta, Rafael, Florencio Lopez-de-Silanes, Andrei Shleifer, and Robert W. Vishny. 1997. "Trust in Large Organizations." *American Economic Review Papers and Proceedings* 87 (2): 333–38.

Loury, Glenn. 1977. "A Dynamic Theory of Racial Income Differences." In P. A. Wallace and A. Le Mund, eds., *Women, Minorities and Employment Discrimination.* Lexington, MA: Lexington Books.

Milanovic, Branko. 1994. "Determinants of Cross-Country Income Inequality: An Augmented Kuznets' Hypothesis." World Bank Policy Research Working Paper No. 1246.

Mueller, Dennis. 1989. *Public Choice II.* Cambridge: Cambridge University Press.

Murphy, Kevin, Andrei Shleifer, and Robert W. Vishny. 1991. "The Allocation of Talent: Implications for Growth." *Quarterly Journal of Economics* 106:503–30.

Narayan, Deepa, and Lant Pritchett. 1999. "Cents and Sociability: Household Income and Social Capital in Rural Tanzania." *Economic Development and Cultural Change* 47 (4): 871–97.

Olson, Mancur. 1982. *The Rise and Decline of Nations.* New Haven: Yale University Press.

Platteau, Jean-Philippe. 1994. "Behind the Market Stage Where Real Societies Exist." *Journal of Development Studies* 30:533–77, 753–817.

Putnam, Robert (with Robert Leonardi and Raffaella Y. Nanetti). 1993. *Making Democracy Work.* Princeton: Princeton University Press.

———. 1995a. "Bowling Alone: America's Declining Social Capital." *Journal of Democracy* 6:65–78.

———. 1995b. "Tuning In, Tuning Out: The Strange Disappearance of Social Capital in America." *PS: Political Science and Politics* 28:664–83.

Sachs, Jeffrey, and Andrew Warner. 1995. "Economic Reform and the Process of Global Integration." *Brookings Papers on Economic Activity* 1:1–95.

Solow, Robert. 1995. "But Verify." *New Republic,* September 11: 36.

Stolle, Dietlind, and Thomas R. Rochon. 1998. "Are All Associations Alike? Member Diversity, Associational Type and the Creation of Social Capital." *American Behavioral Scientist* 42 (1): 47–65.

Sullivan, Michael J. 1991. *Measuring Global Values.* New York: Greenwood.

Summers, Robert, and Alan Heston. 1991. "The Penn World Table: An Expanded Set of International Comparisons, 1950–88." *Quarterly Journal of Economics* 106:327–68.

Taylor, Michael. 1976. *Anarchy and Cooperation.* New York: Wiley.

Taylor, Charles, and David Jodice. 1983. *World Handbook of Political and Social Indicators.* 3d ed. New Haven: Yale University Press.

Uslaner, Eric. 2002. *The Moral Foundations of Trust.* New York: Cambridge University Press.

Wallerstein, Michael. 1989. "Union Organization in Advanced Industrial Democracies." *American Political Science Review* 83:481–501.

Weingast, Barry. 1993. "The Political Foundations of Democracy and the Rule of Law." IRIS Center Working Paper no. 54, University of Maryland, College Park.

White, Halbert L. 1980. "A Heteroskedasticity-Consistent Covariance Matrix Estimator and a Direct Test for Heteroskedasticity." *Econometrica* 48:817–38.

PART 4

Conclusion

CHAPTER 11

Is "Wising Up" Enough? Special Interests and Institutional Reform

Stephen Knack

> No historical process that is understood is inevitable.
> —*Mancur Olson (Power and Prosperity, 2000)*

Mancur Olson claims that "the best thing a society can do to increase its prosperity is to wise up" (chapter 2, this volume). This advice suggests that ignorance rather than incentives is the binding constraint on policy and institutional reform. Several of Olson's earlier writings—including most notably the closing passages of his *Rise and Decline of Nations* (1982)—confirm his optimism regarding the power of ideas and the influence of example. Unless this optimism is misplaced, research on political economy and governance sponsored by USAID (including the studies in this volume), the World Bank, and other aid agencies can have sizable payoffs. Successful reform would be at least partly a simple matter of disseminating research findings to policymakers, or to interest groups and voters in less developed nations.

At least at the margin, reform often can be facilitated by wising up. The example of Japan's economic success undoubtedly influenced the policies of other East Asian nations. Chile's reforms and subsequent success similarly provided a model for Latin America. Socialism was not so long ago widely considered a viable system for generating rapid and sustained growth, but has been discredited by its demonstrated failure to provide an adequate level of economic welfare in the long run. The current consensus that socialism has not worked surely makes it more difficult for its advocates to gain support. In addition, forms of government that engage in or fail to restrain predatory behavior are being similarly discredited today, as knowledge of the costs of predation accumulates and is more widely disseminated. The spread of democracy has also benefited from the example of neighbors and "the active propagation of political ideas across borders" (Carothers 1999, 63).

However, wising up is not always sufficient, as Olson himself recognized, arguing, for example, that "in dramatic contrast to Keynes's view, vested interests do a much better job than the level of economic thought does in explaining the pattern of relative growth rates" (1989, 288). Ideas are most efficacious when there is a balance of power or stalemate among opposing organized interests (1989, 298). The paragraphs following Olson's "wising up" advice in chapter 2 suggest it reflects merely a careless turn of phrase rather than an overly simplistic view of reform.

As Olson notes in chapter 2, world income could be dramatically increased through a seemingly simple policy change in developed nations—namely, allowing freer in-migration of labor. However, an individual nation has no incentive to take world income into account in designing its policies. Free immigration is hindered by more than just lack of information about its benefits; unskilled labor recognizes that its interests would be harmed. Similarly, incentives of certain occupational, regional, ethnic, or other interests prevent efficient reforms within many countries that could drastically increase *national* incomes. These interests do not block reform solely, if at all, because they lack information about its efficiency impacts. This argument also implies that donor-sponsored anticorruption initiatives emphasizing public awareness and freedom of information will often be ineffective.

In chapter 5, Olson provides further reason for pessimism, in this case regarding the feasibility of lasting democratic reforms. Historically, the emergence of democracy from autocracy is an "improbable transition" dependent on particular historical conditions and dispersion of resources. The evolution of democracy and the rule of law in the West occurred over a period of at least several hundred years. In England, the Magna Carta and the Glorious Revolution are the most prominent events in the process of increasing accountability of monarchs to elites, followed eventually by gradual extension of the suffrage (North 1990, 113–14). In several other countries, the adoption of democratic institutions was a precondition for regaining independence from democratic occupying powers following a losing war. As has been said, Douglass North has written fewer constitutions than Douglas MacArthur. The paths taken by nations that are wealthy today provide limited guidance for promoting rapid political and economic progress in less developed nations.

Foreign aid potentially can promote democratization, either through conditionality; through technical assistance programs targeted at strengthening parties, civil societies, or election processes; or by increasing income and education levels, which in turn have been linked to democracy. However, empirical evidence fails to demonstrate any links between higher aid levels and progress toward democratization (Knack 2000). If Olson (chapter 5, this volume) and other scholars are correct that the emergence and maintenance of democracy owes much to a balance of power among factions that prevents any one leader or faction from overpowering its opponents, then the limited success of democracy assistance is unsurprising.

At a minimum, successful democracy-promotion requires a thorough understanding of the configuration of interests and power, combined with an analysis of how aid can change the perceptions and knowledge of key actors and help build alliances for reform (Carothers 1999). Training judges, holding corruption workshops, and so forth may be politically and technically easier to implement, but will often be ineffective in the absence of more fundamental political and social change.

Further grounds for caution regarding the potential or efficacy of reform efforts are suggested by evidence that institutions are determined in large part by unalterable exogenous forces. In the case of Italy, Putnam (1993) traces the cultural factors determining poor governmental performance in the south to the twelfth-century Norman regime centered in Sicily. Similarly, some of the cultural traits responsible for Britain's early transition to democracy and leadership of the Industrial Revolution can be traced back many hundreds of years (Macfarlane 1979). Across the American states, trust and other dimensions of social capital are strongly predicted by ethnic and religious composition (Rice and Feldman 1997; Knack 2002). Weingast (1997) argues that the rule of law is ultimately dependent on appropriate attitudes and behavior on the part of individual citizens, and emphasizes the importance of homogeneity of preferences for the successful adoption and implementation of constitutional rules under which the state protects the rights of all. Cross-country studies point to the importance of ethnic heterogeneity (Mauro 1995; Keefer and Knack 2002; La Porta et al. 1999), legal tradition (La Porta et al. 1999; Berkowitz et al. 2002), religious composition (La Porta et al. 1999), climate (Acemoglu et al. 2001; La Porta et al. 1999; Hall and Jones 1999), factor endowments (Engerman and Sokoloff 1997), and colonial heritage (Mauro 1995; Hall and Jones 1999). The latter appears to be most important of all: democracy has been most durable and the rule of law strongest over the last few hundred years in Britain and in societies that were governed and heavily populated by settlers from the British Isles. However, sending wooden boats full of English convicts and religious fanatics is hardly an option available to aid agencies today.

Finally, our knowledge of what specific reforms work, and how to implement them without undermining local capacity, is limited. Knack (2001) presents cross-country statistical evidence that donor efforts—as measured by aid received—have on balance weakened rather than strengthened the quality of governance in recipient nations. As noted in chapter 1, existing research showing that governance matters for development does not often point the way toward specific reforms, because it is based largely on very broad and aggregated indicators of institutional performance. "Still to be undertaken is systematic empirical work that will identify the costs and *underlying institutions* that make economies unproductive" (North 1990, 135, emphasis added). Continued progress in measuring specific aspects of government processes and institutional arrangements, and in various aspects of government performance, should gradually fill this gap in knowledge. Experimentation by governments and by donors with various types of public sector reform programs and democracy assistance—which tend to be relatively inexpensive by aid industry standards—can provide data useful for such research.

More problematic is the concern that was at the core of Mancur Olson's entire career, that of identifying and overcoming special interests facing incentives to maintain socially inefficient policies and institutions. Olson originally applied his insights on the evolution and impact of narrow and "encompassing" groups to the stable, developed democracies (1982). However, the last decade of his career was spent broadening and adapting these insights to explain the declining economic performance of socialist nations over time (Murrell and Olson 1991; Olson 2000), and persistent poverty in much of the world (chapter 2, this volume). A fundamental conclusion of his work is the crucial importance of structuring institutions "in ways that give authoritative decision making as much as possible to encompassing interests" (2000) rather than narrow interests.

Unfortunately, Olson is no longer around to assist reformers in operationalizing his insights. Relatively little is known about effective methods for co-opting narrow interests or for building broader constituencies that eventually accumulate enough power to overcome narrow ruling interests. Despite the widespread recognition of the fundamental importance of governance for development within agencies such as the World Bank and UNDP, the country assistance strategies of donors are rarely based on a thorough political economy analysis that identifies the binding political and social constraints on development and proposes ways to overcome them or work around them effectively. Technocratic fixes that often differ little from those of past decades are prescribed in the areas of civil service reform and budgetary management, only now under the heading of "governance" rather than "capacity building." While these programs are certainly needed and sometimes even effective, their efficacy is too often undermined by resistance within government and key interest groups. Before implementing such "top down" reforms, assistance strategies must analyze the likelihood that any benefits will be sustainable in the absence of "bottom up" reforms that increase the demand for good governance in business and civil society.

Not only is our understanding of how to build coalitions for reform limited, but the limited mandates of some multilateral donor agencies can create hesitancy in engaging fully on "political" issues. There is already some controversy over whether the World Bank's anticorruption activities violate its charter (Kapur and Webb 2000).

Wising up is therefore not enough, for reasons Olson understood as much as anyone. However, knowledge can matter at the margin, and information about the efficiency costs of institutions and policies—at least when these costs are very extreme—may sometimes lead to small but decisive increases in the perceived benefits of participating in collective action against a regime. As the costs of socially inefficient policies and institutions accumulate, a nation's potential military, diplomatic, and cultural influence—and that of its leaders—will gradually be eclipsed by more rapidly growing competitors. Even if better understanding about the policies and institutions favorable to development stimulates reform in only a few countries, the power of example coupled with the force of international competition can in turn stimulate reform by other autocrats intent on maintaining power. Thus, although incentives obviously matter, they can sometimes be altered by improved understanding of what makes economies grow.

So, not only does governance matter, but research contributing to our understanding of governance matters. And, in Olson's words, "if those of us who are professionally concerned with ideas about how society should be governed . . . work hard enough and well enough, there may be further understanding" (2000, 199).

References

Acemoglu, Daron, Simon Johnson, and James A. Robinson. 2001. "The Colonial Origins of Comparative Development: An Empirical Investigation." *American Economic Review* 91 (5): 1369–1401.

Berkowitz, Daniel, Katharina Pistor, and Jean-Francois Richard. 2002. "Economic Development, Legality, and the Transplant Effect." *European Economic Review* (forthcoming).

Carothers, Thomas. 1999. *Aiding Democracy Abroad: The Learning Curve.* Washington, DC: Carnegie Endowment for International Peace.

Engerman, Stanley L., and Kenneth L. Sokoloff. 1997. "Factor Endowments, Institutions, and Differential Paths of Growth among New World Economies." In Stephen Haber, ed., *How Latin America Fell Behind.* Stanford: Stanford University Press.

Hall, Robert E., and Charles I. Jones. 1999. "Why Do Some Countries Produce So Much More Output Per Worker Than Others?" *Quarterly Journal of Economics* 114:83–116.

Kapur, Devesh, and Richard Webb. 2000. "Governance-Related Conditionalities of the Ifis." XII Technical Group Meeting of the Intergovernmental Group of 24 for International Monetary Affairs, March 1–3, Lima, Peru.

Keefer, Philip, and Stephen Knack. 2002. "Polarization, Politics and Property Rights: Links between Inequality and Growth." *Public Choice* 111 (1–2): 127–54.

Knack, Stephen. 2000. "Does Foreign Aid Promote Democracy?" IRIS Center Working Paper 238.

———. 2002. "Social Capital and the Quality of Government: Evidence from the States." *American Journal of Political Science* 46 (4): 772–85.

———. 2001. "Aid Dependence and the Quality of Governance." *Southern Economic Journal* 68 (2): 310–29.

La Porta, Rafael, Florencio Lopez-de-Silanes, Andrei Shleifer, and Robert W. Vishny. 1999. "The Quality of Government." *Journal of Law, Economics, and Organization* 15 (1): 222–79.

Macfarlane, Alan. 1979. *The Origins of English Individualism: The Family, Property, and Social Transition.* New York: Cambridge University Press.

Mauro, Paolo. 1995. "Corruption and Growth." *Quarterly Journal of Economics* 110:681–712.

Murrell, Peter, and Mancur Olson. 1991. "The Devolution of Centrally Planned Economies." *Journal of Comparative Economics* 15:239–65.

North, Douglass. 1990. *Institutions, Institutional Change and Economic Performance.* Cambridge: Cambridge University Press.

Olson, Mancur. 1982. *The Rise and Decline of Nations.* New Haven: Yale University Press.

———. 1989. "Is Britain the Wave of the Future?" *L.S.E. Quarterly* 3 (4): 279–304.

———. 2000. *Power and Prosperity: Outgrowing Communist and Capitalist Dictatorships.* New York: Basic Books.

Putnam, Robert, with Robert Leonardi and Raffaella Y. Nanetti. 1993. *Making Democracy Work.* Princeton: Princeton University Press.

Rice, Tom W., and Jan L. Feldman. 1997. "Civic Culture and Democracy from Europe to America." *Journal of Politics* 59 (4): 1143–72.

Weingast, Barry. 1997. "The Political Foundations of Democracy and the Rule of Law." *American Political Science Review* 91 (2): 245–63.

Contributors

Omar Azfar is Research Associate at the IRIS Center, University of Maryland, College Park. He has published several articles on applications of the New Institutional Economics on labor economics, profit sharing, collective action problems, and corruption. He is coeditor (with Charles A. Cadwell) of *Market-Augmenting Government: The Institutional Foundations for Prosperity* (2002).

Christopher Clague is Professor Emeritus in Economics, the University of Maryland, and lecturer at San Diego State University. He was Director of Research at the IRIS Center, University of Maryland, from 1990 to 1997, and has edited *Institutions and Economic Development* (1997) and *The Emergence of Market Economies in Eastern Europe* (1992). He is coauthor of *Capital Utilization: A Theoretical and Empirical Analysis* (1981).

Philip Keefer is a Lead Economist in the World Bank's Development Research Group. His research on social and political institutions in economic development has been published in the *Quarterly Journal of Economics,* the *Journal of Economic History,* and elsewhere. He is a coauthor of the World Bank's Policy Research Report on state-owned enterprises, *Bureaucrats in Business.* Prior to joining the World Bank in 1994, he was Associate Director of the IRIS Center at the University of Maryland.

Stephen Knack is a Senior Research Economist in the World Bank's Development Research Group. In addition to his research on the social and political determinants of growth and effective governance, he is the author of numerous studies on American political participation and elections. Before coming to the World Bank in 1999, he was a Research Associate at the University of Maryland's IRIS Center, and Assistant Professor in American University's School of Public Affairs.

Young Lee is an assistant professor in the Hanyang University Department of Economics in Seoul, Korea. He was a Research Associate at the IRIS Center from 1997 to 1999. His work on taxation, transitional economies, and corruption has been published in the *Journal of Public Economics, Economic Inquiry, Journal of Comparative Economics,* and *Journal of Development Economics.*

Mancur Olson was Principal Investigator of the Center for Institutional Reform and the Informal Sector (IRIS), and Distinguished Professor in Economics at the University of Maryland. He is the author of numerous articles and books on collective action and economic development, including *Power and Prosperity* (2000), the *Rise and Decline of Nations* (1982), and *The Logic of Collective Action* (1965). He was named a Fellow of the American Academy of Arts and Sciences in 1985.

Anand Swamy is Assistant Professor of Economics at Williams College, in Williamstown, Massachusetts. His research interests are in the economics of institutions, especially in the context of factor markets in developing countries. He has written "The Hazards of Piecemeal Reform: British Civil Courts and the Credit Market in Colonial India" and "A Simple Test of the Nutrition-based Efficiency Wage Model" for the *Journal of Development Economics.*

Author Index

Koshechkina, T., 219
Kraay, A., 19, 192, 202–3, 209, 211
Krueger, A. B., 51, 52, 53
Kyriacou, G. A., 262

Lake, D., 128
Lambsdorff, J. G., 219
Landes, D., 51, 53
Lane, P., 22
La Porta, R., 70, 254, 278, 293
Lee, J., 74, 94, 105, 113, 262, 267, 282
Lee, Y., 198
Levine, R., 50, 75, 92, 95, 100, 101,
    102, 105, 264
Lewis, K. A., 154
Lewis-Beck, M., 154, 189
Lichbach, M. I., 175
Lipset, S. M., 154
Loayza, N., 75
Londregan, J. B., 59, 166
Lopez-de-Silanes, F., 70, 278, 293
Loury, G., 252
Lucas, R., 33, 41, 42, 52

Macaulay, S., 229
Macfarlane, A., 293
Madison, J., 138, 172, 175, 181
Mankiw, N. G., 6, 64, 75
Matland, R., 212
Mauro, P., 13, 14, 90, 218, 293
McDermott, J., 191
McGuire, M., 175
McMillan, J. R., 57, 75
McNeil, W., 249
Meguire, P., 12, 57, 74, 75
Meltzer, A. H., 181
Merton, R., 249
Milanovic, B., 283
Mill, J. S., 1, 21, 25, 181, 225
Miller, G., 229, 237, 239
Miller, W., 219, 229
Mitchell, B. R., 52
Mokyr, J., 52
Moore, M., 191

Moreno, A., 218
Mueller, D., 268
Mukherjee, A., 198, 220
Muller, E. N., 189
Murphy, K., 281
Murrell, P., 134, 294
Myerson, R. M., 212, 220
Myrdal, G., 230

Nabli, M., 228
Narayan, D., 258
Nelson, R. R., 187
Nguyen, D., 22
Noh, Suk Jae, 144, 167
North, D., 1, 2, 11, 12, 13, 32, 35, 36,
    41, 46, 47, 56, 59, 78, 107, 119, 133,
    212, 237, 292
Nugent, J. B., 228

Olson, M., 2, 3, 4, 5, 8, 10, 11, 12, 21,
    25, 26, 50, 51, 52, 53, 59, 74, 107,
    111, 112, 113, 114, 133, 134, 175,
    218, 226, 230, 238, 252, 269, 270,
    271, 277, 283, 291, 292, 293, 294,
    295
Orbell, J. M., 249
Ozler, S., 12, 74, 76, 178

Parrish, C. J., 218
Paternoster, R., 216
Paukert, F., 183, 185
Persson, T., 113, 178, 181, 182, 183,
    185, 187, 188, 189
Phelps, E. S., 187
Pinker, S., 221
Pischke, J.-S., 53
Pistor, K., 293
Platteau, J.-P., 261, 275, 283
Pollard, S., 249
Poole, K. T., 59, 166
Posner, R., 249
Pritchett, L., 107, 258
Putnam, R., 17, 226, 252, 253, 255,
    259, 269, 270, 271, 273, 274, 276,

Subject Index